Experiencing Ritual

University of Pennsylvania Press
SERIES IN CONTEMPORARY ETHNOGRAPHY

Series Editors
Dan Rose
Paul Stoller

A complete list of books in the series is available from the publisher.

Experiencing Ritual

A New Interpretation of African Healing

Edith Turner
with WILLIAM BLODGETT,
Singleton Kahona, and Fideli Benwa

PENN

University of Pennsylvania Press
Philadelphia

Third paperback printing 1998

10 9 8 7 6 5 4 3

Published by
University of Pennsylvania Press
Philadelphia, Pennsylvania 19104-4011

Permission is acknowledged to reprint published material.

From Ralph W. Burhoe, "The Phenomenon of Religion Seen Scientifically," in Allan Eister, ed., *Changing Perspectives in the Scientific Study of Religion*. Copyright © 1974. Reprinted by permission of John Wiley & Sons.

From James Dow, *The Shaman's Touch: Otomi Indian Symbolic Healing*, pp. 107–10. Copyright © 1986. Reprinted by permission of the University of Utah Press.

Library of Congress Cataloging-in-Publication Data
Turner, Edith L. B., 1921–
    Experiencing ritual: a new interpretation of African healing / Edith Turner, with William Blodgett, Singleton Kahona, and Fideli Benwa.
        p. cm. — (Series in contemporary ethnography).
    Includes bibliographical references and index.
    ISBN 0-8122-3119-8 (alk. paper). — ISBN 0-8122-1366-1 (pbk. : alk. paper)
    1. Ndembu (African people) — Rites and ceremonies. 2. Ndembu (African people) — Religion. 3. Ndembu (African people) — Medicine. 4. Shamanism — Zambia.
5. Healing — Zambia — Religious aspects. I. Title. II. Series.
DT3058.N44T87 1992
299'.6839 — dc20   91-38993
                                                                         CIP

*To Singleton Kahona, Fideli Benwa,
and their Ancestors*

Contents

Preface

This is a different kind of anthropology, the story of a visible spirit form among the Ndembu of Zambia, and it has a different point to make.

When I first worked with Victor Turner, I felt there must be a more humanistic way to explain human behavior and events than the methods we were supposed to be learning in the world of anthropology. It was lucky for me that the academic world was mediated through Vic, and this made a difference. It was not I who sat in the classrooms. I could not sit through the classes myself because I had five children to look after. I learned through him. And this was an informal "him," not a classroom one. The result was that anthropology was peculiarly alive for me, never dead. As I went through life with Vic, we followed research ideas into a wide variety of human experiences, both in the field and back home, and I found I was able to keep my own viewpoint.

In the field, Africa in 1951, I was dropped straight in front of the "material," that is, human beings. The ones I saw most of were mothers with babies basically in the same position as me, a mother with babies. Obviously, my viewpoint was not strictly academic. In a way I *was* somewhat nearer to an African than most, though what credibility that gave me I do not know. I had been a pacifist in World War II and therefore was considered a kind of second-class citizen. In that respect, I resembled the Africans under their colonial government. Also I was extremely poor, almost like the Ndembu by American standards. During the war, I lived for two years with Vic Turner and a couple of young children in a small gypsy caravan. Later the arrival of three more children precluded further education for a impecunious Englishwoman like me with a desire to see the children grow up healthily. I educated myself and had Vic educate me. That meant freedom; we learned together, and there was no authority system.

This is partly why my book is odd. I didn't feel particularly strange when I went out to the Ndembu with the first three children. I rarely looked with horror on the Ndembu's lack of hygiene, and I tended to agree with their taste in music, storytelling, child-raising—almost everything. The exception lay in my use of quinine and modern medical aids. It should be stated that I was no master of Ndembu culture in any way, being not much good at Ndembu singing and dancing. Gardening I loved and could grow a mean tomato. Otherwise, I was rather a klutz at everything. Yet the women and I often loved each other. My children ran around in common with their children, and I danced (badly) at initiations, busily writing everything down that happened because I liked doing so and because Vic was interested. Monica Wilson had once given me a course on rites of passage and initiations, which gave me a handle on Nkanga, the Ndembu girl's initiation.

The following might explain how, long before I met Victor Turner, I became interested in anthropology and symbolism. It was through riddle-telling while hoeing kale in Rutland, England, early in World War II. There were Mr. Plant and Mr. Want on either side of me—all of us striking our hoes into the soil—and they were asking me riddles; and of course, they had to tell me the answers—I couldn't guess them. I can see those seedlings now, in thick lines running to the left with weeds among them everywhere, and clear earth to the right showing one neat seedling per foot in the row. We did a good job, with wide sharp hoe blades like skate blades, and we were walking sideways to the left as we hoed. Mr. Plant, a burly man, said:

> There was an old woman with but one eye
> And a long tail that she let fly,
> And every time she went over a gap
> She left a bit of her tail in a trap.
> Who is she?

I hemmed and hawed until he said, "A needle."

This rhyme resonated with the seedlings in neat array like sewing stitches, but nowadays the tail of the old woman also connects in my mind with the continual pulling along of a thread of a story that joins various themes and elements. Is the kale field the anthropological scene of this book, its method? That might be going too far, but there are correspondences.

Particularized experiences were then my life. So later, when Vic Turner hit on anthropology as his avocation and it looked as if we really might go to Africa, it was my wildest dream coming true, bringing into reality among other things the Henty stories of my childhood. I might actually smell Africa, I might feel the touch of another batch of blessed reality, all the better for being in an altogether strange milieu.

Indeed, we found a complex world out there, and in our precious two years of hard work, the fieldwork was undertaken and completed. Then thirty-one years passed in rapid succession—too quickly it now seems. The time came when I was able to visit the Ndembu once more. But by then many changes had taken place; years had gone by, I had raised the children, and Vic was dead. Just after Vic died my philosophy was different from what it is now. For instance, then I argued every which way that Vic had not "gone to heaven" or anywhere, just that there remained this "time that was no time," which was nothing more than those liminal times we had together. And for me that was it.

It's true that I once had an experience of religion, after which I didn't see the point of disbelieving other people's experiences. It gave me something else to be inquisitive about. For instance, I was fascinated when I read of the Moslems' ritual of baring their heads to God on the Mount of Arafat at Mecca—their experience of God. I had also once attended an Umbanda trance session and had seen an actual trance. This was good anthropological material, and later Vic and I enacted that ritual and others with our students. I felt there was some human birthright that we possessed, which like sex in the Victorian age seemed taboo to anthropologists. But I was beginning to think that we no longer had to forego it. It was in this bold mood that I went to do my restudy of the Ndembu. What happened is told in the book, which is anthropology of a different kind.

Acknowledgments

My thanks are due to the Wenner-Gren Foundation for Anthropological Research and to the Carter-Woodson Institute for African-American and African Studies at the University of Virginia, for grants-in-aid to make a restudy of the Ndembu. I am particularly grateful to William (Bill) Blodgett, whose unstinting help made the enterprise possible, and to his father William Blodgett III, who funded Bill's trip; also to Singleton Kahona and Fideli Benwa and their ancestors who were the true owners of the Ihamba ritual and to whom this book is dedicated; to Benwa Muhelwa, Fideli's father, who was a wise teacher in matters of ritual; to Stephen Moyo and the Institute for African Studies; and to Cecile Clover, Irene Wellman, Roy Wagner, and many others in the States for their help, advice, and encouragement. Finally, I acknowledge the intellectual legacy of Victor Turner, which is beyond price.

Introduction

When anthropologists do fieldwork, they try to participate in the life of the people they are studying, but there appear to be limits. Geertz wrote: "We cannot live other people's lives, and it is a piece of bad faith to try. We can but listen to what, in words . . . they say about their lives. . . . We gain [our sense of other people's lives] through their expressions. . . . It's all a matter of scratching surfaces" (1986, 373). This is partly true. Indeed, it would be valuable if we possessed their memories, if we had the same personal background in the culture: we did not have that background. But there are times when an ethnographer involved in an event of ultimate concern to the subjects of her work goes deeply into an experience herself—something which at least may be said to parallel theirs. Such an event is the focus of this book: a moment when I actually saw a spirit manifestation.

The story is complicated. To record it fully requires scenes of different kinds and at different levels (including my own personal drama) to be laid out as in a play, complete with social process and inner meaning; because this event, which was the moment of healing of an African woman, was nested in a complex social milieu consisting of the overlapped contexts of both the Africans and myself. The healing was effected by taking out the tooth of a dead hunter from the sick woman's body. As we shall see the Ndembu ritual theme was "coming out," just that, a theme played over and over again. It was a theme that affected the entire style of the ritual. In keeping with this I will come out with the whole story. "Coming out," "laying out," "speaking out," "revealing"—such opening work was essential to the cure, and the same frankness had to include both myself (Edie) and my co-researcher Bill Blodgett, who were the anthropologists. Bill, an American, was about to finish his undergraduate degree majoring in anthropology and was later accepted in the graduate department of anthropology at the London School of Economics. The African doctors were Singleton Kahona and Fideli Benwa, and in fact, they have been named in the credits of authorship of this book since it is their material, their work of ritual, and their exegesis upon which the book is based. I myself was a widow of two years standing and a mother of five, who had studied and researched in anthropology in collaboration with her husband for thirty-seven years.

The ritual, the Ihamba tooth ritual of the Ndembu of Zambia, was recounted and analyzed by my husband Victor Turner in *The Drums of Affliction* (1968), using his and my field observations, photographs, and inquiries made from 1951 to 1954. The Ihamba affliction runs like this: The patient has been bitten by the tooth of a dead hunter, an object normally kept as an amulet helpful for hunting. When the tooth is neglected, so the Ndembu told us, it enters someone's body and travels along the veins, biting and inflicting a unique disease. This thing is both a spirit and a tooth, as the actions of the doctors attested. It is removed by means of cupping horns after a lengthy ritual. In 1985, thirty-one years after my 1951–54 fieldwork, I returned to the same area with Bill Blodgett and attended two more of these rituals. In the second one I participated instead of merely witnessing. At the climax of the second one, to my surprise, I saw with my own eyes a large afflicting substance, some six inches across, emerge from the body of the patient under the doctor's hands. It happened at the moment when the participation of the whole group became total. Because of my previous fieldwork in the 1950s, I shared with the participants much of their consciousness of the complexities and meaning of the ritual and of the social field in which it took place. Conversely, the older Ndembu present remembered my earlier participation and were relatively comfortable with my presence in their midst.[1]

In his 1968 book, Victor Turner wrote a long account and analysis of the Ihamba ritual, discussing its social context, the psychological state of the patient and the psychological skill of the Ndembu doctor, the social reintegration achieved by the lengthy curative process, and the symbols. When in 1985 I returned to the Ndembu to restudy them, the two rituals of Ihamba affected me personally in a way that they had not done before, culminating in the spirit experience; this event was unique for me and shed a new light on my research. It was then that I knew that my conclusions would have to be different from those of most African research.

How have anthropologists dealt with such material? The vast majority have not reported any experiences of their own in the way I am doing. In the history of anthropological work, the ethnography of ritual was usually presented as if it had been witnessed from the outside. Even in the case of Malinowski, certainly one of the most sympathetic fieldworkers, who used to watch the story of humanity in Melanesia unfold with fascination, it did not concern him whether or not the beliefs of the Trobrianders might be true, for he was interested in the way beliefs, kinship, and practical life all linked together coherently. This style, concerned with "the living integument," influenced Vic Turner's approach. Basically for Malinowski, survival, that is, practical life and its needs, were primary, and religion served that end. Safety at sea and agriculture were uncertain, so these were guarded by ritual. He was a functionalist.

Now, modern anthropologists have learned to regard the tales told by the fieldwork subjects about spirits and powers as greatly significant. They study the cultural forms surrounding such magical events—that is, symbols—and trace their hermeneutic paths, how each symbol expresses various social or mental structures and relates to certain social or psychological characteristics. In the spirit of genuine respect for the earth, they see ethnic cultures from the grass roots up, even from the standpoint of economic conditions such as capitalism or the situation of neocolonialism.

Anthropologists study the manifestations that the people they are studying feel to be spiritual in their *cultural* aspect, how they originated from those peoples' experiences of living on this earth. One writer exemplifies this and carries it almost to a breakthrough. Godfrey Lienhardt in *Divinity and Experience* (1961), writing on the Dinka people of the Sudan, came near to seeing eye to eye with his Dinka people when he described the process of *actual* divinity developing from the people's experience. He also gave a glimpse of how it was born—a glimpse not often found among many works on Africa, for they do not include that moment of birth, nor are they particularly concerned in its implications. Victor Turner briefly developed Lienhardt's thesis in a passage in *Blazing the Trail* (1992)—but he was never to follow it up.

Anthropologists in the past have sometimes argued that underprivileged people were prone to self-hypnosis owing to a deep need for psychological compensation, which induced hallucinations or made it easy for them to make false statements about strange events. Strange ritual effects were imagined, it was said, owing to a need for mystical reassurance, which in turn was created in the ritual by the focusing of symbols and meanings. When strange events did happen, as field subjects would sometimes give warning that they would, the anthropologist's reaction was often to stay quiet about them. The people themselves pointed to these events as significant, but most anthropologists did not take them in the same way. The fact that they themselves occasionally had something like the same experience did not seem to alter the case. But supposing the astronomers had failed to believe the evidence of their senses when they found Pluto. The reason they looked for such a planet in the first place was because their measurements of orbital deviation had pointed the way. They did in fact find it and were proud of their success. Some of us have had visual evidence of strange events, ones with which traditional peoples are more familiar than we. But we find it hard to accept their knowledge, nor do we like to use our own experience. Why is this? It is said to be embarrassing, I suppose, just as sex used to be embarrassing; in fact, just as there exist euphemisms for defecation and orgasm, there exist a number of euphemisms for the experiences I am talking about, such as my own term "strange event."

A "hierarchy of authority" has been argued by some in academia who believe that trained anthropologists supposedly understand aspects of a culture better than the field subjects, but nowadays many have problems with this notion. Which world of logic is the correct one, theirs or ours? We are gradually discovering that there are as many logics as there are cultures, and we are encouraged at least to dialogue with them, if not adopt their way of thought. Advances have been made in symbolic understanding. Numerous hermeneutic anthropologists have achieved beautiful work on the ritual of the people they studied as metaphor and poetry (see, for example, Alan Campbell 1989), since the patterns of ritual symbolism in many societies possess both esthetic and intellectual as well as symbolic depth. Occasionally, written work is produced actually using the field subjects' way of thought, as with Robin Ridington (1987–88).

At all events what I decided to do when I returned from my 1985 research was simply to describe what I saw, my own reactions, and the reactions of the others (as Bill and I saw and heard them) to the events they were bringing about, and also their reactions to my presence. It was clear that the events had their effect upon me—such anthropological events are full of echoes back and forth creating new situations as they progress. This effect has been called "reflexivity." Echoes, reflections, and transformations are surely the stuff of social process. The memory of a past that was richer in symbols was a major reflexive factor for the Ndembu of 1985, and that was enhanced by my bringing to them Victor Turner's books on their culture, so that they, the subjects of those books, could look at them. It was plain that looking at them moved them deeply.[2]

Therefore, in order to lead up to the climax, I have laid out both the dramatic scenes and also the exegetic and analytic material Bill Blodgett and I gathered on relationships, objects, and spatial layout—every possible aspect of the healing ritual, the gathering of which enabled me to get a sense of and document "orbital deviation," as I put it above, that is, my own way of measuring and locating a hidden object. This way of gathering and using material is how Victor Turner and I worked with notebook and camera among the Ndembu in 1951–54. Having given the context and exegesis, I will continue on through and recount the outcome of the second Ihamba of 1985, the "finding of Pluto," that is, the discovery of what the Africans' knowledge and my own studies were indicating, the existence of a spirit.

It can be seen that for such a thing to happen it was essential to be an actual participant, not just an actor going through the motions. On my return I found I was not willing to push what happened to one side as Evans-Pritchard did in connection with his experience of a spirit among the Azande (1937, 11), Peter Huber with his similar experiences in New Guinea (personal communication), and Ramanucci-Ross in Mexico (1979, 57–58, 60), though she did complain at having to do so. Laura Bohannon, though writing professionally on her research among the Tiv, saved her own experience of spirits for a "novel" with a deceptive title under a pseudonym (*Return to Laughter* by "Eleanor Bowen," 1954), and Larry Peters in Nepal, who underwent a classic shamanic experience, wrote a book giving a reductionist psychological explanation of the events (1981b). These are some notable examples, and there are others.

In the case presented in this book, it is not I but the Ndembu who need the defense, for it is their turn to have their voice heard. Although, of course, I only experienced what *I* experienced, it was nearer to the Ndembu's own idea of taking out a harmful object than anything I had come across before. Therefore, I was willing to make the tooth-spirit event central to my account, just as whatever it was the sick patient experienced was central to the Africans involved in the healing ritual.

Two Books on Ihamba: The Effect of Victor Turner's Study

Victor Turner's book on the original Ihamba ritual (*The Drums of Affliction*, 1968) has exerted an influence on anthropologists, psychologists, and students of religion. In this book, Turner exposed the social context of the Ihamba ritual of an Ndembu named Kamahasanyi and showed the political forces played out in the drama of events. Anthropologists found this exposition to be a key to the understanding of the dynamic sources of this ritual and to the interpretation of the sociology of healing rituals generally.

Psychologists were interested in the personality of the patient named Kamahasanyi, a man under stress, and appreciated the African doctor's skill in resolving the sick man's conflict, albeit by means of what seemed to be sleight of hand. Religion scholars saw the confession of grudges (an indispensable condition of cure in Ihamba) as a cleansing of the spiritual community.

Since certain contradictions exist between Vic Turner's writing on Ihamba and his other work on the Ndembu, the reader will need to know how his Ihamba book came about. In 1951–52 and 1953–54, he and I lived among the Ndembu with our three young children. When we began fieldwork in Zambia, then known as Northern Rhodesia, we expected to be occupied with the social and political structures of the Ndembu, for we had been trained in the structural-functionalist school of British social anthropology.

The Ndembu were part of the matrilineal Lunda group of northwestern Zambia, on the upland watershed of the Zambezi and Congo rivers. Vic and I found the Ndembu to be a turbulent, highly conscious community, continually performing ritual. As we lived among them, we began to doubt the dominant paradigm of the structural functionalism we had learned. We began to see that it had limitations. It did not seem the right instrument for evaluating the negotiations, conflicts, rites of redress, transitions, and initiations in Ndembu life—all *processes* that changed social structure or resulted in social structure, and thus it was process that appeared to be primary—structure becoming secondary. We began to steer away from structure to processual anthropology, encouraged by the example of Max Gluckman's work on the judicial process among the Barotse.

Our ritual-laden environment changed us further, and we took the step of changing our focus to ritual and rites of passage. We became rather hooked on ritual. The seeds of our future view of it were planted but had not yet grown. Soon we were to see the inadequacies of the functionalist explanation, which holds that ritual is basically designed as some kind of all-purpose social glue for mending broken social relationships. Vic was already arguing that ritual did not merely preserve and reflect social structural laws, it often broke them. For a time, ritual created an antistructure, a temporary liminal world of reversals that was oddly satisfying, something different from the everyday laws of social custom and political strategies, a special phase in which "sacra" were revealed, that is, sacred objects that were keys to the religion.

Vic handled Ihamba differently. It seemed as though this ritual had an impossible claim—that a tooth should wander in anybody's veins. He and I never saw any Ndembu spirits in our fieldwork during the 1950s, and the only explanation we could find for a ritual like Ihamba was a social-psychological one. Vic went ahead on these lines and patiently related the Ndembu's reports of their Ihamba experiences to social process. He had also become interested in Freud, and he delighted to fathom the depths of African symbols that seemed to echo the concepts of psychoanalysis. These he described in the case study of the illness of Kamahasanyi and his treatment in several Ihamba rituals. "His symptoms are partly self-punishment, but they are also an expression of his concealed aggression against others" (1968, 182).

The Ihamba rituals, like those of the 1980s, consisted of long sessions at the end of which the doctor drew out the harmful tooth from the back of the sufferer—a tooth that had come from the skull of a dead hunter. Vic documented the main ritual in a blow-by-blow account in *The Drums of Affliction,* naming and explaining all the medicines and symbols employed. Owing to his reading of Freud, he discovered in the ritual symbols the dynamism residing in their "polarization": the orectic, or sensory, pole (the savagery of a tooth) energizing the ideological pole (piety toward the dead). He described the complex multivalence of the symbol of the Ihamba pole shrine (1968, 183–85) using Edward Sapir's concepts of condensation and multivalence. In the narrative of the event, he struck a social-psychological note, telling how the doctor sensitively "felt after the points of stress and strain in the social field he had been invited to operate in" (1976, 47). (Such stresses and strains of varying kinds still occur among the Ndembu today in the context of an Ihamba ritual.) Turner took the reader through:

> the therapeutic process itself, its ups and downs, the symbolic substances used, the ways in which Ihembi [the doctor] built up and released tension, and how finally he produced the ihamba tooth itself from a medicine pot in which he had been washing the blood-filled cupping horns his assistants had been applying to Kamahasanyi's body to suck out the elusive biter and gnawer. . . . Ihembi succeeded in building up a climax, so that when after many hours of drumming, washing, cupping, etc., he finally produced the tooth, relief in the village was so great that normally hostile individuals warmly exchanged handshakes, while everyone smiled and indicated extreme relief. (1976, 47–48)

In my narrative below, a difference of emphasis will be noted, for I saw and also heard in the tape replays how the doctor of 1985 *listened* to and addressed the spirit in the patient's body, and found in the condition of the spirit and in *its* relationship to the social body the reason for delay and finally the occasion of climax.

After I returned from the 1985 field trip, I started working on comparative healing systems. I discovered a book belonging to the burgeoning nonacademic movement interested in healing that started to develop in the 1980s. It contained a criticism of Victor Turner by Richard Grossinger (1980, 46–47), who takes up Vic's remarks in an earlier work on healing, *Lunda Medicine and the Treatment of Disease* (1964, 61–62):

> There is a tendency to define tribal medicine, on the supposed evidence of firsthand viewing, as primitive first aid mixed with magic. . . . Victor Turner's writings on African religion, especially of the Ndembu Lunda of Zambia, are much admired in liberal academic circles. He is considered one of the more sympathetic observers. Generally, he is, but not in matters of medicine, i.e., of practical science. He concludes that "medicine is given to humor rather than to cure" and that "a rich and elaborate system of ritual and magical beliefs and practices provides a set of explanations for sickness and death and gives people a false sense of confidence that they have the means of coping with disease." Why do such beliefs persist? he wonders. And his answer is that "they are part of a religious system which itself constitutes an explanation of the universe and guarantees the norms and values on which orderly social arrangements rest." In other words, they are stuck with their medicine because they are stuck with the symbols which back it up and which their survival has come to require. The author goes on to prescribe a big dose of Western medicine and an extension of Western-type hospital facilities.
>
> So much for African medicine. There's nothing happening but hocus-pocus, delusion, and placebo. And this from a person who knows more about the subject than the author of this book and 99.9 per cent of his readers. Knowledge, it appears, doesn't make the difference.

This criticism was disturbing. Vic had indeed treated Ihamba as a ritual of psychology, not religion, performed under the aegis of an African traditional doctor extremely skilled in social psychology. Vic regarded the symbolism of Ihamba as a mixture of moving poetry and undoubted hocus-pocus.

What is curious is that Turner had already written a much more "emic," truly sympathetic account of another Ndembu ritual, Chihamba (1962). It was well after this that he turned once more to the sociological and psychoanalytic explanations he used in *The Drums of Affliction* (1968). (He did not stay long in that mood either.)

In *Chihamba, the White Spirit: A Ritual Drama of the Ndembu,* he had already begun to relate Ndembu ritual experience to the general characteristics of religion itself. In his description of the Chihamba ritual, a cult ritual differing from Ihamba and centering on the demigod of the thunder, he compared its ritual symbols to those of his own new religion of conversion, Catholicism. It is interesting to note that he identified the demigod Kavula with the "Act-of-Being" itself (1975a, 179–80, first published 1962), using relevant concepts of Etienne Gilson in his writings on Thomas Aquinas. Turner showed how in matters concerning spirits it is hard to speak directly: one finds oneself in a nonverbal world. The Ndembu, like the Jews, never *named* their god. Vic compared the whiteness of the Chihamba spirit with the unearthly whiteness of Moby Dick, Melville's whale, and with the whiteness of the resurrection angels in Christianity, whiteness seen as the absence of color, as dumbness is the lack of speech. On page 187 he put it this way: the Ndembu ritual of Chihamba "is the local expression of a universal human problem, that of expressing what cannot be thought of, in view of thought's subjugation to essences." He argued:

> A strictly sociological explanation of the white symbolism we have been discussing would appear to be inadequate. One has to consider religious phenomena in terms of religious ideas and doctrines, not only, or principally, in terms of disciplines that have arisen in connection with the study of secular institutions and processes. White symbolism is but one genus of religious symbolism, which gives us actual clues to the nature of realities we cannot perceive by means of the senses alone. It is not a question of setting the intellect to work at reducing the religious symbol to sensory terms. Our task is rather, like T. H. Huxley's in quite a different context, to sit down before the facts as a little child, be prepared to give up every preconceived notion, follow humbly wherever and to whatever abysses nature leads, or we will learn nothing. . . . That is why the attempts of such scholars and philosophers as James Frazer and Durkheim to explain away religious phenomena in naturalistic terms have been so obviously unsuccessful. . . . We must go to school with the Ndembu. (pp. 195–96)

It is obvious that this kind of thought did not enter Vic's later interpretation of the Ihamba tooth ritual. Vic oscillated all the time from one philosophical position to another using psychology, social drama, and religion in an incessant dialogue.

I had many viewpoints in my own epistemological background too. When I decided to return to the Ndembu in 1985, I did not plan to do a Chihamba-type reanalysis on what I saw but intended to go deeper into the impact of ritual on the people generally, especially the initiation of adolescent girls (see E. Turner 1987b). (Initiation was also the main concern in my

Wenner-Gren grant proposal.) When Ihamba was offered, I seized the opportunity to find out how the ritual had fared during the disturbed history of the intervening thirty-one years. I remembered the tooth ritual. Ihamba would be a hard nut to crack. Should the purely psychological explanation hold? This was no profound "Act-of-Being" ritual; it smacked of mumbo jumbo. A tooth wandering in the veins?

I was going to have to pay careful attention. The ideas about liminality and *communitas,* warm fellow feeling, that Vic and I had so often discussed were relevant. I was not unaware of the at-oneness that had occurred at the end of the Ihamba in 1953, as described in *The Drums of Affliction* "a spontaneous outburst of friendly feeling" (p. 173).

It should be noted that, for some time before my 1985 fieldwork among the Ndembu, I had been working with Vic Turner on the anthropology of performance. We and our colleagues and students performed Ndembu rituals, especially the girl's initiation rite, and usually found that they "worked," that is, the student being initiated did become more mature. It was beyond me to explain why. Certain puzzles were pushing at my mind. In November 1983, I joined in a session conducted by Roy Wagner enacting the Jivaro shaman journey. Furthermore, after Vic died, I wrote (1993) on a Jewish miracle shrine I had visited and on the Jewish mystical tradition exemplified by the Baal Shem Tov—wondering how the "peak experiences" in that history came about. Finally, in 1984 as I worked on my old manuscript on the Ndembu fieldwork of the 1950s, entitled *The Spirit and the Drum* (1987), it occurred to me to go back to the Ndembu and see if I could find out more about how their rituals worked, to put my finger on the process, as it were. So I went.

After my return at the beginning of 1986, having seen the surprising result of my attention, I was free to ponder anew certain features of anthropological theory and found that these features appeared to vindicate my venture into personal participation and merited further exploration. They were found in the works (among others) of Lévy-Bruhl, Lévi-Strauss, and again, Victor Turner.

Theorists of Ritual

Lévy-Bruhl's *How Natives Think* (1985, first published in 1910) was for me the most important of the early school; I now saw that his "law of participation," the discovery of the ambience of mystical meaning that surrounded the senses of "primitives," went beyond partial categories such as "sympathetic magic" and "contagious magic" and included all senses and meaning in one world of ancient tradition in which everything had a "soul" and humankind was bathed in it while life lasted. Healing was effected in relation to that sense of "participation mystique." Lévy-Bruhl was a master theorist of what we might call total perception. He termed that primitive mentality "prelogical." It didn't have much to do with logic, but it made sense to itself, as most anthropologists now see. Like other anthropologists, sometimes Lévy-Bruhl seems to have been seduced into believing in that world. At first, he constantly used the term "collective representations," a term he employed in keeping with the conceptual framework of the French Année Sociologique school of anthropology. According to these theorists, the mentality of "primitives" was ruled by symbols, "collective representations," which became impressed by force of custom into the likeness of reality, bearing some of the awe pertaining to society's ancient authority and resulting in real effects, but which were themselves, nonetheless, unreal. However, Lévy-Bruhl later discarded the term "representations." In his characteristically cautious way he circled around his subject, then plunged in:

> In aggregates of the type furthest removed from our own, the collective representations which express the mentality of the group are not always, strictly speaking, representations. What we are accustomed to understand by representation, even direct and intuitive, implies duality in unity. The object is presented to the subject as in a certain sense distinct from himself; except in states such as ecstasy, that is, border states in which representation, properly so called, disappears, since the fusion between subject and object has become complete. Now in analysing the most characteristic of the primitive's institutions—such as totemic relationship, the *intichiuma* and initiation ceremonies, etc.—we have found that his mind does more than present his object to him: it possesses it and is possessed by it. It communes with it and participates in it, not only in the ideological, but also in the physical and mystical sense of the word. *The mind does not imagine it merely: it lives it* [my italics]. In a great many cases the rites and ceremonies have the effect of giving reality to a veritable symbiosis, that between the totemic group and its totem, for instance. At this stage, therefore, rather than speak of collective representations, it would be wiser to call them collective mental states of extreme emotional intensity in which representation is as yet undifferentiated from the movements and actions which make the communion towards which it tends a reality to the group. Their participation in it is so effectually *lived* [italics in original] that it is not yet properly imagined. (Lévy-Bruhl 1985 [1910], 362)

Lévy-Bruhl's slight qualifiers, such as "not yet," imply the evolutionist idea that natives are not as advanced as we civilized people. Yet he is clearly deeply involved—also for instance, in the Huichols' holistic vision of the unity and mystical participation of peyote, corn, and plumes (p. 125). His book seems to corroborate neurobiological ideas about left and right brain thinking:

> Ideas and relations between ideas governed by the law of participation are far from having disappeared. They exist, more or less independently, more or less impaired, but yet ineradicable, side by side with those subject to the laws of reasoning. (p. 386)

These contrasting faculties are now believed to exist side by side in the two hemispheres of the neocortex. Lévy-Bruhl cleared the way for those anthropologists who have experienced trance or sorcery, such as Michael Harner (1968, 28–33, 60–61), Larry Peters (1981a, 37–54), and Paul Stoller (1984), and also possibly for the kind of ethnography and theory that might one day succeed in coming close to what indigenous field consultants would accept as true. We may even have to begin to regard the field subjects' criterion of truth as a fundamental one.

Then I found that Lévi-Strauss himself, questionably self-styled a structuralist, had by means of his rather questionable words, "myth" and "symbol," often managed to bridge the gulf that separates us from the world of primitive knowledge.

Lévi-Strauss's structuralism did serve to grant some kind of logic to peoples whom Lévy-Bruhl considered had none, terming them "pre-logical." Lévy-Bruhl had committed a solecism by claiming that they had "not yet" learned the principle of noncontradiction. But Lévi-Strauss broke through this arbitrary limit set on their minds, by means of his famous analyses of kinship and marriage rules, dual organization, and regularly varying forms in myth, claiming structural logic for a widely misunderstood sector of humanity. However, today we see Lévi-Strauss stuck with that one logic, basically, the logic of binary discrimination. He was a "cognitive absolutist," as Littleton put it in his introduction to the new translation of *How Natives Think;* that is, Lévi-Strauss was

> fundamentally committed to a *single,* all-pervasive model of how the human mind works, while the author of *How Natives Think,* like most contemporary anthropologists, was committed to the proposition that there are multiple (or at least two) modes when it comes to the ways our minds work. (1985, xxxvi)

Yet Lévi-Strauss himself, when dealing with shamanism, also oscillates between the two levels of reality. In "The Effectiveness of Symbols" (1963, 186–205), which is the analysis of an eighteen-page transcription of the incantation at a Cuna medicine ceremony, one can trace the two levels of consciousness. His word "structure" originally connoted the deep laws of binary discrimination, but in this essay it describes something nearer to the shaman's world. Lévi-Strauss refers to the powerful curing effect of what he here calls outright the shaman's "other order of reality" (p. 200)—a concept he usually terms "myth." (In using "myth" he is simply using word *X* for thing *Y*.) However, the word "myth" is a stumbling block because educated persons are not supposed to regard myth as real. Also in common parlance it means "a lie." In "The Effectiveness of Symbols" Lévi-Strauss seems to be taking that slender bridge to the shaman's own realm, even though he is not a member of the shaman's culture. For, as Lévi-Strauss seems to have established, his "other level of reality"—what he also calls myth—belongs to all.

The bridging of the two levels of consciousness is clear in this passage, in which I substitute "the other order of reality" for "myth":

> [The situation of healing] sets off a series of events of which the body and internal organs of the sick woman will be the assumed setting. A transition will thus be made from the most prosaic reality to [the other order of reality], from the physical universe to the physiological universe, from the external world to the internal body. And the [other reality] being enacted in the internal body must retain throughout the vividness and the character of lived experience prescribed by the shaman in the light of the pathological state and through an appropriate [ritualizing] technique.
>
> The next ten pages offer, in breathless rhythm, a more and more rapid oscillation between the themes of [the other reality] and physiological themes, as if to abolish in the mind of the sick woman the distinction which separates them. (1963, 193)

From this viewpoint we can see that Lévi-Strauss is quite aware of the oscillation from one side to the other that is taking place in the shaman's therapeutic chant, and one can intuit that he truly understands his "other reality"—and what is interesting, that he understands it in the sense that this slightly changed passage highlights.

It is said that Lévi-Strauss does not regard ritual highly, but "The Effectiveness of Symbols" belies this notion. Anthropological field material has provided many detailed accounts of dramas of healing and the effects of the spirits in action—and it is in action that the spirits come alive. They originally exist in the experience of Lévi-Strauss's "other order of reality." Victor Turner began developing his concept of ritual as process. The ritual process, usually containing some revelation of communitas and the world of the spirits, is the key to the locked door of structure. Lévi-Strauss was troubled by the triviality of particular occasions of ritual. He yearned toward general forms, away from the particular, toward the discovery of the structural rules of the symbolic system in question, or of narrative or of social order, whose *"form* takes precedence over the *content,"* as he said (1963, 204). It is true that mental structures may become numinous. Religious texts are often considered to be holy, but not merely because of logical forms based on some philosophical, sociological, or political impact that they possess but because of something that releases them from these. However, we are not dealing here with a written text or spoken myth. We are dealing with matters beyond language, born in the world of antistructure and liminality, a world of which the processes of *ritual* are the language.

As for Victor Turner, he taught that process was the basic condition of life, and this is how he became interested in liminality. He was first preoccupied with the exigencies of the human potential in the multitudinous circumstances in which different cultures operated. A major universal was adolescence, for which many cultures have developed rites of passage, rites that came to be expressed as a doorway (a limen) into a strange world of sacred objects, monsters, ludic or humorous recombination, status reversal, and communitas. These particularities, said Turner, could not be reduced to laws, they flowered in the realm of antistructure, a realm that seems to be an analogue of the "other reality" of the shamanistic curing rituals. He recognized the "synthesizing and focusing capacity of ritual symbolism" (1968, 185). The chishinga shrine, examples of which appear in the account of the Ihamba rituals below,

> is regarded by Ndembu not so much as an object of cognition, a mere set of referents to known phenomena, but rather as a unitary power, conflating all the powers inherent in the activities, objects, relationships, and ideas it represents. What Ndembu see in a chishing'a, made visible for them in its forked and awe-inspiring nakedness, is the slaughterous power of Wubinda [ritualized huntsmanship] itself. (1968, 185)

Symbols are thus more than ritual markers or statements about the ritual world but rather effectors, triggers of the set-aside condition (*chakumbadyi* as the Ndembu called it, from *mbadyi,* "side"), or openers through the *chipangu,* literally a "hedge" that encloses a secret. The set-aside condition creates around itself liminal hedges or protectors; from the point of view of practitioners, that set-aside condition is of ultimate concern.

Turner's interest in the set-aside, which he called "liminality," was fueled by his own experience of it, as a poet and a pacifist and, later, in the circumcision camps of the Ndembu where the novices were taken for their initiation.

Although Turner used psychology in *The Drums of Affliction,* that did not make him a structuralist. When documenting Ihamba his emphasis was on the social, on process, on performance. He headed his chapters on Ihamba in *The Drums of Affliction* "Field Context and Social Drama," "The Social Setting of the Ritual Sequence," and "A Performance of Ihamba Analyzed"—this was clearly a social and symbolic analysis. His attention to the *process* of ritual was minute. He regarded myth as static and bypassed and tended to ignore Lévi-Strauss. He understood what it was the Ndembu were trying to reach, "the hidden animosities of the village" (1968, 172) and showed the Ndembu doctors at their work in *The Drums of Affliction.* The result was not a static text but the record of an activity field, the record of social process, not custom, containing a detailed and seamlessly integrated portrayal of the living social and symbolic forces playing in the field of ritual. In addition to the percipient analysis, the field material itself was extraordinarily useful during my later restudy of the ritual in 1985, when the knowledge stored in the book stood me in good stead. For instance, Vic painted a word portrait of the Ihamba doctor Ihembi, which I discovered to my surprise was very similar to the temperament of my new consultant and doctor, Singleton Kahona.[3]

And coming to the present book, it is intended as a continuation of the investigation into Ihamba, a further delving into the puzzle of the tooth itself and an attempt to face the issue of the "spirit object."[4]

The Groundings of the Present Ethnographic Method

In its tone and style this book is part of the movement to bring the presence of the anthropologist into the ethnographic account. It is now recognized that "more and more person-centered ethnographies, concerned with subjective experience, are being written" (Shweder 1989, 19). Here it should be noted that I do not claim a sophisticated method or style in the fashion of the extreme postmodernists nor the stance of critical anthropology that highlights political power pressures, neocolonialism, and the like. It seems that there is power emanating from Western intellectuals that interprets the traditional religion of fieldwork subjects as an oppression to them, a wasteful substitute for real action, or at best a metaphor for resistance (which, of course, it is as well as what it is actually all about). Is there a kind of critical anthropology that is concerned to curb this sort of power, a hands-off-the-people's-culture-movement? This might be something more than the cultural survival movement, more of a trust-the-people ethic. There are growing signs of it. We might yet grant traditional peoples credit for their own kind of religion instead of translating it away.

My method is fairly simple: along with many modern ethnographers I employ in the narrative section of this book a more intimate style than in older anthropological writing. The style also derives from the kind of technology Bill Blodgett and I brought to the field in 1985—particularly Bill's tape recorder and his skill and tact in operating it. The recorder became a lucid channel through which many minds made their mark, with much spontaneity. My whole account took its color from this spontaneity. I found that the consciousness of my own emotional situation in Mukanza Village was the same kind of consciousness with which I might be able to understand Nyakanjata and Meru, the two main patients in the sickness cults, and also to understand the doctors. Indeed my own consciousness sometimes seemed to be on the same continuum as their own consciousness. After all, we were often present together and interacted a great deal. I therefore needed to retain the narrative style, showing where I myself became most deeply involved and why, for these delicate networks of interrelationships can indeed be delineated. Thus a fuller perspective of the Ndembu themselves could emerge with a truer view of the ebb and flow of the social consciousness.[5]

In the account the "field context" and "social setting" required clarification as the story unfolded; I needed to backtrack sometimes and draw in further elements to conjure up the environment, both social and geographic. The writing is allowed to echo the character of fieldwork—episodic, in the grip of events, not having achieved wisdom until it was achieved. My theoretical underpinnings can be seen here and there in the web of the narrative. I remember chapter 12 in *On the Edge of the Bush* (Turner 1985): "the problems are not resolved, as in cold blood, at the cognitive left-hemispheric level, but directly in that nonverbal noetic mode known as 'ritual knowledge'" (p. 289).

Thus when we untangle the strands of theory and the methodological form of this book, the following emerge: In the writing, I aim as I have said to reveal social context as it matures in the narrative, layer after layer. This could be called Victor Turner's "social drama" method (1957), or more generally the "recursive process," as described by Kevin Dwyer (1982, 281). In the present book, conflict analysis is combined with ritual analysis, in keeping with Vic Turner's method in the social drama entitled "The Expulsion and Return of Sandombu" at the death of Nyamwaha, where conflict was resolved by means of a tear tree ritual (Turner 1957, 116–120).

A further strand I note in the rites is how in the hands of a skilled ritualist the ritual's needs make *themselves* known, the source of selection being the ritual itself. That is, the ritual builds the symbols and not vice versa.

It will also be seen how there is a difference between (1) representational symbols, (2) spirit triggers to actuate the climax of the ritual—sometimes as a series of jolts, and (3) sacramental objects that *are* the numinous—they *are* the spirit, and do not stand for it. Such an object is the tooth that afflicts the Ndembu sufferer. (It is unfortunate that the word "symbol" so strongly connotes "representation.")

Further, we see not only how the genres that ritual employs are multiplex as regard to the five senses but also how ritual requires its particular range of traditional elements to be linked in special combination in order to be effective. In the case of Ihamba, all the following elements were indispensable: the patient, the doctor, medicines, tutelary spirits, participants, the particular social state of the community, singing, drumming, dancing, "words" or deep outbreaks of grievances, divinatory propositions (questions put to the spirit), shrine, spirit-objects, ritual paraphernalia, and ritual performance itself with its impeded form and delayed climax. It would be impossible to discriminate between any of these for primacy over the outcome. Ihamba was a multigenre ritual. My aim in what follows is to raise a sense of these genres on paper, in two dimensions, an enterprise that will only succeed if the reader lets his or her mind retranslate the limited medium back into the multiplex one.

1. The Field Context of the Ihamba Rituals in 1985

Time Factor: History Continues Separately for Ndembu and Turners

After Vic Turner and I left the field in 1954, a gap of thirty-one years elapsed before I was to see the Ndembu again. Much history on all levels overtook the Ndembu and also myself during the interval. The events altered both sides, gradually and inexorably. Signs of the differences emerged in the new field material and in the way I took the field experience; it is all the more necessary to contextualize the rituals in the milieu created by the personalities involved and, even more importantly, in the historical context. When I was back among the Ndembu in 1985, both they and I were again coevals, as Fabian put it (1983, 31), that is, we actively shared the same time.

When Vic and I finished our fieldwork in 1954, we returned to England, not without many pangs of nostalgia for the old village. I wrote a narrative about my part in the fieldwork and put the manuscript away in a drawer. The children grew up. Our progressive ideas about politics and Marxism changed as the "people's struggle" of the Marxist countries seemed to become more and more structured. Vic and I became Catholics, using some of the Catholic teaching to understand symbolism. We developed our own framework for analyzing symbols, and thereafter, Vic's work began to get known. In 1964 we emigrated to America, the same year that Zambia won independence from the British; the latter was an outcome for which we had always hoped. Vic and I, at the very juncture of our own change of country, were suddenly able to write down what real comradeship was—the comradeship of liminality, communitas, the direct sense of "I-thou," more a treasure of the people than the communists ever realized. Communitas was religion, and religion was communitas: this led us on, as we shall see.

Our work became intensive. We began to pursue research on pilgrimage systems, which we identified as authentic manifestations of ritual in Western societies. Meanwhile in newly independent Zambia, copper prices were high, and the country was booming. In Mukanza Village, our old field base, our erstwhile translator Windson Kashinakaji found himself in the wrong political party and narrowly escaped a violent attack. Kasonda, our assistant, who comes into this story, was in the clear politically—a state of things that represented a difference between Kasonda and the lineage of Kashinakaji that we could see developing in the form of jealousy, even in the 1950s. The Ndembu would often tell us very seriously "We Ndembu are a very jealous people."

In the period of the boom in copper, Zambia's main industry, Zambian self-respect at last had a chance; a fine socialist constitution was created with schooling for all, excellent medical facilities, a small but thriving nationalized factory system, and a nationalized distributive industry. The Christian values of fairness, justice, and love for all humankind were promulgated. The era became a heroic, even utopian, one in which the United National Independence Party, government administrators, and all the people built a fine working system. Our district of Mwinilunga even boasted a large well-equipped agricultural station and a pineapple canning factory, preserving what are surely the finest pineapples in the world.

Soon the population of Zambia doubled and even tripled in some districts including our own. The infant mortality rate dropped from 250 to 140 per thousand, and an era of ten- or twelve-children families set in. Such a population boom does not end in the natural way of things until after a generation, according to demographers, so that on my return in 1985, twenty years after the copper boom, I found my genealogies noticeably increasing in size as I compiled them.

But in the mid-1970s, copper prices crashed all over the world, causing ruin to the Zambian economy. This happened to be the time when Vic and I were turning to the study of performance and putting to one side the study of ritual. We traveled extensively but not to Africa. Nevertheless, history went on there, a disturbing history. What, one wonders, is the value of anthropologists' work when world economic forces overtake the little local area one remembers, a world of "micropolitics," as Vic called it in the paper that analyzed headmen's quarrels over circumcision roles (1985, 43–52)? A threat of greater tragedy makes the small Greek-like tragedies of virilocal marriage versus matrilineal descent seem insignificant.

Let us look more fully at the story of Zambia and the Ndembu up until the 1980s.

In the era of our first fieldwork, missionary influence was slight, claiming converts among only 5 percent of the population. At that time, the Ndembu still retained a complex ritual system including full-scale initiations, a wide repertoire of healing rituals, an elaborate pharmacopeia of herbal medicines, and many categories of spirits. The high forest easily supported the scattered population, which lived in temporary pole and mud huts they rebuilt in fresh forest areas every five years, thus managing to rest the soil in a rotation cycle of cassava growing from about 14 to 26 years. This system had been working for centuries in a self-renewing way. As we knew, the Ndembu were under the absolute rule of the British colonial government, headed locally by an English District Commissioner and implemented by the traditional chiefs under a cunning system of "indirect rule." Medical facilities were exiguous, and the infant mortality rate stood at 250 per thousand. But the people had enough to eat, at least in the way of a staple crop, and their indigenous agricultural practices were not exhausting the soil as present practices are exhausting it. One may ask if it was the almost total neglect of the system by the British that in fact enabled the system to continue much as it had done for thousands of years, thus keeping the ecological balance. However, what the British bequeathed to the Zambians before they left was their "civilized" value system so that in both urban and rural milieux an overriding desire for Westernization took hold of the people. There is an ominous side to this trend, for the territory consists of an important sector of the world's forestland on whose vegetation the earth depends for its oxygen.

The legacy of the British worked itself out. The new independent Zambia fell into the capitalist trap awaiting a country that had to rely on a single main industry. It suffered the fate that overtook many third-world nations supplying raw materials to the first—that of collapsed prices resulting in economic disaster. In Zambia what happened was partial layoffs in the copper mines and the closing of many of the factories that produced consumer goods, while on the farming front there were insufficient funds for fertilizers with which to replenish the depleted arable soil to supply the cities with food. Thus a further effect of the copper crash was uncontrolled deforestation to clear fresh fields and the misuse of the soil by farmers in an effort to wrest from their land any crops they could. It is hard to envisage the contrast between the bad times of 1985 and the good ones after independence in 1964 when the plans of the new nation had first gotten under way.

In 1985 the birthrate remained enormously high yet food was scarce. As soon as I arrived in 1985, my services to sick children with tetracycline and acetaminophen were very much in demand. I helped children to survive, while at the same time, out in the scrubby fields, the last trees were being felled for that extra scrap of land and fuel. People were hungry. This was the bitter social milieu into which the Ndembu were plunged and in which Bill and I temporarily found ourselves. Neither we nor any of the experts we later consulted could find an answer to the problem. Without funds, no plan however praiseworthy could be implemented.

By 1985 the old ritual system had also suffered change. Initiations had come under strong attack from the missions and government schools and were severely reduced. Nevertheless, they persisted in an underlevel of the community, manifesting themselves at initiation time in drunken dance-fests characterized by popular songs whose subject matter consisted of ironic commentary on sex, crime, prostitution, disease, and death. The songs were belted out with relish, along with skillful harmonizing and counterpoint to the sound of drums. It was at this level too that healing rituals were increasing despite the fact that the assisting ancestor spirits had been branded as demons by the missionaries (who were wondering why the young no longer respected authority). In adaptation to this interdict, some traditional healers redirected their prayers to Nzambi, God, who was formerly a distant creator figure, otiose and rarely in touch with humanity. What was now happening was a change in the watershed of good and evil: the ancestors now were all "evil"; many of the healers had moved up under the umbrella of Nzambi and added prayers to him during their proceedings. There was an increase of witch and ghost affliction, and the use of leaf medicine continued with an additional knowledge of its effect. Personal helper spirits of the patients themselves were now unknown. It was only healers who could claim tutelary helper spirits, and these spirits might form a chain in the healer's genealogy in a kind of apostolic succession.

It seemed that everywhere in Africa indigenous doctors had been improving their techniques during these years, gauging well which cases would respond to African treatment and which would not, and were curing a greater proportion than formerly. Perhaps owing to lack of laws and control, there was a chance for these skilled people to experiment, develop, become more sure in their spirit work. We are able to trace over the continent of Africa a varied patchwork of cults of affliction by spirits (see Appendixes 1 to 6). There is a tendency for certain characteristics to repeat throughout the continent: washing with herbal decoctions; drum and song performance, often dance; community concern in the case or actual participation in the ritual; tutelary spirits who help and guide the doctors; and the idea of witchcraft or ghosts as causes of affliction. The variability in style of healing has gone on ramifying. Healers are becoming more individualistic, not less, and their numbers are increasing (see Appendixes 1 and 9).

Partly because of the high value set on everything originating from the West, Christianity in Mwinilunga grew to reach a figure of 40 percent. The beginning of class distinction based on religion could be observed around Mukanza Village, with the Christian class bemoaning the backwardness of the sinners, who were generally poorer than they and often their distant relatives. These people were considered as "lost" because they did not come to church. In Christian eyes they were drunkards, fornicators, thieves, and witches, and that was the reason they were poor.

The first missionaries had been old-style fundamentalists of the Plymouth Brethren sect, originating in England. Their mission organization was called the Christian Mission to Many Lands. During the thirty-one years' interval between my field trips, a breakaway group known as the Christian Fellowship had become the most popular church in the area, now with a black preacher and a beautiful form of hymn-singing; there was some sense that a hopeless character could find help from alcoholism within its walls, for the members made an attempt to provide warmth and support for each other. A few years prior to our visit miracles of healing were performed in this church, and joyful scenes of speaking with tongues took place. By 1985 the church had been advised by its central organization that these activities were unseemly (see also Haar 1987, 475–93, and Milingo 1984 for a similar interdict upon the healing activities of the Catholic Archbishop Milingo of Lusaka in 1982). The Christian Fellowship had clearly had time to become structured, after an inspired beginning when the congregation ventured into a faith that preached the powers of the weak. For many Ndembu, the great world religions were exotic and gave contact with some kind of world communitas as well as a promise of protection from witchcraft.

The Mwinilunga Christian Fellowship, unbeknown to me when I planned my return to Mukanza Village, had attracted into its fold Kasonda, our previous interpreter, cook, and friend. His three wives and almost his entire surviving family of twelve children, fifty-five grandchildren, and five great-grandchildren had also joined the Christian Fellowship. Thus both Kasondas and Turners had become Christians, but of different denominations. Kasonda was now the headman of Mukanza Village and was known as Mwanta ("Master") Mukanza. He had succeeded the old headman Mukanza by an election of twenty-two votes to one, so he told me, the one vote being that of the sorcerer Sandombu, who voted for himself. Master Mukanza was now a noted judge in the area and head of the school board.

In 1983, back in the United States, Vic died of a heart attack. I needed to work and so turned to my old manuscript on Africa, my *tale* of what happened, and prepared it for publication. This not only jogged my intellectual appetite, but I began to want to hear that singing again, to stroke the soft hair of the babies. All my children were gone from home and lived hundreds of miles away. It seemed a great idea to do a restudy of the Ndembu. I seriously wanted to get back to ritual and religion, to get closer to the emotional roots of the people, to sense them and perhaps at last to describe them for what they were. I was fit and decided to go; a friend supplied me with her son as helper—greater love hath no woman than this, for he seemed to become a fifth son of my own, although I didn't look after him very well. Bill worked and starved alongside of me, ending the trip with a horrendous attack of malaria and trichinosis.

I had read a good deal about the changes in Zambia before embarking on the fieldwork, and I knew that initiations had gone downhill, and heard of the nationalization of the distributive industry. But for some reason the growth of Christianity had not come home to me. It never occurred to me that Kasonda might have converted, so I arranged to go back to Mukanza Village hoping to continue to learn rituals from him much as I had done before.

Returning to Mukanza Village

What did I find when I returned to Mukanza Village after an absence of thirty-one years? Bill Blodgett and I were riding in the municipal truck from Mwinilunga Township down a reddish dirt road, very familiar to me—but wider than before with almost continuous bare deforested land on either side. I tried not to look at that. "Here's the turn-off," I said, and we swerved to the right, then to the left. In a dizzy flash we were there, but the village was sparse now, there was no ring of fifteen huts, simply four brick huts behind trees and a large brick thatched house, which I did not look at. I had eyes only for the traditional meeting shelter which had meant so much before. It was surely in exactly the same position. Kasonda struggled out from under the low thatch as we approached. He was an old man now, with sunken cheeks and high cheekbones, and he was terrifyingly aged. I had to realize that this was just ordinary old age. At once we were shaking hands, my arm on his shoulder—I was moved to see him, my old friend Kasonda again. So he had survived in this somehow disunited village where there were few elders to gather and make greetings. Swarms of children gravitated to the spot. Kasonda seated me in the shelter, and children gathered at my feet, immediately charming me and drawing out my forgotten words of Chindembu. Mika, Kasonda's second wife, approached—I did not recognize her at all. They led us to the hut they had prepared for us, along a path and beside a shady tree. There they sat us down on dining chairs carried from the brick house, and old Mangaleshi, Kasonda's senior wife, came forward with an enormous rooster which she gravely presented to me.

I remembered how they valued those large breeding roosters, so important in the struggle to improve the stock. Were we to *eat* this one?

"Don't, don't," I said. "You'll need that rooster for breeding good chickens." It was translated.

Mangaleshi's face was crossed with mortification.

I rapidly changed my mind. "Oh, thanks, thanks, I accept," I said, comforting her. "What a splendid bird!" I bit my lips and kept smiling at her.

Thus my relationship with Kasonda enters the picture. My liking for him even showed in my fear when he caught malaria and lay longing for a sweet cup of tea in his large but bare mudbrick house. When I went with the tea and chloroquin it was sad to see the honored judge lying so ill.

Kasonda did not get on too well with his Christian wife, Mangaleshi. She was from a chiefly matrilineage centered in the village of Shika, and she was the mother of Morie, a personality central to the events leading up to and during the Ihamba rituals I describe. Morie hated his Christian father; Morie was the one son who was a freethinker—not that he was a traditionalist or animist, but like his father's classificatory brother Sandombu, he tended to be cynical about his own people's culture, whatever that was. Nevertheless, there was also a sweetness to his character. Like Sandombu, he was an alcoholic. The anomie of many literate young men who have no choice but to live in their home villages seems to lead them to alcohol; it may become a means to forget the loss of the outside world that education had once opened up for them. Or was Morie simply bad (*bajama*) as the Ndembu would say? Had he reacted to the pressure, then disappointment, of his mother, who wanted him to become chief? Who can explain alcoholism?

As soon as we arrived Mangaleshi, ambitious as ever for Morie (she had indeed always hoped that he would succeed to the senior chieftainship, as his kinship position promised), appointed Morie as our interpreter, and indeed he was easily the most educated person in the neighborhood apart from the busy headmaster and the head of the branch committee of the local government (a committee that had not existed in the 1950s). Morie's sister Lessie, who was a schoolteacher, obligingly helped me during my first experience of the new-style shortened girl's initiations, but she could not bring herself to translate the songs, those "sinners'" songs. Most of Kasonda's people were helpful when they could be, but they noted how I was going downhill into paganism and they gradually became distant, as we shall see.

Bill and I soon discovered that there was an old-style seclusion hut within the nest of villages. Morie informed us that a woman called Maggie was having treatment there for miscarriages. Maggie's doctor was Philip Kabwita, a man with a permanent tutelary spirit. He later managed to cure her. Up the road was a very sick man, a friend of mine from the 1950s, also undergoing ritual and herbal treatment, a combination which again proved successful. Philip also succeeded in curing a recalcitrant case of ghost-induced insanity (E. Turner 1986b). Apart from these major cases, the people often had malaria and with greater frequency than I had known before. A young man would hole up in his mudbrick house and quickly find himself helpless. He would have to be taken to the hospital by truck and given a blood transfusion.

People sought treatment in the village or hospital according to the kind of disease, "African" or "European," without much soul-searching about what was "right," just what would work. Witchcraft, as in the old days, was suspected in two of the cases I have mentioned, but now the culprits did not seem to be locals but strangers. This was partly because populations were now higher and more mixed, and much traveling was taking place. An urban character was developing even in the rural areas. In such a milieu the only people who were not scared were the healers.

Map 1 in Appendix 10 shows the vicinage of the Kawiku subgroup and some of the many tiny villages and farms of the area. The location of rituals and the position of churches are marked. Kasonda's village, Mukanza, was central to the group of villages, and his sphere of influence spread throughout the vicinage.

In the course of my enquiries into the existing state of initiation ceremonies, I often found myself on the other side of the tracks — that is, a dirt road that seemed to divide the Christians from the pagans — among a group of semipagan villages. To reach them I had to pass by the home of Rosa Matooka, the mother of the Zambian ambassador to Zimbabwe and grandmother of my second assistant Jennifer Matooka. Mrs. Matooka's house had a tin roof. Kahona, further on, was a true circular village of thatched houses such as old Mukanza Village used to be, as shown in Map 2. Here lived an assortment of relatives, linked mostly through the mother's line in the old style, with some added complexities that are part of the story. A table in Appendix 9 shows that matriliny was gradually giving way to patriliny among the Ndembu, partly because of the adoption of the European custom of taking the father's name as a surname and partly because of a new dependence on the wage earner of the family, who was likely to be male.

The full genealogy of Kahona Village and its offshoot Mulandu, the villages concerned in my story, would be impossible to reproduce in an ordinary publication, because of the enormous numbers of children born. A shortened genealogy appears in Appendix 11. Nyakanjata, a big breasty old woman who became one of the two main protagonists in this account, had eleven children, forty-five grandchildren, and twenty-four great-grandchildren, while her son-in-law's brother, from a linked matrilineage, had twenty-two children, which was not considered an extraordinary number. The village genealogy can be regarded as a combination of two matrilineages descended from a couple of women, Nyakanjata and her sister. Long ago Nyakanjata married the prosperous headman of the village, Kahona Sambumba (C5 on genealogy in Appendix 11), who was the mother's brother of the headman of Kasayi village that Vic Turner and I used to visit in the old days.

Kahona, later headman of his own village, eventually died, leaving the village with two of his sons in powerful positions. These were Singleton (D7), an Ihamba doctor, and Timothy (D8). Timothy had business interests in town and was also often absent hunting game, an occupation that he pursued as a secular hunter, that is, outside the semireligious hunters' guild. Which of these two brothers was actually headman was hard to determine.[1] Since the departure of the British, the concept of headmanship was somewhat diminished, so these two men lived without a great deal of conflict, each considering themselves masters of their own lives and families. In 1985 the authorities no longer held a headman responsible for his villagers' tax payments. The nuclear family was in fact growing in importance as compared with the extended family or lineage. Many men interacted more at their work place than in their tiny villages or farms, and acted independently of their seniors, except in law disputes which were settled by a court of elders led by the most experienced man in the area. Even the clothes of important men showed the difference in the two eras. No longer was there a headman easily distinguished by his long white waist cloth, no longer did he go about accompanied by his deputy similarly clad. Who indeed was headman was often uncertain. An elder in a Western-style shirt and long pants might offer a visitor a seat in a village, but beer and a chicken were becoming rare as presents. These items were now offered at a price, not in an exchange of gifts.

I had some friends in Kahona Village, particularly Singleton's younger brother's wife, Zinia (D10), a fairly young woman with a lightsome step and a funny sense of humor. She loved smart clothes and odd hairstyles. She was teaching me dancing, medicines, and songs. I used to dance with her at crowded initiation celebrations at night. At one of these events I also made friends with an old woman who had been dancing bare-breasted beside the drums, a woman with a keen sense of enjoyment, liked by all. This was Nyakanjata, the relict of the former headman Kahona. The two women proceeded to light up the darkness with ephemeral torches made from thatching grass. Nyakanjata, Zinia, and I enjoyed ourselves hugely (Figure 1).

Fideli (E2) was a mature grandson of Nyakanjata, an educated man who professed the religion of Baha'i. This is one of the lesser universal religions but not a Western one, being derived from Islam. It was the only local nonindigenous religion that was free from narrow exclusivism. Fideli was at liberty to be both an animist and a Baha'i.

My relationship with these people was more normal, less constrained by imperialism than in 1951. It was now 1985, and Zambia was independent. These Africans were proud, and my dealings with them were on a personal, business, or research basis, not an imperialist one as perforce in the time of the authoritarian British. The Kahona people remembered Vic and myself and our presence at the neighborhood rituals over thirty years earlier (1951–54), and when they saw Vic's books they outdid me in drawing attention to the continuities and the changes.

The rest of the genealogy will come into focus as we use it. On October 19, 1985, about seven weeks after our arrival, at a hunter's conference organized by Bill Blodgett, we first met Fideli (E2). He informed us that there was going to be an Ihamba ritual in Kahona. We were surprised because on the Christian side of the tracks we had received the impression that Ihamba was obsolete, along with most of the rituals except anti-witchcraft exorcisms. "That is not so," said Singleton, who was present along with Fideli. Then Fideli, who spoke good English, told us that he and Singleton did, in fact, perform Ihamba "often." At the hunters' gathering

Figure 1. Zinia and Nyakanjata at a night dance.

Singleton took a long look at the book I had brought out from our hut—
The Drums of Affliction. His finger jabbed down on my photographs, he
peered at the medicine names, looked up, and smiled. "You know it," he
stated. On further acquaintance he said I should serve as *chiyanga* ("doctor") at the ritual.

Before the day on which the Ihamba was scheduled, Bill and I turned
again to the book and checked over the medicines and ritual action. I read
once more where Vic had written that Ihamba is "a compensatory form of
unification . . . taking flight into a world of symbolic compensations" (1968,
197). Even so, I remembered how in that other book, *Revelation and
Divination* (1975a), he maintained:

> The ritual symbol had its own formal principle. It could be no more reduced
> to, or explained by, any particular category of secular behavior or be regarded
> as the resultant of many kinds of secular behavior, than an amino-acid molecu-
> lar chain could be explained by the properties of the atoms interlinking it. The
> symbol, particularly the nuclear symbol, and also the plot of a ritual, had
> somehow to be grasped in their specific essences. In other words, the central
> approach to the problem of ritual has to be intuitive, although the initial
> intuition may then be developed in a logical series of concepts. (pp. 186–87)

These inconsistencies sounded like the ambivalence of anthropology itself, ever swaying between rationalization and deep understanding. I remembered how Vic's thought often changed, how he used to be on the watch for psychologically derived behavior, yet he had his own visionary experiences that he could not help but trust. I resolved to go ahead on my own behalf, to be mistrustful where need be, and to simply experience what I must.

The Ihamba Tooth

What is the ihamba tooth?[2] (In my account I refer to the ihamba tooth/ spirit without a capital letter to distinguish it from the name of the ritual, Ihamba.) It is the tooth of a dead hunter that is wandering about in search of meat; it is also his spirit. In the course of the ritual, this ambiguity was continually demonstrated—complicated often by the memory of the living presence of the person who had later died: a human husband, father, uncle, relative, with a particular personality. Although dead, a spirit afflicts the living until they treat the spirit with respect and feed it meat, satisfying its desire, the same great desire for meat that drove the living hunter out into the bush. And once the spirit dwelling in the human tooth is thus humanely treated, the tooth itself becomes a talisman for its hunter descendants.

How does the ihamba tooth come to a person? Old Benwa the gun hunter (B1, about 80 years old) told his neighbors of his own experience:

> At first I didn't know whether it was true, but one day it came to me. I was very surprised. If ihamba comes to you, you can't even eat your porridge. The ihamba just gives you pains. You'll think it's ordinary pain, but the way it hurts you is significant. You'll hear something biting. If it comes through the arm, leg, ear, or eye, you'll see it moving through the veins of the body. I am telling you the truth; you can't even eat your porridge.

After being cured of his ihamba, Benwa became an Ihamba doctor himself. He assisted in the first ritual of the two I saw, actively engaged in the task of taking out the tooth.

Soon the day of the Ihamba was upon us. At this stage we did not know the villagers and their problems very well, and learnt as we went along.

We discovered that Singleton and Fideli had a patient with an ihamba tooth wandering in her body. They were going to treat and cure her in this daytime ritual. First, they planned to collect herbal medicines from the bush and then set up a shrine area where the combined efforts of song, medication, and ritual action would draw out the tooth that was troubling her.

2. The Medicine Quest for the First Ihamba[1]

Medicine Collection

At 7 A.M. on the morning of October 21, 1985, Bill and I presented ourselves at Kahona Village. Fideli had warned us not to bring our assistant Morie since he was in no way connected with the Ihamba cult as I was, and as Bill was too by association. I believe that Morie's alcoholism, his severe manner with the people on the other side of the car track, and the fact that he used to be a member of the local constabulary presented problems for the Kahona people.

When we arrived at Kahona, the village was damp and chilly from a brief rainfall and nobody was about. After a time Vesa (D12), a slender young man, emerged from one of the houses carrying a long kayanda drum (see Appendix 5), the first and most important requisite for a ritual. Because "drum" means "ritual," this act was the signal for the beginning of Ihamba. Vesa set the drum upright on the ground. On the top of it he placed an old flat winnowing basket with ragged edges. Singleton and Fideli appeared and made their greetings to us; we knew them a little by now. Fideli's face shone with the health of early middle age. He was an able man of thirty-seven, a thinker with a knowledge of Western science. Fideli was a true short-nosed southern African, with a round head and the manner of an interested person well in control. He carried himself this morning with the buoyant air of one looking forward to a procedure with which he was familiar. He knew we would do no harm to the ritual by joining in. He once told me he used to play with my son Fred back in the 1950s.

The senior doctor Singleton, Fideli's mother's brother, was a tall man with a long, lined face—a conscious face, capable of unearthly flashes of irony and mischief, a man who said what he thought, who was used to being a *mukulumpi*, an elder. He had touches of gray in his hair and the hint of a gray straggle on his chin. He was thin, and habitually wore an old pair of blue coveralls, carrying himself with limber ease even though he must have been nearly seventy years old. Ihembi in *The Drums of Affliction* (Turner 1968) was about the same age, I remembered. I had felt in Ihembi the sense of a similar firm, practical, authoritative mind: he was a highly skilled man. Vic Turner tells how Ihembi "went into the bush whence he swiftly returned holding both hands behind his back. He put the leaves he held into his mouth, chewed them, and spat the juice on Kamahasanyi. . . . He was building up suspense. . . . With a smile he took over. . . . He pronounced . . . he said firmly . . . he shouted . . . singing with a sad smile" (pp. 168–72, 292–93). Singleton had the same natural firmness.

Singleton, Fideli, and Vesa (D12, Singleton's brother-in-law, whom we discovered was an apprentice doctor) gathered together a small hoe, a long hollow wooden rasp (aptly termed a "stridulator" by Victor Turner), complete with a new reed for playing it, a small tin can containing honey beer, a small well-worn bag made of cloth, another small pouch made of mongoose skin containing *nsomu* medicine (Turner 1968, 28) the ingredients of which are described below, a very small horn from a blue duiker antelope, just large enough to fit on a finger, tucked into the string tie of the skin pouch, and an ax. These were assembled on the wide basket atop the standing drum. They were our medicine-collecting equipment (Figure 2).

All was ready. Fideli and Vesa between them took the loaded basket and lifted it high above the drum—"drum" (*ngoma*) being the instrument that would be played during the "*ngoma*" (the word for any ritual) which was now beginning. The connection of the basket and the ritual was thus signaled. Then Vesa placed the basket on one shoulder and we started off, Singleton leading the way between two huts and out between the cassava mounds to the main dirt road, which we crossed to reach the scrub country beyond, an area all wasted with overcropping. Vesa followed after Singleton carrying the basket containing the ritual equipment, then came Fideli with the ax. I came next, then Bill with his long legs and youthful goodness of expression bringing up the rear (Figure 3). In front walked Singleton playing rhythmically on the wooden rasp, singing a plaintive little ditty in which we all joined:

Mukongu, katu-katu ye,
Mukongu, katu-katu ye,

in a falling repetitive rhythm. Fideli said it meant "Hunter spirit of the medicine tree, stand up and let's go." Singleton was walking swiftly, weaving toward a bush he had spotted among the mounds. It was *mufungu*,[2] the

Figure 2. The Ihamba equipment.

ishikenu, literally, the "you-have-reached-home" tree, the greeting tree (the first). *Mufungu* means "the gathering together of a herd of animals." Singleton squatted down before the base of the tree trunk and took out his mongoose skin bag from which he drew a lump of red clay; he rubbed this in a broad vertical line down the west side of the trunk, then in a line from the foot of the tree to himself, and then on the east side of the tree (Figure 4). He drew the lines to call ihamba to come soon, directing it along the

Figure 3. The doctors in search of medicines.

lines. When this is performed ihamba knows "I am soon going to be out of the patient." Then he took the cup of beer and poured it out at the foot of the tree, on both sides. He barked out, "Maheza!" Instantly, I recognized the old slogan.

"Maheza!" we shouted back.

"Ngambu!"

"*Yafwa!*" we returned—with special emphasis on the last word. It was the hunters' chant from the old days (Turner 1968, 167). It means, "Friends!" We answer, "Friends!" He says, "Sudden death?" And we answer, "It's dead!"

Singleton addressed the tree; his tone was urgent and harsh. "This medicine was brought by Kamawu, it came down from him to Koshita, and from him to Sambumba, and from him to Chisanji, then to Muhelwa Benwa. Me, I have it now. Really and truly." He addressed the spirits and indicated the red lines: "You were the first people using this medicine. See? We're putting this red clay of yours on the west side of the tree. I admit it's a pity we haven't done the tooth-removing ritual more often. Listen, you'll

Figure 4. Singleton marks the greeting tree.

have your honey beer, just give us your blessing; come on, give me the power to cure this woman well. And hurry up about it. You others, you guys who made it hard for us. You're the bad guys, I've given you your drink on the other side. You really fucked up, didn't you? Besides, you couldn't kill animals" (he used the pejorative word for having sex, *kusunja*). In this address Singleton named each one of his chiyanga ancestors who had handed down the ritual, finally reaching him.[3] The train of names was a kind of apostolic succession or tooth doctors' guild (see Appendix II). He was talking to those old healers, even including the bad lots, the *ayikodjikodji* (literally, "those who gulped everything"), as they used to be called in the old days (Turner 1967, 138). Singleton's voice was grim and strong as he spoke into the tree. When he had finished, he rose to his feet and sighed with satisfaction. I was watching his actions and prayed in my own way, although I was not a member of the family as my companions were, not even of their culture.

Fideli told us that we were not going to take any medicine from this tree, because it was the mother tree. "You don't cut your mother, do you?" he said. I shook my head.

In those open fields in the cool morning, I was beginning to relate to the men focused on their task, rather as I had done working on an old-style farm in World War II. It was a task with which they were familiar—a task that was now my business too. I hoped I could actually help. We resumed our medicine quest. Once more taking up the song, and accompanied by the gentle rasp of Fideli's reed as it swished over the musical bar, we went on to a musengu tree[4] from which we took some bark to make drinking medicine and some leaves for washing the patient's body. This tree meant "blowing on the food and blessing it for the ancestors," from *kusengula,* to bless.

We went to a mututambulolu shrub[5] which Vesa dug up, then Vesa squatted down and proceeded to tear open the whole root, while Singleton spoke down into the ground and said in a throaty voice, "Old folks! Old folks! Are you really dead down there?" He was remembering the old hunters who had taught him, wild man Chisanji, and his own father whom Nyakanjata used to love. Then he said to Vesa, "Chop some medicine." The root was large and plump. He took the entire system of roots, then filled up the hole again afterward until the dirt reached the surface. The tree means "to swarm," as bees do around flowers. This root is bright orange inside; when mixed with beer it makes ihamba obey. "See how it works?" said Fideli. "The medicine passes into the bloodstream, then it goes throughout the body and kills the germs that make the person sick." The scientist again. We came to a tall anthill looking for a chikwata thorn tree. Chikwata[6] was added so that it would "catch" (*kukwata*) the ihamba with its thorns. We picked its branches carefully. In the old days, chikwata was used because the spirit caught the patient, the reverse process. Pregnant women with stomach pains steep the roots in water and drink the potion for relief.

Off we went singing and sizzing with the rasp to a mukombukombu tree[7] from which we took leaves and roots that have the power to sweep (*kukomba*) bad things out of the blood. Now we came across another mufungu, and this one supplied the necessary bark and leaves that were used in medicine to call a large gathering of people. We took bark and leaf medicine from the mucha tree,[8] often used for ancestor rituals because "its pit never decays" but resists time. The wood is hard, especially the pit of the fruit; the fruit is sweet, it too wants people to gather.

Then Singleton took off from the path and circled around a bed of what looked to me like bracken with broad double leaves, which I then recognized as the stems of the bright red tuber called nshindwa. These aboveground tuber knobs are thirst-quenching with a very tart lemony flavor. The plant itself is called mutungulu[9] and possesses a wandering mass of fine black roots. Singleton sometimes cured malaria with the roots by rubbing them into cuts on the left shoulder of the sufferer, or using them in a poultice. I wondered if they contained bitter quinine. But there was more to mutungulu. Singleton told us that ihamba may have little children inside the patient's body. The drum ritual may successfully bring out the mother ihamba, but her children may remain inside, as indeed even the afterbirth may. However, scraped mutungulu roots, put into a cupping horn with other ingredients—a mixture called nsomu—can kill the afterbirth inside the body and make the entire ihamba come out. Accordingly, the men got to work on the roots and sorted out some long tangles for the basket.

Singleton circled around another shrub with fixed attention. "This is the tree which I didn't think we'd be able to find. Go easy on the leaves. Take them from the eastern side, not the west. It's musoli." With musoli[10] the ihamba would appear quickly and would not be able to hide; it was the tree of revelation, from *kusolola*, "to reveal," but it was now rare. We took a few of the big leaves and also some bark from the east side, the side of the sun's revealing, and went on singing—"Mukongu, katu-ka-tu-ye."

Here we stopped again and looked around. We were on a path above a long derelict garden without a bush in it. "It's all been dug," said Singleton to Vesa disgustedly. "You look carefully in this area, or we'll never find the tree I was telling you about." He caught sight of a mufungu. "Ah, here we are back where we started, at the first mufungu. Wait. I think I saw the tree we're looking for when we came this way just now. It's somewhere here." He grumbled, "I don't want to go all the way over to Mindolu Village for it."

They gazed around. Vesa said, "Look! Over there!" We went over to some scrubby trees and searched among them. They found what they were looking for, a small tree called *mukosu,* "soap root." This tree needed extra care in the cutting. Singleton took the ax while Fideli held the basket beside

Figure 5. Cutting the soap root lid.

the trunk. Singleton very neatly cut grooves into the bark outlining a 4 × 6 inch vertical rectangle, with Fideli squatting beside him to catch the chips in the basket, careful not to touch any of the chips. Fideli explained, "If any of them fall on the ground you can't have Ihamba." Singleton then levered off the rectangle of bark with his ax and let it drop safely into the basket (Figure 5). Singleton told us afterwards,

> This way ihamba permits us—right?—to catch it without running away. So the piece of bark must be caught in the basket. Ihamba keeps

trying to fly away, so we have to be strict and make ihamba honest. Mukosu has a strong smell; we use the piece of bark for a lid. It comes in useful when we take the ihamba tooth out of the patient's body and put it into a can. We need a lid. Ihamba doesn't like mukosu, it has this strong smell, so ihamba won't try to come out of the can and escape.

Similarly, we saw that when the ritual was over and the medicines were dumped into a hole in the ground, the bark lid was used to cover over the place to stop anything getting out. *Mukosu* is derived from *kukosa,* "to wash." This medicine when well infused becomes a lotion to wash all the bad things out of the body.

Now we were joined by the young woman Etina (F1), the basket carrier of Ihamba, whose ritual name was Nyamakola, "the strong." She should have been with us before and turned up late.

She immediately inquired, "Have you already done Maheza?"

"Yes. We've been looking for you."

"Maheza!" she said, and we joined in, "Maheza!" "Ngambu!" "Yafwa!" Together we continued on our way, now searching for an ironwood tree[11] to provide fuel for the ritual fire.

But before we found one Singleton spotted a kapepi sapling.[12] He set himself beside it, and with rapid deft strokes of his ax he cut it down and made it into a chishinga forked shrine pole, sharpening the branches into tines exactly as Mundoyi had done in 1951 (Figures 6 and 7). Kapepi sets one's teeth on edge with its bitterness: as a result bad teeth drop out—a major desideratum in the case of the ihamba tooth. Its name derives from *mpepela,* "the wind," which is ubiquitous and invisible, which all hunters desire to be so that they can find game everywhere, and also not be seen by the animals (Turner 1967, 290).

We went on singing, with the chishinga pole balanced on the basket that was now atop Etina's head. The doctors were concerned about the ritual firewood; it had to be ironwood because this wood is strong and unbending, and has no stringiness in its bark to tie up huntsmanship. At last we came across an enormous felled ironwood tree just as we were turning back home. Fideli got astride the trunk, already bare of bark, and hacked patiently at the wood with his ax, careful to let none of the firewood fall to the ground. When they collected enough they searched among saplings until they found a termitary made by a species that produces small mud towers about eight inches across and a foot high.

"We're lucky," said Vesa. "Here's one of those small termite towers, a big one."

Figure 6. Cutting the chishinga shrine pole, 1985.

"Let me see it," said Singleton. They gathered around. "Yes, that's the one for us. Take it. We won't find another like this. Take it out whole, right from the bottom."

They lifted it out and carved it into a house shape, a cube, and put it into the basket (Figure 8). It was going to be placed at the base of the chishinga shrine pole and would become the grave for ihamba, that is, of the dead hunter who was troubling the patient in the form of ihamba as spirit. I told Fideli I knew that in the old days the body of a hunter would be buried sitting upright, with many small termite towers heaped around his

Figure 7. Cutting the chishinga shrine pole, 1951.

head. The head was positioned so that it protruded from the grave, enabling the dead man's spirit to see between the pieces of termitary and gaze forever on the bush. Fideli was indeed familiar with this custom. There had been hints in the early interpretation of Ihamba that the ihamba termite tower was in fact the little house of the spirit, set there so that the spirit could visit its house during the ritual. Some overtones of fertility existed, connected with the swarming life of the termite tower (Turner 1967, 294) and with its erect appearance.

Singleton said he would go off alone later to collect the leaves of

Figure 8. Finding the small termite tower for the spirit's grave.

muhotuhotu[13] and the leaves and roots of mutuhu. This corresponded to the 1951 Ihamba, when Ihembi went off on his own to collect unnamed ingredients (Turner 1968, 160). Muhotuhotu was gathered because its leaves fall all at once; similarly, everything would come out if the patient were given this medicine, even malaria. Thus the ihamba inside the patient would come out. Mutuhu used along with mututambulolu calls ihamba to come out. It is a potent, dangerous coming-out medicine, used for abortions.

Muneku, a leaf for expelling the placenta, was not to be found, so mukandachina[14] with similar powers was substituted, taken from a tree that grew atop a giant termitary. Singleton wanted the leaves so that he could chew them and spit the pulp into the cupping horn to "call ihamba to enter the horn."

"There are medicines for the below and the above and inside—every medicine to make ihamba come out," declared Singleton, and then, "Let's go back to the road."

At this ritual Bill and I were watching and learning. Much of the action up to this point was the same as in Victor Turner's "Ihamba." Now in 1985 I was the main observer, eagerly taking in all those properties that referred to "coming out" and especially childbirth. (It will be recalled that I am the mother of five children. Here one's personal viewpoint alters what one notices. Victor Turner's work showed little on childbirth.)

We returned to the village. I stood by at the edge of a growing circle of people while the shrine materials were assembled, watching the empty dirt of the plaza change into a complex ritual scene. The place became something between an operating theater and a temple, for they were going to extract something, and yet it was done before a ritual shrine. Not only did I watch in wonder while all those small preliminary rites that I remembered from thirty-one years ago were performed, but the fact of the repetition, the consciousness of my recognition, drew me doubly into the ritual and made me happy, as any extra awareness will do for me. Yet on this fresh occasion,[15] I still had to record anew, connect meanings, get to know personalities.

Singleton was tired. When I lifted my camera once more to photograph the medicine preparation and setting up of the shrine, he grumbled—so the transcript says—"There she goes snapping again. I offered her a stool, but she won't sit down. If she doesn't sit down sooner or later the ihamba will fly into her. Give your father a stool, will you? I'm tired." He had the main work before him, dealing with a level of the human psyche that our psychologists do not handle. How hard that work was will be shown below.

Medicine Preparation

The doctors had chosen a spot under some small trees in the middle of the village plaza around which lay the ring of mudbrick huts. They settled down in the shade and were soon busy preparing for the ritual. Singleton spread an antelope skin on the ground between the trees, upon which Etina the Nyamakola placed the basket. They dug a hole with rapid skill and planted the chishinga pole, settling the anthill in front of it in a little pit.

"Meya, meya, meya!" called Singleton, demanding beer, then went off on his mysterious errand for medicine.

Fideli separated all the roots, leaves, and bark into different piles and proceeded to cut the bark into small pieces, save for the mukosu bark lid which he put aside.

"Where's the pounding pole?" asked Etina. Snodia (D11, Nyakanjata's middle-aged daughter, who was named for a church synod) then told a child to go and fetch it, along with a mortar. Fideli started shoving medicine roots into a pot wholesale. At this point Singleton returned and admonished Fideli.

"What are you doing there? Don't put the medicine in the pot as it is, peel it first."

"Shouldn't it be this way?"

"I thought it was like that too," said Luka (E4), a young assistant of twenty-four. The child arrived with the mortar which turned out to be white and floury from cassava pounding. "Wash it," said Singleton. "There isn't any water. Bring water, water, water, for your grandfather!" Water was soon brought and the mortar washed. A villager came forward and dropped the equivalent of five cents into the basket. Another added two cents.

Fideli put the leaves in the mortar, and then arranged a can containing beer a little behind the chishinga pole on the right, ready to receive the tooth when it came out. He flattened a bunch of castor oil leaves into a pad and placed it atop the can, then covered the pad with the mukosu bark lid (see Figure 5). The castor oil leaves were there because they have a pungent smell. As with the mukosu bark, ihamba is afraid of the smell and keeps inside. "In the old days you would have had to pay a gun for this knowledge," said Singleton. A gun was the most valuable object they had.

Before they started Singleton and Fideli shooed off the village children. Fideli started scraping the orange mututambulolu roots. "This knife isn't sharp," he said. He turned to old Benwa who was now with us. "Father, lend me your sharp knife."

"Mine isn't sharp either," quavered the old man. "And I don't know where the sharp one is."

"You mean this one behind me?" said Morie.

"Yes. Thanks." Fideli got back to work.

He put the orange mututambulolu pieces into an orange mug when they were done. Some dog had defecated in the area of the new shrine. "Remove that stuff," said Snodia. "Someone might step in it. That dog looks just like my grandfather's dog, the one we used to call Shit." Everyone laughed.

Singleton was absent looking for something else, the final mutuhu. He returned and proudly displayed a bunch of herbs (Figure 9). "Have you explained this one to Edie?" he asked Benwa.

"Yes—I told her that it will make ihamba come out quickly." *Tuhu* means "for no special reason." The plant is said to leap unexpectedly out of

Figure 9. Singleton displays a bunch of herbs.

the ground like a mole, for no special reason. The disease leaps out of the patient in the same way; the "no reason" adds the sense that there would be something nonrational about the cure.

The cloth bag from the basket was hung on the tines of the chishinga. Singleton saw to it that his mongoose skin pouch was ready on the basket, with the tiny finger horn tucked into the mouth of the pouch. One cupping horn was found and put on the basket. It was a goat's horn. "We used to have four horns in the old days," complained Benwa, he who had taught Singleton the Ihamba. He was remembering the old days just as I was.

A vital medicine, a key medicine for Ihamba, was now on hand to medicate the horns. This was nsomu, part of a hunter's *mpelu* ("organic residue") medicine that he is accustomed to keep in his wallet. (Victor Turner held nsomu in awe and described it in 1968, p. 28; Singleton also explained its power, impressing me with its importance.)

Nsomu is a pellet made of the inside nerve of an elephant's right tusk mixed with reed salt. This nerve is a limp object, a "flaccid penis"—signifying masculine impotence. In divination the nsomu nerve signifies a sorcerer, for a sorcerer can blast the fertility of his victims. The nerve must be taken from an elephant that has been recently shot, it must be fresh "living" tissue. An ax is used to break into the tusk, then the soft and hidden nerve fiber is gently pulled out. The nerve is so deep inside the tusk that kapwipu medicine[16] is utilized to find it and get it out. Kapwipu medicine is bitter and hot and is regularly used to stimulate a strong sexual erection. It also contains within itself the meaning "affliction followed by success in hunting." The wood is hard, and gives health and strength—thus within the process of preparing nsomu there is revealed a powerful conjunction of secrecy and flaccidity (meaning also sorcery and the effects of sorcery) on the one hand, and a strong symbol of erection, the kapwipu, on the other, the latter being utilized to extract the substance that is so hard to extract. So we find two opposite effects written into the nerve medicine—the trouble and its cure in one.

Vic Turner quoted a diviner about nsomu: "Diviners use nsomu to see secret things which crop up unexpectedly when they are divining, just as a hunter expects to come upon animals by chance when he is hunting. Nsomu is like a torch at night whereby he can see witches openly. This is because nsomu is a secret thing that has been brought into the open" (1968, 28).

There is another connection with the elephant as well as the tusk nerve: the animal makes a great trumpeting which calls an ihamba out. An ihamba in any part of the body can hear it. And the softness of the nerve, mixed with salt consisting of an ash of the reeds called *mabanda,* the "bending ones," makes ihamba obey (*kwovwa,* "to be soft and pliant"). There are also other connections of this salt with compliance: One of them concerns the boys' circumcision. Boys at their circumcision are taught to be obedient, compliant. The pain that taught this, the pain of the cutting of the foreskin, is connected with an old tradition, that the first boy ever to be circumcised was cut by accident. He was down by the river and was cut by a sharp reed. It is the ash from burning these reeds that constitutes *mbanda,* "salt." Hence, the obedience of ihamba to the salt in nsomu. Furthermore, the salt itself is used when cooking cassava leaves—it softens them.

Nsomu then is a pellet with complex implications, containing something hard to get out (as the ihamba is), success being implicit in the very presence of the nerve in the medicine, a success owing to the hardness of kapwipu; then nsomu is a secret thing brought into the open, thus its possessor can see spiritual evils clearly; it contains the strong trumpeting of the elephant whose tusks were so resistant; yet again nsomu has the ability to soften ihamba's hard will into obedience, for the soft nerve is included; then there is the curious connection with the obedient circumcision boys whose first boy prototype was so hurt by the bending reeds now used for salt in the nsomu mixture; and then salt itself, which is a softening agent. There are implicate powers enfolded and reenfolded into this tiny pellet—now we understand something of the awe.[17]

The nsomu substance used to be kept in a small calabash. Now it resided in Singleton's mongoose skin pouch. At the beginning of this Ihamba ritual, Singleton inserted a pellet of it into the tiny finger horn that would be used—as we saw later—to draw the ihamba out. The cupping horn itself was a capacious goat's horn, now set on the basket, but this other little horn of the blue duiker antelope, called *musengu,* was very slender. It could be fitted onto the finger of the doctor and would serve to draw lines on the patient's back to lead the ihamba tooth to the surface.

The musengu horn was a rare object in itself for, as Singleton explained, it had to be taken from a blue duiker antelope killed by a predator—a lion or a leopard, or eaten by a hyena (any of which might be an ancestor). The horn had to be the one from the right side, the stronger side. This horn and the nsomu stuffed inside it were thus the certificating objects, the trademarks of the doctor, his shingle as it were, without which he could not practice his skill. A special blue duiker horn like this, and the elephant's tusk nerve pellet to go in it, imparted the character of a patent to the doctor's work; only he who possessed these rare patents could practice, thus no one could steal his trade.[18]

Fideli was still seated on an upturned pan hard at work scraping the mutuhu roots (Figure 10). I watched him as he very carefully peeled a black root. My notes say, "It *comes out* white."

Now Nyamakola took the pounding pole to pound the leaves in the mortar so that their juices would be extracted. She first struck the ground with the pole on the left of the mortar, then on the right, then into the mortar, pounding and crushing the leaves. And in the same manner, before she poured cold water into the mortar when the pounding was done, she

Figure 10. Fideli prepares the medicine basket.

poured some first on the ground to the left, then to the right, then into the mortar—so that ihamba would come out. When she had done all her pounding and mixing, the cold medicine was ready for use.

Two cone-shaped cups made from milk leaves now lay on the basket. They were to be filled with the juices of the orange mututambulolu ("a gathering") and mutuhu ("leaping out quickly") and used during the treatment to call ihamba to come out. They would prevent ihamba from hiding in the fingertips and toes. The primary role of the milk tree, *mudyi*,[19] from which the leaf cups were taken, was its use as the central bush-shrine for the girl's initiation celebration. It was a tree specially honored in her transition from girl into woman. Here, what was important about the milk tree was that it was the food of antelopes—this was its "dominant" mean-

Figure 11. Medicating the doctors.

ing for Ihamba, in Victor Turner's sense. By extension, therefore, we may trace a connection with huntsmanship.

It was time to medicate the doctors, in case the ihamba should escape from the patient and enter one of us (Figure 11). Fideli started by drinking a cupful from the leaf infusion in the mortar. He handed both Bill and me a cup. "It will protect you from ihamba," he said. "It will think you are powerful gun hunters." I drank, happy to experiment and also to experience the Ihamba ritual myself.[20] The potion tasted freshly of leaves and made my head swim a little.

Then we were given a touch of reed salt to eat, tasting of ash, sulfur, and salt, as in the old days when I tasted the salt medicine from my Chihamba rattle (Turner 1987a, 131–32). A flat pan was brought and the orange mututambulolu from the orange mug was put into it and also some of the black mutungulu roots, now peeled and white. The medicine mortar stood one foot to the left of the chishinga. Fideli crushed some long peeled roots on a log of ironwood and added them to the basket.

Fideli belonged to the Baha'i religion. He had been thinking and said to me, "Many people here have quit doing this because of Christianity— but you yourself know it can cure people."

"True, it can," I said, remembering Kamahasanyi's cure in the 1950s.

Singleton then lit the ironwood fire with thatching grass. He was careful not to let anyone else touch the fire because it was the ritual fire. When Morie, now standing among the crowd, attempted to light his cigarette from it, Singleton scolded him and he desisted.

Fideli looked into the basket. "Only one horn?" he asked. It appeared that Timothy's wives had the other horns in their safekeeping, but the wives were absent and the horns could not be found. Meanwhile, we watched the fire grow; Fideli set the flat pan upon it with some water to stew the mutungulu roots. I thought, "It's mundane—it looks like ordinary cooking. Yet it's not."

Meanwhile, Singleton was complaining that Vesa and Luka (E4, the youngest assistant) had not paid the half-dollar for their drink of leaf medicine. I had virtuously given two dollars—but then I could easily do it. The men handed the money over, and it was put in the flat basket, alongside a wrapped razor blade, the orange mug, the leaf pokes, and the mongoose skin pouch (see Figure 10).

All the bark fragments were now stewing in another pan on the fire.[21] Luka went off to find some beer and a rooster, which turned out to be a lengthy task. Luka was still only at the helping stage of the cult. While the doctors were waiting, they discussed Vic Turner's *The Drums of Affliction*. Fideli balanced the book in his hand. "This is our history," he said. That volume was much in demand.

Honey beer arrived and was given solemnly to the doctors, that is, only to those who had gone on the medicine quest. We had a full cup each for which we had to pay a quarter, or else we were in trouble from Singleton. "Drink it all up," barked Singleton, and I did so: it was quite strong. I wrote down, "Beware of notes from now on," but when I read the notes later no change was discernible in my writing control.[22] On the contrary, I felt proud to be an apprentice doctor, and the beer tasted good.

We were still waiting for the rooster, but there was time to fetch the drums, one big one, *kayanda,* a medium one, *monfusa,* both in the bongo style, and a small wide one, a *musenki.*

"You know what? I used to play with your sons Freddy and Bobby when I was a kid," volunteered Fideli. "So did Zinia's husband, Bakston. We were named Edena and Kawewu then."

I looked at him trying to recognize the boy in the muscular male before me—father of many children, my scientific friend Fideli. A picture of a gang of small boys formed at the back of my mind, scouring around after a soccer ball, the freckled boy and his brother with the straight dark hair, and

Figure 12. Fideli and Snodia bring Nyakanjata to the patient's seat.

perhaps a black kid who was especially enthusiastic, with a round face? The common memory knit us closer together.

Now Singleton went to fetch some mukandachina; he chewed it and spat into the cupping horn. He stuffed the tiny horn with nsomu. When the rooster finally arrived, Singleton took the bird and cut off the end of one of its claws with his knife and let the blood drip into the medicine mortar. He put the bird down; it could stand, more or less. "The crowing of the cock is like the trumpeting of the elephant," said Fideli. "No one can sleep through it, get me? Both of them call ihamba to come out."

Fideli and Snodia left us. They returned supporting between them a very weak and suffering old woman (Figure 12). It was Nyakanjata; she was the patient, my old big-breasted friend of the initiation dance-fest, my favorite old lady! We learned she was suffering those ihamba pains in different parts of her body. Her daughter and grandson eased her gently on to the antelope skin and seated her with her legs stretched out toward the east. Her legs needed to point east to prevent ihamba escaping through her toes where the doctors would be unable to catch it. Just as the rising sun comes out from the earth in the east, so ihamba must also come out, Fideli explained later. (My own logic fails to combine these two reasons.)

Figure 13. Two lines are made on Luka's right wrist.

Nyakanjata sat with her hands open on her knees, with the palms facing upward. The doctors started by tucking the tiny horn between the toes of her right foot—her first protection. Then Singleton put red clay from his skin pouch on her face beside her eyes as they used to do in the old hunting cults, then along her forehead and down the length of her nose. He put similar marks of red on the face of Luka the assistant, adding two lines of red on his right wrist, to deceive ihamba into thinking he was a full doctor (Figure 13). Luka was an apprentice, learning by doing, and was likely to become a doctor in the line of succession.

Luka brought ax heads ready to strike with the *kenkumwina* clinking music, a deafening sound which causes the patient to shake and which calls the spirit out quickly (see Turner 1968, 175). Nyakanjata was now set apart, seated on the antelope skin that was touching the spirit house—a sick and weary woman with something bad wandering inside her. Around her the stage was set in a ritual space that had been quickly organized and filled with objects where before there had been nothing but plaza sand. The hunter's chishinga pole was behind her, the medicine mortar behind to her right, the can ready to receive the tooth to her left at the foot of the pole, the medicine basket away by her left knee, then the ironwood fire behind the basket, with the pan for hot medicine beside it, along with another pan for cold roots, while the rooster lay trussed beside the hoe well off to the back. The cloth bag hung on one of the tines of the pole. The shade tree was undoubtedly a mukula blood tree, a teak that oozes red sap. Once the crowd had collected, it could be seen that the men were sitting around in the eastern semicircle, with the drums at the northeast quadrant of the circle, and Bill and I and our assistants on the southeast, while the women sat or stood completing the circle on the west. Two of the women refused to clap and kept their heads lowered in an attitude of disapproval. (They may be seen in the background in Figure 15.)

3. The First Ihamba: The Performance for Nyakanjata

The First Tooth

The women gathered around Nyakanjata. Along with Singleton they raised their hands in unison and waved them in a circular motion above the suffering woman's head, saying "Shww—shww—!" Thereupon, Singleton, Fideli, and Luka each in unison with the others made a fist with his left hand, licked his fist, placed a castor oil leaf on it, raised his right hand high, and all together clapped down on the leaf, crying "*Paya!* Come out!" (Figure 14). I saw this rite, called *mpandwila,* in former times (Turner 1968, 167). The clapping-down activates the ritual. The singing started, also the sprinkling of the patient with medicine: the rites had begun. We sang in vigorous keening harmony alongside a syncopated medley of rasp, drums, and clinking ax heads. Nyakanjata's back was wet and speckled with leaf medicine above the scarf that she wore tied around her breast. We sang:

You've revealed it, you've revealed it.

The heady rhythm infected me and rolled my own head about. Nyakanjata began to sway, her hands rising above her knees (Figure 15). It was the spirit beginning to work. However Singleton stopped us and brought the episode to an end. Nyakanjata's hands sank back onto her knees, whereupon Vesa gave her a cup of the leaf infusion to drink. Singleton crouched beside Nyakanjata with a razor blade in his hand, considering. He changed his mind and decided to use the leaf cups. He filled one with the anti-ihamba liquid (mututambulolu, for a gathering, and mutuhu, for leaping out) and held the leaf cup to drip liquid over Nyakanjata's right fingernails, then over her left, in case ihamba were hiding under her nails; then he dripped all her toenails, her shoulders, between her breasts, on her wrists, and on every joint—it seemed to me like a plumber sealing possible leaks. The proceedings throughout were marked by the same kind of ritual practicality.

Figure 14. Clapping on a castor oil leaf.

Singleton smiled his long smile and started another sequence, straddling about and singing while he played his rasp bar:

> Wrap your clothes around you,
> Divine with the pounding pole,
> There are witchcraft familiars—

accompanied by the syncopated drums and irons and our mournful exuberant chant (Figure 16). When Ndembu harmonize they produce a richly
woven shout rather than a reed sound. Another song went:

> I am Yapi who hunts alone,
> Today I walked alone and found a witchcraft lion by a tree.
> Welcome the guest hunter. Hunter, you've hit it, wo-o.
> I went off hunting, but you killed my child,
> You had witchcraft spirits, you hated my family.

Here they stopped again. Luka cut a quarter-inch slit in Nyakanjata's
back with the razor blade and drew red blood; Nyakanjata grimaced with
pain. Singleton took the cupping horn and showed it to everyone to verify

Figure 15. Nyakanjata begins to sway. Two nonparticipants hang their heads.

Figure 16. The mournful exuberant chant.

that it was empty—like a conjurer, I thought, as if he were saying, "There is no deception." Luka placed the horn over the cut and sucked vigorously, sealing the top end with wax. But it soon fell off, in fact it kept falling off and was a great nuisance. It was because the cut surface of the horn was jagged. It was not until later when Singleton carved its wide end smooth that it adhered properly and could draw out blood by suction.

A wealthy elder named Paulos (D1) made his appearance from a village five miles away. This man wielded much influence in Kahona, being a member of the Kahona family. He was respected as the head of a large family village of his own in an area which boasted of exceptionally good soil conditions able to support fifty cattle and many fruit trees. Paulos now came forward and addressed Nyakanjata's body possessively: "If you're Matunka, you're going to have to come out today." Paulos could remember Nyakanjata's maternal uncle Matunka who had been a hunter (B3). Matunka, now a tooth/spirit, was there inside the body before him; for Paulos at that moment, Nyakanjata's body was just the envelope for the tooth/spirit.

Singleton regarded Nyakanjata closely. He could sense it too. He barked "Maheza!" And the people shouted back "Maheza!" Then the reply "Ngambu!" and the people's triumphant "Yafwa!" Luka, Fideli, and a smaller man started another drive on the drums—Singleton working on the rasp and singing. Now Singleton stepped and stepped, leaning forward while keeping in place, holding his rasp and reed stretched out before him. He was dancing the antelope dance and loudly sang his plangent song. Ihembi had done the same thing skillfully in 1951, old though he was. Luka's ax heads took up their blinding rhythm, which induced Nyakanjata—or the spirit inside her—to jig and sway. Singleton went with the pounding pole behind the mortar and beat the ground with it. After about five minutes, Nyakanjata of her own volition slowed her pace and stopped. They took off the horn and emptied the sucked-out blood into the receiving can: "Ihamba mwos!" No ihamba. Singleton washed the blood off the horn in the flat pan containing mutungulu water (for bringing out the entire ihamba), then handed the horn to Fideli, who cleaned out the nozzle with a needle, finally blowing it through. He set it back on the same cut on Nyakanjata's back, which was now exuding. He sucked hard, and the horn stuck. He twice applied a drip from a leaf cone exactly onto the point of horn contact—the duplicate of the action in 1951 (Turner 1968, 172), then once on the tip of the horn itself. Singleton revived the fire with more thatching grass while the drummers tightened their drumskins by warming them at the fire.

Suddenly everyone was looking behind. Through the village trooped a procession; it was Philip Kabwita the ghost doctor with his two patients, Maggie and her baby (Turner 1986b), along with sundry relatives. Philip was renowned for his active tutelary spirit; such a spirit was called a kayongu and was usually won through a Kayongu ritual. This new ritual party was returning from the river where they had been treating the baby's fever with Wubwangu medicine (Turner 1969, 44–93). I scribbled a reminder to myself to take the baby some medicine later; meanwhile, the consciousness of the crossing of the two rituals was strong in everyone's faces until the procession had wound its way across the village and disappeared up toward Kajila Village. There was no open conflict, but something had happened.

The men took the drums away from the fire and tapped. The pitch was good, it was sharp and clear, so they struck up for a new round. Singleton was still troubled however. He sang:

Food for the kayongu spirit and its healers? Sheer waste.

He touched his mongoose skin bag and leaf cones to the forehead of Nyakanjata, and said, "You're kayongu. Get out of here, I don't want you, I want ihamba."

It appeared that Philip's kayongu spirit had jumped the gap while his procession was passing. Singleton immediately crossed the circle and elbowed aside the drummer. He bestraddled the big drum and whacked out a rousing rapid beat, the true Ihamba rhythm, in order to get back to Ihamba. Then he showed the player of the small drum how to do it. Luka clashed his ax heads—those sounds unique to Ihamba—then took the ax heads toward Fideli who was playing the rasp, played them at him, then went to Nyakanjata and struck the ax heads together by her ear in the same heady syncopation. I saw how it made her shake more, writhing and jerking strongly. But Singleton broke in just as the horn fell off and he stopped the sequence; obviously, he was still not satisfied.

Fideli decided to set the horn this time above Nyakanjata's left knee, first quickly making a cut, then retrieving the horn from the pan where it had been put and sucking it on the cut. He then gave Nyakanjata a cup of the mixture from the larger pan. Singleton addressed Nyakanjata's body: "Ihamba, come out quickly because time is going by." Nevertheless, he soon took off the horn himself, emptied out the blood, and dipped it into the hot medicine in the flat pan on the fire, ready to put it on the leg again.

While at the fire he heated the ball of wax that was used to block the small end of the horn, in order to soften it. He licked the wax, added more wax, and warmed it in his hand.

He spoke sharply to Vesa: "There're supposed to be two or three horns. This is no good."

"Timothy's got them and he's away. We've asked his wives. None of them knows where they are. I think they've hidden them." Singleton frowned. He and his brother Timothy had a hidden rivalry for ascendancy in the village.

In the next drive he beat the big drum and sang while Luka took the middle-sized drum, but Nyakanjata stayed quite quiet. Etina the Nyama-kola pounded in an empty mortar to increase the sound. Singleton took the rasp from Fideli and stood in front of Nyakanjata with his eyes shut, quiet. He listened to something, then sang loud, above the other voices. He saw a pushy group of children quite close and drove them off; after that they watched from afar with wide eyes. The horn had fallen down so he put it in the pan. Nyakanjata was shaking violently; he took the slender finger horn and stroked it repeatedly up her back toward the circular mark left by the horn. He looked up and called, "If any of you women are pregnant, get away from here!" He warned them because the coming-out was set to occur.

He took the tiny horn and blew across it making it emit a high flute sound to call ihamba, then leaned over Nyakanjata and ordered the spirit harshly, "Matunka, come out of there! We've been calling you to come out through the horn, Matunka. You don't seem to want to come out with the blood. If you want to come out through bloodletting, start to shake, but if you're refusing because the horn fell off, then die in the receiving can. I've called you brother: now you'd better be quiet."

This was *makunyi,* a kind of test or shaking oracle—divining by means of two opposite propositions: "If you want to come out, shake, but if you're refusing, die down, don't shake." (I call this kind of oracle "the divinatory proposition.")

Now Singleton cried, "Maheza!"

"Maheza!" we responded.

"Ngambu!" "Yafwa!"

Then Nyakanjata spoke. Her voice was old and raised in complaint; it was rapid, in a "getting it out" tone:

"I don't see my children here. My sons and daughters ought to come around." It was the stage of *mazu,* the "coming-out-with-grudges," literally, "words." This expression, *words,* connoted a certain action of prime importance to the success of Ihamba, the act of "coming-out-with" whatever was secretly bothering the patient about her fellows, or bothering any member of the community (also called *chitela,* "grudge"). It was as if dark things *ought* to come out of the soul in this ritual. An almost perfect translation would be "psychoanalysis," which itself literally means "soul-un-loosen."

Johnny, the classificatory brother-in-law of Nyakanjata's dead brother Sakutoha and a resident of Shika Village where Nyakanjata had lived as a child, approached the old woman. Bending down he talked to her, then looked around. "This woman is calling for Smart [E1], her grandson," he said. In Ihamba participants sometimes spoke on behalf of their kin; in this way, they became a vehicle for the patient's *words.* Singleton disappeared and returned, not with Smart, but with another of her sons, Bakston (D9). Snodia her daughter (D11) was seen approaching. When Snodia reached her mother, Johnny told Snodia, "She's saying that if you don't like to be here let the ihamba come out."

"It's Timothy. He's the one who likes her," said Snodia. "The others don't care."

Nyakanjata raised her head and said her *words:* "I'm telling you, I'm going to have to leave this village and go to Kabompu to die because you don't like me in this village. What I say is, if you like me, that's all right, but if not, this ihamba had better come out. I'm telling you"—her voice rose to a crescendo—"I'll have to leave this village and go someplace else, I'm suffering too much here. I'm only loved by two people: my youngest child Snodia, and Timothy, but the others don't look after me."

A high tranced voice arose from among the women. "Ask God to help her. Take her to the mission, to the Apostles of Maranke. She ought to go to hospital—"

A growl of disagreement broke out and the voice died down.

"Where *is* Timothy, anyway?" questioned Fideli. Timothy was a hunter, so he was probably far away. He was not an Ihamba doctor, a chiyanga, nor had he joined the Wuyanga hunters' cult that had connections with the Ihamba ritual. (Even Singleton, who was a chiyanga, was not an initiated Wuyanga hunter, for that cult was rarely honored now.)

Singleton ordered his nephew, "Come here, Fideli, and get on with the cupping." Fideli bent his black head to the horn and sucked on hard.

"This is a really big drum," announced Snodia. She meant *ngoma,* "ritual."

Morie said, "Snodia, can't you put some *words* on this drum? Your mother wants you to."

"No, it would just be repeating what she said."

"It's your mother who wanted you here."

"She only wants me here because I'm the one who's looking after her. My brothers and sisters do nothing."

Singleton was fiddling with the cupping horn. Benwa had a good look at the horn and said, "Let me show you: there's a notch in the wide end, air's getting through."

"It'll need trimming again," said Etina.

"Give it over here, come here, I'll trim it down smooth," said Singleton, and he worked on it with his knife.

Benwa looked around; "You kids, I told you before, get out of the way."

"You're jostling the grownups all the time," complained Snodia.

"I'll beat the child that takes the first step," said Fideli. The children retreated a little.

Fideli fitted the cupping horn to the same cut on Nyakanjata's leg, and sucked really hard—I could hear the whistling sound. He blocked the end; it stood up, and held when he wobbled it. However the doctors were still bothered about the effectiveness of the horn and argued at every turn.

Fideli was looking at my hair, which had turned gray over the years. He sighed. "Everybody changes year by year," he said. "Every time you look at the babies, they've changed. Some people don't realize this. You might think you're at the same stage, but you're changing, see? The next time you think about it your hair has grown white, and all the time you never realized how old you've been getting." There were many white hairs on Nyakanjata's head, and on Singleton's. I thought to myself, "It's only a short time that we three will live." I was tired of holding the camera and being nice to everybody.

I heard the sudden "Maheza!" and joined in, "Maheza!" "Ngambu!" "Yafwa!"—Friends! Sudden death! It's dead! That helped, it was so vigorous. There were many fluctuations of weariness, emerging rage, or sudden spells of pure bliss in this ritual.

Singleton addressed the spirit. His speech was rapid and flowing: "Listen Matunka. This person says she'll have to leave the village and go into the bush to die because some of her children don't like her. Only two love her, Snodia and Timothy." His voice was nostalgic. "It's the same with me, I've lots of children myself, but none of them looks after me either.

Were these two the only ones who ate her food and were looked after by *her* when they were kids?" He'd hit on an important point and his voice grew harsh. "Now she says she'll go and die in the bush. Matunka, if you're annoyed at what she said and you're asking, 'How can I come out when the one I went into is annoyed?'—*come out* from this woman. When you come out you'll see what we're going to do for you. I'm one of the children who don't look after you"—a correct statement—"but even so I've come to take ihamba out of your body." Singleton was going to have to do that.

This address is obviously very complicated. Singleton, who was Nya-kanjata's own son after all, was hurt by his mother's exclusion of him when she said only Snodia and Timothy loved her. Singleton did not receive attention from his own family. And now he has to speak for his mother. He sees that being looked after when you are a child brings later obligations. Furthermore, he is speaking to the spirit rather than the possessed one, and this can release and disinhibit one's own hidden pains and guilts. The spirit is feeling the subject's anger as well: "If you're annoyed at what she said." Singleton himself was annoyed, but in Ihamba the spirit and you may be one, and you may speak to the spirit or speak to the person as the need arises; flexibility is increased enormously throughout. The beginning of another divinatory proposition emerged in this address also, "If you're annoyed . . . come out." It also had the nature of a challenge.

At the impact of the address everyone burst out with "Maheza!" "Maheza!" "Ngambu!" "Yafwa!" and a new episode began. Singleton circled around Nyakanjata with his mongoose pouch. They sang "Ihamba, twaya, come out, come out, we can see you," and Singleton shouted his fierce command into the body of his mother, "Twaya! Twaya! Come out!" at which we all called "Woo-oo" in falling tones quickly breaking into the song:

Where's the path where the cows go by?
What went by? Are you ihamba or a disease?
Kakuwe-e-e, your friends can sing.

The drums suddenly shifted their rhythm and we began to harmonize in a sorrowful song:

When I sowed seed I thought I was sowing pumpkin,
Instead I planted calabash.
This year the people are going to suffer on the plain of Mayawu.

This year there'll be no entertaining of guests.
O sister, I thought I was planting food
But it only grew into an empty gourd.
This year we're going to be hungry on the plain of Mayawu.
And yet you ought to welcome the guest with respect.
My liver wants to do it, ye-e-e,
Wants to welcome the guest, the hunter, ye-e-e.

Singleton was dancing the hunter in full run, sweat pouring from him, the music beating, Nyakanjata swaying, Bill with water starting in his eyes, my voice with theirs, everything coming together. We advanced to the center and chanted "Maheza!" "Maheza!" "Ngambu!" "Yafwa!" Singleton took off Nyakanjata's horn and emptied the blood. "Mwos, nothing." It was disappointing.

Children crowded around, scattering the firewood.

"Get out of the way, you kids," Singleton shouted at them. "You'll burn the patient. And you're dropping the flowers from the mango tree."

"I tell them but they simply won't listen," said Morie.

"Move back," ordered Luka.

Benwa said, "Their mothers pretend to be Christians and they know nothing about the old Ndembu customs. *You will see, if ihamba comes to you.*"

Old Johnny approached Nyakanjata again. Morie exclaimed, "Get away from there, uncle, look, you're even touching her body. Did you get to go into the bush with them for medicines, eh? You know it's forbidden to touch."

Fideli came to Benwa. "Father, you're wanted."

Zinia (D10) called, "You kids get out of my kitchen."

Snodia felt the mood. There had been another mounting and release of tension, another oscillation. "Those backbitings are from herself, not us," she said, meaning her mother.

"The children say they're not backbiting her," said Singleton. "But they still refuse to give her food." His irritation was coming out in plenty.

"Let's just agree, can't we?" said Benwa.

"And there's Timothy: none of his three wives gives her food."

Snodia sighed. "I have sorrows because you've put mother into my hands, and I'm the only woman looking after her." She looked around. "Does that mean I'm the only daughter of Nyakanjata?" It seemed true. Ngeni (D5) was always away, and the other daughters were dead. If you counted the daughters-in-law, the wives of Timothy and Bakston, they had as much as they could manage as it was in these hard times, with their large families. The same applied to Nyakanjata's sister's daughters, Meru (D2) and Liza (D4), who ought to be like real daughters to Nyakanjata. Snodia had a large family of eight herself. And again, the word "backbiting" was curiously apt.

Many of us were afraid that something might come out of Nyakanjata's back and wander around. And I thought, what was I doing here with Vic dead, in an ambiguous position in Mukanza Village under the aegis of Kasonda the Christian convert, with his son Morie as assistant who was sometimes all right and sometimes very frightening when he was drunk? Singleton knew better than to allow Morie on the medicine hunt. As for me I was trying to learn a closer feel for ritual, to feel what was going on, with young Bill as helper, Bill who was both the son of my friend Ceese and the friend of my own son Rory. I felt for Nyakanjata. You give your life up to the service of your children, then you're left alone and want to go off and get your feelings out somehow. This was my own affair, but I knew what Nyakanjata felt like.

Benwa considered his mother-in-law. "She's been wanting to fall down in trance, but she hasn't done it. Does that mean she's got something on her mind she hasn't come out with?"

Now the grudge burst out of Snodia in *mazu,* "words."

"I've been named by God as the one to look after mom. Thank God for giving me a husband who looks after my mom too and brings her firewood, and I do the cooking for her every day. Of course, I have a great many children and my husband to feed. If my mother sleeps without food, it's because I've slept without food as well. When I eat, she eats too. My husband brings the firewood and I bring water for my mother. However, it seems my brothers and sisters can't do any of this. I'm very annoyed; why should they leave mother to me as if it was only me who used to eat the porridge she gave us when we were little? The others say they don't have any porridge for her. Timothy has three wives, Bakston has one, Smart has one, Fideli has a wife, and there's Ngeni too. We all ought to be looking after her. If I give her food in the afternoon, you should do it in the evening, or if I give food today, you ought to do it tomorrow. But no, they leave it all in my hands. See how I'm suffering with the children? Is that the way you ought to go on?"

On hearing Snodia's words the crowd chanted, "Maheza!" "Maheza!" "Ngambu!" "Yafwa!"

Singleton addressed the spirit: "Matunka, if you're annoyed because

Figure 17. Nyakanjata points and waves her hands.

Nyakanjata said she'd go off and die in the bush, look, she did say it, and she shook and swayed. We're happy at what she came out with, and we said, 'We're about to catch Matunka.' But to our great surprise we didn't. Instead, you were just pointing and waving your hands [Figure 17]. So Snodia felt the sorrow in her liver because she's the only one giving her anything to eat. We all received food from her as children, not only Snodia. Smart, your mother Ngeni walked out on her own sister Snodia while Snodia was looking after Nyakanjata and father; father and the others asked Ngeni, 'When was your child born?' No one here knew. Ngeni and Benwa were in another country, in Salisbury [Harare, Zimbabwe]."

"That's a grudge of your own," said Fideli. "It's not my fault." (Fideli was this child of Ngeni.)

"Be quiet about that," said Benwa.

Singleton admonished them, "You're going to have to be careful to give Nyakanjata food from now on."

"Which of you hasn't been giving her food?" persisted Snodia. She was going to pin them down.

Singleton turned to Matunka in Nyakanjata. "Matunka, if you're annoyed with what Snodia just said, you're right to be, we heard her. Each and everyone in the village heard her. This village is yours, and you came to your own niece here. Everyone here calls you grandfather. We're going to sing one song, and you must fall down so that we'll know you've come to your own folks. Maheza!" And they responded.

Fideli, still irritated, said, "Come on, the cupping." He applied the horn, this time to Nyakanjata's shoulder. Meanwhile Singleton tightened the drumskins over the fire and tested the sound. He turned to the company, "You guys, come on, keep on helping. We want Ihamba songs! You know them all right, everybody knows them. You can't leave it all to me. Do you think because I'm the doctor I'm supposed to sing the songs alone?"

"You'd best try songs that are easy," said Benwa. "Then they'll help you. It's hard to sing those difficult ones."

"Sing 'Porridge for Mukongu is different,'" suggested Snodia. Johnny struck up the new number. But although Nyakanjata started shaking, this time the rhythms were unsteady and the drummers had a struggle to find the groove. Ultimately, the song gave way to:

Chikungulu will come.
You'll go and see the origin of huntsmanship,
Wuyanga.

This happened to come out very strongly; we were warming up, and I began to clap and sing. Another pair of ax heads was clashing in addition to Vesa's—Singleton came and played his rasp by Nyakanjata's left ear—often the praise sound of trilling was heard from the women—Nyakanjata shook and swayed violently—Singleton shouted "Twaya, twaya!" sharply. There were sounds of "Maheza!" and a chant of the hunters, "ayanga-ayanga-ayanga-ayanga-ayanga-ayanga" again and again until it became hypnotic.—And Nyakanjata was down on the ground on her left side—she jerked there as we sang, "Your friends shrill their praises!" Singleton put his mongoose skin pouch to her neck with his left hand as she shook and in his right hand he took the thin horn with its extract of elephant's nerve, drawing lines on her back toward the erect cupping horn, while the music continued in a long long urge. He drew and drew, then pounced on the horn with the pouch, wrenched it off, and rushed to the receiving can, where he poured out the blood. There was no tooth.

Breathlessly Singleton addressed the spirit: "If you haven't come out we have you beaten. If you're no longer there, don't shake." This was the true divinatory proposition, which was answered when they started to sing again, for Nyakanjata did shake; so the horn was sucked on again. Now

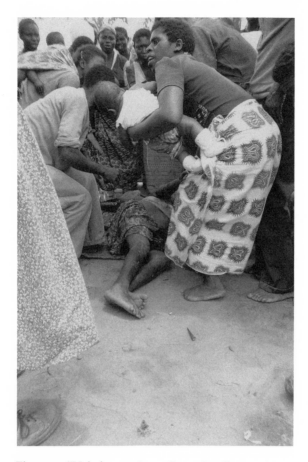

Figure 18. "Help her, can't you," says Snodia.

once again they took castor oil leaves and clapped them on their fists in the mpandwila rite, "Paya! Come out!"

Snodia was anxious every time her mother fell. "Help her, can't you?" she said piteously (Figure 18).

"Put your *words* on again, Snodia," said the onlookers, while Paulos said, "Pour some water on her." Paulos laid on *words* that repeated those of Snodia. Here again was a respected elder giving the *words* of the patient or protagonist on her behalf, to lend her his own weight. This ritual was collective in that way too, a network supporting its aims.

There followed an unsatisfactory round, until Benwa took over the rasp, and Daudson from Mukanza (married to a Catholic) came into the circle to drum. At this, everyone exchanged ribald jokes with the sense of,

"You'll catch it, Daudson, your old watchdog is coming!" Then they sang again the sorrowful hunger song and the origin of hunting song. The women were all gathered in a circle, and started to move with a dancing walk, swaying and clapping in a counterclockwise direction around Nyakanjata. Singleton bent over his mother, then carefully touched his skin pouch to his finger horn, then touched the pouch to the very end of the cupping horn protruding from the old woman's back. He took shredded castor oil leaves and placed them between Nyakanjata's thumb and forefinger. He was clearly afraid that Matunka would escape. Again came the end of the round and again the Maheza slogan.

Benwa was ready to put on his *words,* starting as befits a fourth-degree[1] hunter: "The animal is dead: it's me saying *words* to you now and you must attend to these *words.* I was the one who introduced Ihamba to Sakutoha Village. I was the one who first gave you the medicine of vomiting. All these children gathered here have been treated by me. But I don't understand why they're rude to me nowadays; these things stay in my mind. Our medicine came from Kamawu, then to Koshita, then to Sign Chisanji; then Chisanji gave it to me. Now I've become a Christian, and I've handed it over to you, Singleton, and it's up to you. It's for you to heal the village people just as your forefathers did." His voice was cracked and old. He said to his suffering mother-in-law, "I used to feed you once. When I realized I'd grown old, I quit because your own people were feeding you. You've had plenty of food from Snodia's hands, but most of your children hate you. If that's why you are annoyed just topple over, do it, and let ihamba come out. Otherwise, if it's not true stay quiet. Maheza!"

"Maheza!" "Ngambu!" "Yafwa!" we responded. Benwa had come out with his truth. At the next round Nyakanjata did not shake, but looked around complacently at those nearby. There followed a hunting song and then this:

Oh mother, Nyanshinga and Nyayifolu wo-o eye-ye-e,
They left troubles in the path where Katayi and Mpeza wanted to walk.
Father, let me walk where the elephants went by.
Ihamba, you must come out, you needn't be afraid.
The sun's setting, let's go find the hunting path.

Nyakanjata showed irritation at the sight of a small girl who was distracting the crowd with her dancing. She was too young to be there.

Another song broke out:

Figure 19. Nyakanjata's arm moves convulsively.

> Chief elephant, my brother,
> Today I'll go with you.
> He's gone to find medicine for hunting.

Benwa played the rasp and sang aloud in a cracked voice, calling "Ihamba! Come out!" Nyakanjata fell again—would it be this time?

All I could think of was "Can I get a shot?" I pointed my camera impotently toward the gaps in the crowding bodies, trying to catch it. I see Snodia grab hold of her mother by the shoulder as she falls, singing loudly while she holds on and eases her down. Benwa's hands are busy stroking the ihamba toward the cupping horn. All of a sudden Nyakanjata's right hand along her side spreads open convulsively, while Snodia, Singleton, and Benwa crowd around her where she lies (Figure 19). What's happening? There seems to have been a shift, a kind of rift in the social atmosphere.

Now they're taking castor oil leaves to make the mpandwila clapping on their fists—they raise their hands, "Paya!" Smack! Singleton addresses the body: "If you've come out don't shake, if you haven't, shake." They're starting to sing again, and now she's quiet. But who knows? Fideli dances, Benwa plays the rasp by her left arm as she sits, and they sing. Nyakanjata looks up consciously at Fideli, then nods her head deeply. She looks sleepy and sways forward a little. And puts her tongue between her lips; then looks up at Fideli again. Singleton looks terribly knowingly at me writing here (he knows that I caught the change). They all stop. "Akaa! Something surprising has happened."

A voice says, "It's finished." It's Morie.

"Give me some water, Snodia," says Singleton. They start to sing and drum again, testing for the presence of Matunka. Nyakanjata moves her head and flicks with her hands in ordinary fashion.

"We want Matunka," says Singleton. "*If you are still there, come out!*" speaking into Nyakanjata's body. Nyakanjata continues to look about her in ordinary fashion, seeking her children; now she nods low and shakes her head deeply. At this juncture she appears haggard from her long effort, with bags under her eyes. Still there's no real shaking. Singleton smiles at Nyakanjata; Luka and the others discuss the matter while finding grass to make fire to tighten their drums. They discuss with Singleton standing in the middle; great bursts of laughter come out, and Fideli is now within the circle. Fideli says, "When ihamba goes into a horn you should feel the horn vibrating." But it didn't vibrate. What happened to Matunka?

What Fideli was saying was this: "You see? We're sneezing already. Smart here's crying with pain, look at him crying. This ihamba is so difficult to control, so difficult. Bakston had to have an ihamba taken out of his ear, Liza had one taken out of her eye. Uncle Matunka will cut us all into pieces." They doubled over laughing. The whimsicality of that tooth, though a serious matter, showed a large element of silliness. It seemed that Matunka escaped and they had fumbled and missed him, since he was already buzzing Smart and Bakston.[2]

Benwa warned them, "When you cup blood, you have to notice everything.[3] Ihamba, if you're in that horn, start quivering so we can see you."

And they chanted the Maheza slogan. At the next song Nyakanjata shook, but the horn fell off. They sang:

My friend the hunter's wife,
Nyanjingu Balilanga, she's gone.
They might tattoo us.
If you go out with a hunter, you go eating.
Don't keep thinking about beehives and honey.

My father left me a gun.
You suddenly come upon a lion walking in the path,
You're startled by an elephant walking in the path.

Nyakanjata was uneasy. She put on the *words:* "I'm annoyed with Paulos, and I'm annoyed with Seti. Why doesn't Seti come?" Was Nyakanjata jealous of the well-to-do Paulos? I wondered. As for Seti (D6), Nyakanjata's son at Shika Village, he had been caught thieving on the copperbelt: a bad lot, no one liked him. Before Nyakanjata said any more, Fideli inserted the finger horn into the crop of her hair. They suspected that something was still inside her.

"Listen, Matunka, if you're there," said Singleton. "We don't want kayongu, that's a different spirit. We refused him before because we didn't want to be distracted from what we were doing. Listen, kayongu, if you're Matunka in this woman, get out of here. We've taken you out. If you're not dead, come out; otherwise, this woman must stop shaking." Nyakanjata did not stir. They sang, starting again at the opening song:

Go and bless the source of huntsmanship.
The owl's coming.
Wrap your clothes around you.
An elephant has drunk water from the spring.

Then they uttered the "Maheza!"
The ritual frame was still intact.

Commentary

In the middle of this ritual, then, there was a turn toward a whole new endeavor, starting with the same song, "Wrap your clothes around you." The first part of the ritual was a complete whole. We saw Nyakanjata, closely operating with all of them, in a patient trance that fed on music, on being a central figure, on pain, on a deep connection with the doctors and people, on the loosening effect of the leaf infusion, and on a growing consciousness of what it really was inside her, like nothing that you can describe: Matunka the tooth-spirit—and apparently somebody else as well. What had just happened was that the long application of these episodic pushes to remove Matunka, aided by the stroking of the finger horn, by the flow of blood outward through the cupping horn, by the myriad "coming-out" effectors, had actually allowed a kind of spirit synapse (or a group of synapses) to open somewhere in Nyakanjata when she stretched her arm—except that what came out did not emerge in the horn as they wanted, but escaped and flew away. This is what the doctors said, and they had laughed at the anomalous situation, the mess they were in. The question was, where had the tooth gone?

In this treatment of Ihamba I am taking the statements of the protagonists as truth, and now that I have become accustomed to it, it looks strange when anthropologists do differently.

Reviewing what has come out so far we see first the basic effect of focusing in the ritual. Singleton's act of drawing the horn always toward the cupped area, focusing again and again upon it, was paradigmatic of the method itself. Again the "coming-out" effects of medicine after medicine and rite after rite, bringing to bear a wide lens-like sensorium of different means and genres, finally plunged us toward one moment, in which something did come out. Because they knew it was in there they knew how to draw it out. This is different from the way Lévi-Strauss or Durkheim look at ideas about spirits—in a sense, as the "crystallization" of structure—that is, the idea that mental or social structures have crystallization points which are the origin of nonscientific notions of "spirits" and the like. For the Ndembu the focusing is to find something, to enable something to happen. Benwa's focusing was on something not of himself or Nyakanjata; he, a human being, was causing to come to birth an independent being, rather as Lienhardt described the birth out of experience of something divine. Here, I quote Victor Turner (1992 [written in 1980]):

> Godfry Lienhardt (*Divinity and Experience* 1961) shows this calving process in Africa on pages 147 and 148. Just as a single cell divides and produces its mirror image—seen on TV as a swelling trembling object, pausing on the verge of self-birth, then performing the act unhesitatingly before your eyes—so the Dinka with trouble and pain treat a sick man, to "isolate a particular Power which can be regarded as a subject of activity within him, from the self which is its object." . . . "The process of making manifest an 'image.'"

In cellular, human, and spirit birth—even in the actual formation of crystals in a solution—the future is somehow written into the event of the birth itself. The Ndembu doctors, by focusing, seem to facilitate the organizing into palpable existence of the thing that is troubling the patient, then they get rid of it. The details here are precise and personal, for the ritual is enacted in a context-sensitive milieu, one concerning the catching of a particular entity that lives on flesh and blood as the Ndembu know and describe it. In a sense the Durkheimians and structuralists may be apprehending such processes in their own way from their own direction. It is just that they do not follow across the "social fact" line into the curious realm of "the future developing itself."

It should also be said that Ihamba is not some kind of visualization technique. How does it differ? There is no mild hypnotic voice telling Nyakanjata what to fill her mind with. Work is done by ritual action itself, resulting in actual effects. When Nyakanjata's arm spread out, I was bending over her, saw the spasmodic gesture, and clicked my camera. Vic Turner at the equivalent moment in 1951 "felt . . . that what was being drawn out of this man was, in fact, the hidden animosities of the village" (1968, 172). Vic himself *felt* the "drawing out," then he put it in social and psychological terms. In October 1985, I myself saw that outward sign of the act in the arm. The sensitive procedures had been progressively focused until the ihamba was released. Here symbols and their meanings and the effect of them were one, not one *standing* for the other (compare Roy Wagner's *Symbols that Stand for Themselves* 1986).

The effect of focusing to enable "coming-out" to happen often referred to childbirth—that is, the coming-out of the tooth as an act of parturition (see also Chapter 4). In this Ihamba, childbirth imagery was more pronounced and must have taken a new turn during my three absent decades, since there were no explicit references to childbirth in our fieldwork at the Ihamba of the 1950s.

Next there was the theme of openness. There was a deleterious spirit in Nyakanjata. For it to move and shift out of her, she had to be open in all respects. This follows the general southern African pattern of sickness as a hidden spirit inside harming a person, but when revealed, doing good (see Appendix 1). Ndembu medicine from the musoli tree, used in this ritual, concerns revealing, making things appear quickly, making known what is hidden, naming the afflicting spirit so that it will be remembered by many people, speaking private matters in public, and bringing hidden grudges to light (see also Turner 1975a, 57–58). The coming-out with the *words* was mandatory in the proceedings (see Chapter 4). When Junod (1962, 484–88) described a healing ritual among the Thonga of Mozambique in which the doctors persuaded the spirit to reveal itself and declare its name, he recorded the address: "We salute thee, spirit! Come out gently by the straight way." Here is healing by revelation again.

Next I have been noting the ambiguous nature of ihamba as, on the one side, person and spirit with volition and, on the other, object, tooth. The reader can pick up on these signs as we proceed. There will be more on the ambiguities in Chapter 4.

It was clear that Nyakanjata "came to" afterward, out of an altered condition; during the shaking she had been a blank to me, a body responding to drumming and the crash of ax heads, a thing whose body we spoke *through* to what was within. In this tiny interval she was in normal reality for a time and looked pleased; and this difference, this contrast between trance and ordinary consciousness, was something I was beginning to recognize. You could have waved your hand in front of Nyakanjata's face in the thick of the ritual, and she would not have noticed.

Trance follows a sudden consciousness of pure knowledge, the "I know" syndrome. You enter a world that is complete in itself, where you simply know, you are obedient. You do not hold it, it holds you. The outside world fades, pain does not pain, time is not time, human will is left behind. The ability to enter this state appears to be potentially universal throughout humankind, as Erica Bourguignon has shown statistically (1973).

The Second Tooth

Back in Kahona the ritual work was not yet completed. The doctors went straight on to remove another tooth. More precise knowledge of the identity of this other tooth gradually transpired during the new event, though an ambiguity still existed. Something concrete was going to be given to them. It would be made visible out of the morning's work, and it had not happened yet. Matunka, it seemed, had flown away; Nyakanjata sat there still.

Snodia broke out with: "Here! I want to say more *words.* Yesterday certain people from this village went off into the bush to look for honey. Are you listening, Matunka? When they got back they didn't seem very happy with the honey they found. What they did was to act mean to Smart, just for staying home and not going with them. Those people [she named no names] kept all the honey beer for themselves. They insulted Smart in the presence of his wife, and they insulted everyone who was left behind. I'm not happy with this at all. I happen to know that everyone who stayed behind had a lot of work to do, so I don't know what they're talking about.

We weren't slacking. When I hear nasty talk like that I'm not about to eat anything from their kitchens, meat or whatever. I refuse in the presence of everyone."

At this the villagers broke into angry words from all sides. Singleton's voice rang out with new energy, putting the question to the spirit in the body before him, in a voice of command: "Shake, Matunka, if you're annoyed at what they said. Maheza!"

"Maheza!" we chimed in.

"Ngambu!" he rapped out. "Yafwa!" we rapped back. The drummer struck up a new drive with the special rapid Ihamba rhythm played on the small drum, and we burst into hunting songs:

He went hunting, who will cry for me when I die?
The eyes of an animal appear like lights,
I want to kill it.

Then in an altered rhythm:

Porridge for Mukongu is different.

And then the Maheza.

"Twaya, twaya!" shouted Singleton at his mother's swaying body. "Come out!" And they sang:

Father, you wanted to stay with your relatives
So that they'd give you food.
You found them, father.
I want to come and stay with you too, eye-ye-ye.

But now the response was uncertain.

In the middle of the song Bill and I were accosted by two traveling magicians from Zaire who had been performing conjuring tricks around Mwinilunga District and wanted us to fix up some kind of engagement in Mukanza Village. We frowned as it was hard to switch gears and talk ordinary business. As soon as the song ended Singleton turned angrily to Morie our assistant.

"What's going on?" he growled. "Get those men out of here—they shouldn't be talking to medicine collectors, to ayanga. You guys, I'm charging you a fine of one dollar each for interrupting the Ihamba."

There was much parleying on this issue, and it was finally decided that the magicians were strangers after all and couldn't be expected to know Ndembu custom. But they were made to drink leaf medicine, in order to deceive ihamba into thinking they were great hunters. Singleton turned to Bill and me, "You can drink from a broken bottle and eat the glass without harm because you've drunk the medicine. We'll show you if you like." I thought about that for a time.

We had indeed been so absorbed in the ritual that we felt as irritated as the Kahona doctors by the interruption. We regarded the Zaireans' lack of respect for the ritual as symptomatic of the insensitivity of townsfolk to the traditional people's ways; moreover, they had turned up at the most uncertain moment of the ritual.

Singleton now worked at the faulty cupping horn with his knife and pared the wide end into a shining smooth circle. This improved its suction greatly.

Headman Derek Mulandu (D3), Nyakanjata's classificatory son, was present. He too was reckoned to be a Shika man, though he had set up a farm group away on the other side of Kahona and made himself headman of it. Now he complained, "I've given money for the Ihamba, Johnny's also paid; only two people seem to have paid anything, the rest haven't put down a penny." He was giving a plug for his village of Shika here. He was right about payment: custom decreed that all should pay a little when a doctor danced well.

At this point Singleton announced a short intermission. It was 12.30 P.M.

When we returned after the interval Nyakanjata was seated on the antelope skin with her knees bent and her hands clasped together around them to rest her legs. A tight ring of people was gathered around her. "If you are in there, come out!" commanded Singleton, but when the episode started again she was motionless. She was somehow looking more pleased. She swayed slightly to the song, then went into the real swinging shake, advancing on her haunches off the hide toward where Bill stood with Morie, then she put out her hand to her foot and adjusted the small horn which was falling off: she did that on her own. They stopped the song and took her back to the antelope skin, while Morie whispered to Bill that he had informed the people that the remaining tooth was Sakutoha (C2). Sakutoha was originally from Shika, Morie's own village of allegiance, the home of his matrilineage, as it was also Johnny's. "Sakutoha?" I thought. "That old man I used to know?" Sakutoha had been a respected hunter and

Nkula doctor, one of Victor Turner's consultants. Vic wrote that Sakutoha used to make illuminating comments on the general principles underlying the collection of herbal medicines (1968, 61).

The song began again and Nyakanjata shook deeply, once more sidling toward Morie—the spirit was indicating that Morie was right.

"Come quickly," called Singleton. "If it's you, Sakutoha, if you're annoyed with this woman, come out!"

Morie announced, "Sakutoha had the same mother and father as Nyakanjata, the father was Mpwampu of Shika [B5] and the mother was Kabwangu [B4]." It *was* the same man that I knew; his village adjoined Mukanza in the old days. In fact, I had photographed him firing off his gun in honor of the return of my friend Manyosa from the hospital. So Nyakanjata was the sister of Sakutoha? Things were becoming clearer.

Singleton bent to adjust Nyakanjata's toe horn again. Then he said, "If it's not Sakutoha it's Matunka who must come out." He was puzzled, as we all were.

Derek Mulandu addressed the spirit: "If it's you my *mandumi* [affectionate term for mother's brother], you'd better make an appearance. Sakutoha is now underground. He used to live here, but he went off to Shika and died there. If the ihamba isn't taken out here, it ought be taken out at Shika where he died."

"Then we're going to have to take Sakutoha out here," said Singleton, getting to his feet for more medicines. He disappeared into the bush; meanwhile a middle-aged woman, Meru (D2), Nyakanjata's classificatory daughter who lived on Derek Mulandu's farm, appeared on the scene complaining that nobody had told her about the Ihamba ritual. The company brought her up to date on what had occurred: Matunka was out and Sakutoha still remained inside. Now Singleton returned with fresh medicine and Etina started pounding the new leaves for another round. Singleton had a sense that it was indeed Sakutoha in there. Meanwhile, Morie kept pointing out that it was he himself who had enlightened the group. Morie was becoming quite involved in our Ihamba.

At this point Njesi, the Catholic wife of Daudson the drummer who was back on the drum, came up and summarily despatched her husband back home. She proceeded to quarrel with Zinia, Bakston's Baha'i wife (D10), who was my good friend. In what followed, one could see how Njesi unconsciously joined in with the "coming-out-with-your-grudges" ritual. She began by laying on these *words:* "I came here to buy beer, and Zinia handed me water."

Everyone started arguing. It appeared that Njesi had pressed Zinia to sell her some beer that was not for sale—it was unavailable because all the beer was bespoken for the Ihamba ritual. But Njesi had persisted in her demand until Zinia took a cup and said, "OK, come here and I'll give you some beer." The cup contained water. Njesi was furious and said, "I hate you!" This was a kind of miracle of Cana in reverse and a further crosscurrent in the flow of the ritual, another difficulty of focus, a flaw in unity. But the effects of coming out were obviously strong that day, for even irresoluble conflicts, brought out into the open, were somehow going to purge the social and physical body—the social and the physical in one.

The next episode began. Snodia went up before her mother and danced for her amid song and the most frantic percussion. Nyakanjata shook a little. She was tired and discouraged now and seemed a beaten woman. Singleton squatted down and took red clay from his mongoose skin pouch. He smeared a broad band of it on Nyakanjata's back between her shoulder blades, high up just below the neck. Fideli switched the slender horn from Nyakanjata's left foot to her right. They were going to trap that ihamba whatever else they did.

Singleton announced: "Sakutoha came from Shika Village, then he went to Sameya, and then he went to Mukanza for a time. When he left Mukanza he went back to Shika, and that's where he died. It was while he was lying there ill that Seti lit out for Kakoma. Seti deserted his poor uncle—the no-good!" Then he divined: "We're not hunters like you, Sakutoha, but if it's you, come on out! Maheza!"

"Maheza!"

"Ngambu!"

"Yafwa!"

The round commenced with another song that quickly gave way to yet another. The reference to Seti's cruel act seemed to go through Nyakanjata; she shook in wide arcs and shuffled herself off the hide again, always in the direction of Morie—in the direction of Shika Village. After all her brother Sakutoha's wife was the sister of Morie's mother Mangaleshi. Sakutoha had married an important Shika woman.

As Nyakanjata moved, her hand came out to cover herself with her skirt, which had come loose in the intensity of her shaking. Now she was down on her left side. With his slender nsomu horn Singleton drew repeated lines around the cupping horn on her right shoulder. The singing continued. He bent over her and rubbed the fur of his mongoose pouch up her back to squeeze the ihamba out, and raised the cloth tied around her chest so that he could draw the pouch from underneath upward. Morie said to me, "How they *want* the spirit to come out!" At that moment a hooting of praise arose all around us—I realized that this time it was Morie who caught the sense of the coming-out. For it *was* out. The hooting of praise meant that everyone else had that sense too.

Singleton rapidly emptied the cupping horn into the receiving can, put on the lid, and thrust the horn into his mongoose pouch, then took medicine to splash Nyakanjata. Here they paused. I watched. There were divinatory propositions to pronounce, for there might be a possible after-birth or ihamba children to expel. Fideli applied the cupping horn again and Singleton spoke to the body: "If it's you, Sakutoha, and you're out, your body will not shake." Benwa squeezed Nyakanjata's shoulders, giving them a final check over. The music began but Nyakanjata did not shake. They addressed the body again, they sang and observed. All seemed cleared out. Once more they made the divinatory proposition; listening to their concern, I learned how careful one must be about an organism that has been inside a woman, perhaps breeding inside her. Benwa came behind Nyakanjata and squeezed her shoulders again to make sure it was out. She did not shake at all.

"Sakutoha is out too!" cried Singleton triumphantly and everybody began to laugh and celebrate. Snodia made one more divinatory proposition: "If you're out, Sakutoha, your body won't shake when they play the drums"—at which we shouted, "Maheza!" "Maheza!" "Ngambu!" "Yafwa!" with special emphasis on the last word, "He's *dead!*"—grinning widely. Nyakanjata did not shake at all.

Singleton at last laid his rasp on the medicine basket, and drew up a reed mat for Nyakanjata to sit on—since she no longer needed to be located on the antelope skin, in the hunter's sacred milieu. She moved over to the mat painfully, like a woman after an operation. They turned her to lie on the mat face downward. Singleton went to the hot medicine pot and using cupped hands he dredged out handfuls of bark and roots and pressed them on Nyakanjata's body. They raised her into a sitting position, and he did the same on her chest and sides (Figure 20). Then they hauled her to her feet and guided her tottering steps into her house, where she was to be nursed by Snodia. When I visited her the following day she was fine, if a little shaky. After all, she was quite old, born, so it was said, in the year sweet cassava was first brought to Mwinilunga—around the turn of the century. The man that introduced the cassava was Kasonda's uncle, Mukanza himself, who in mid-century became headman of Mukanza Village.

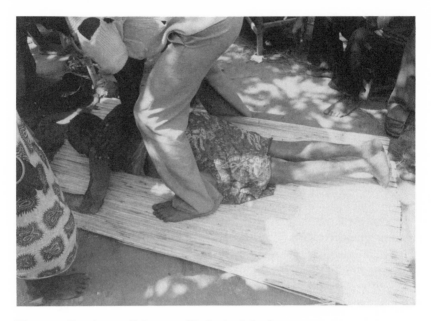

Figure 20. Pressing medicine onto Nyakanjata's body.

Meanwhile, Fideli had been digging a hole behind the shrine pole and a little to the right. After that he drank some of the root medicine from the cold pan and handed the remainder in the pan to a helper to be carried to the patient's house.

Singleton organized the windup: he opened his mongoose skin pounch and took out red powder, which he put on Fideli's fingers for protection. He took the cupping horn out of the skin bag, then poured some water into the receiving can of beer and roots. Then Fideli lifted the mukosu bark lid and the castor oil leaf on the can just enough to put his hand into the blood and beer mixture and extract the roots, which he placed in the freshly dug hole. Now he tried to find the tooth in the can (Figure 21). Everyone in the group went "Ah-h-h." Should there perhaps be two teeth in there? Benwa washed his hands and took over from Fideli, feeling about in the can and looking around puzzled.

Again there was a delay. Singleton himself came around, but Benwa went on dredging. Quite suddenly, Benwa jerked his hand out and every- one in the assembly gave high hoots of praise. Benwa then walked out of the ritual circle and motioned to Bill and me to come over. He opened his

Figure 21. Fideli dredges in the receiving can for the tooth.

hand and in it lay a tooth, an ordinary hard human tooth. It was true about the other tooth, Matunka, it had flown away and may indeed have gotten into someone else.

Here I knew the part I should play: having observed the tooth I turned and said to the company, "Yes, it is a human tooth"—echoing Victor Turner's similar statement to the company of 1951 (1968, 173).

"Too-ooth!" they shouted, in English; great joy reigned, and the clearing up proceeded. The leftover water was poured out in front of the chishinga pole; the cloth bag was taken down from the pole and appropriated by Singleton to hold the tooth; Fideli emptied the contents of the orange mug into the hot pan with the mutungulu roots; Singleton gathered up the money, about forty cents in small coins plus my two dollars; Fideli rescued the razor blade, tried it on his cheek, then wrapped it up. He was careful to put some of the loose medicine into the cloth bag to provide continuity with the next Ihamba; the bag would contain the ravenous tooth safely until the chiyanga doctors could put it into a Vaseline jar and feed it with blood and meal. Singleton went off with the medicine basket to Nyakanjata's house and deposited it there because he intended to come and wash the old lady with medicine during the next two days. Finally, the remaining medicines were buried and covered with the mukosu lid—the safety lid that prevents escape.

There were, of course, various problems with this last event. The hard obvious human tooth that people said had been going around in Nyakanjata's veins, what of that? I knew that Vic had concluded that the doctor did a simple conjuring trick and slipped the tooth into the receiving can by sleight of hand: "teeth do not travel in veins, they are too big," I kept telling myself. I was aware that many shamans do actually perform these conjuring tricks *and* also heal their patients. Was the tooth the outward and visible sign of an inward and spiritual being—albeit the somewhat concrete bulky spiritual being of my old friend Sakutoha? The tooth seemed to have so little connection with him.

I had been writing earlier, before I left England that very summer of 1985 (Turner 1987a, 141), how Vic and I had readily accepted the effigy of Kavula the thunder demigod in the Chihamba ritual of the old days. Of course, it was an effigy, as well as a kind of attractor of spirits. Was this tooth like an effigy? Here it was, here was Singleton's peculiar smile looking at me above it, and I knew at the same time that the tooth was no mere metaphor for the troubles in the village, for the Ndembu in 1951 had caught Vic up in it, he had "felt" it more than one usually does a metaphor. Morie saw the great urge going on and saw when the tooth emerged. Even my camera, like some animate thing, had caught Nyakanjata's gesture when Matunka came out. The nature of the tooth is addressed in Chapter 7 below.

4. Discussion of the First Ihamba

Sakutoha

My mind still revolved around Sakutoha. Why had this old fellow turned into a biting parasitical tooth, a thing of aggression and pain? When I searched in Vic Turner's writings for references to Sakutoha, I found on pages 190–93, in *Schism and Continuity* (1957), a passage about Sakutoha which Vic had used to illustrate his explanation of the role of slavery (pawnship) in the Ndembu society of the 1950s. There I saw in print certain facts that never came out at the recent Ihamba—that both Nyakanjata and Sakutoha had been slaves; they had been given as indemnity for murder to the headman Kahona Sambumba (C5), way back in 1913 while they were still children:

> The father of Kasonda of Mukanza Village, a man named Kahumpu, was an elder of Shika Village, and his wife Nyamwaha of Mukanza Village [also the mother of Manyosa, my best friend in the 1950s] was living with him virilocally. One day, he caught his wife *in delicto flagrante* with a man called Kalubinji, classificatory brother of the headman of Kasayi Village. Kahumpu attacked Kalubinji and killed him with an axe. He then ran off and hid himself in the bush. Headman Kasayi demanded and obtained from Headman Shika Ikubi [C6] a promise to pay two slaves and two guns as compensation for his brother's death. Kahumpu paid two slaves, a young man of about fifteen called Sakutoha and his sister, together with a gun. Kasayi received these....
>
> The compensatory slaves, Sakutoha and his sister, were allocated by Kasayi to his classificatory mother's brother, Kahona [C5].... In the late twenties Sakutoha purchased his freedom from Kahona with a muzzle-loading gun. A few years later he tried to obtain his sister, who had borne Kahona several children, by the offer of another gun. Kahona did not wish to lose his concubine and children, the major part of his following in Kasayi Village; he took the gun, feigning that he would release them to Sakutoha in a short while. Sakutoha, who had returned to Shika Village, was planning to break away and found a settlement of his own with as many of his siblings as he could muster. But Kahona then claimed that although Sakutoha had purchased the enfranchisement of his sister she still wished to remain with him, and he offered Sakutoha bride-wealth to legalize the marriage.... Sakutoha, whom I

knew well, was a simple and straightforward man, traditional in the extreme, and he accepted the bride-wealth, although condemning in round terms Kahona's double-dealing. . . . This case history . . . reveals that slaves, although they might be inherited or transferred like chattel and were compelled to remain in their owners' villages, nevertheless enjoyed certain rights. Sakutoha, for instance, had been able to obtain a muzzle-loading gun of his own with which he bought his freedom. The status of slave could not have been very onerous, for Kahona's slave woman refused to leave him to join her brother, even though Sakutoha had obtained her liberty and guaranteed her an important position as the potential founder of a village matrilineage. (Turner 1957, 190–93)

The position Nyakanjata did achieve in Kahona Village is directly visible in the genealogy in Appendix 11. It should also be noted from this chart and from Map 2 in Appendix 10 how Meru (D2), Derek (D3), and Liza (D4), the children of Nyakanjata's older sister Nyamaleji, also settled near Kahona—incidentally reinforcing the matrilineal principle, that is, if we see Nyakanjata's line as the principal village matrilineage. Since Nyamaleji may have also been an indemnity slave (see Chapter 6), events in this village exemplify the surprising advantage a strong slave lineage can win if it keeps together. Here, Kahona Village's very name seemed a misnomer because it consisted of few of Kahona's matrilineage and many of Nyakanjata's. Later events shown in this book added to the anomaly.

From Turner's background account, it can now be understood why Sakutoha, after he was dead, came back to the village of his sister's powerful matrilineage and struck with vengeance the one who had defied him. Ever since I reread this story, its emotional content has hardened in my mind into something solid and painful and has combined with Nyakanjata's present story, strengthening my sympathy for her. She had disobeyed her brother Sakutoha's wishes for the sake of her children, yet even so her children did not love her.

The desire for influence and the anxiety over its loss in a small group can be extremely strong. My mind goes back to Sakutoha firing his gun at Manyosa's homecoming. Manyosa was the daughter of Nyamwaha over whose adultery the murder of Manyosa's father and the resulting slave-compensation came about. Manyosa and Sakutoha were related, not by blood but by an emotional tie; his interest in her may have been strong because the fatherless child and the banished slave children were linked by that ancient blood indemnity. Then there is the curious fact that the Shika members, Johnny and Morie, evinced interest in this Ihamba. It was Morie who intuited that the second tooth was Sakutoha's. Sakutoha had belonged to Shika Village, but we read that he and his sister had literally belonged to the headman Shika as slaves, even prior to the murder; they had been paid to an earlier headman of Shika (once used as pawns they were likely to be used as pawns again). Yet the fact that they had once belonged to Shika had reinforced the connections between Kahona and Shika.

Slavery had been banned by the British South Africa Company when it took control of the area in 1907. However, this ban only limited commercial slavery, whereas village slavery, or pawnship, continued for some time. Village slaves were paid as a fine to settle debts, to terminate feuds, to clear a person from the accusation of sorcery, or as in Nyakanjata's case, they served as a payment for homicide. As is true in the case of Nyakanjata and Sakutoha, the persons paid as slaves were often young children. While children of male slaves by free mothers were regarded as free Ndembu, children of female slaves continued to have slave status and would marry within the village. The preponderance of Nyakanjata's matrilineage in the village is related to this fact. As Victor Turner (1957) noted, "The slave lineage may be the larger, since most of its members may marry within the village while the virilocal[1] marriage of female members of the free lineage may reduce its effective membership within the village" (190).

Nyakanjata

Using Nyakanjata's ritual history, which she related to me in December 1985, it is possible to sketch in the intervening developments in Kahona Village. As a young girl coming into puberty, Nyakanjata was initiated at Kahona Village by the headman Kahona's sister, Nyamuwila, who was evidently a strong personality, because after her death her name descended in spirit succession to become the Ndembu name of Nyakanjata's son Timothy, the worldly, often drunk, and often absent Timothy—whose several wives considered *him* to be headman of Kahona. The existence of the new Nyamuwila, Timothy, reinforced Kahona's influence in the village but also gave good standing to Nyakanjata's matrilineage. Even Mulandu (D3), Nyakanjata's sister's son, strengthened the Nyakanjata lineage by becoming headman of Kahona for a short time after the death of Kahona Sambumba. Later, he and his family "hived off" to a further group of huts down from Singleton's house, leaving only Timothy in the main circle, a man who sporadically contested the position of headman.

Another event contributed to Nyakanjata's power. When Nyakanjata's first child Ngeni, a girl, was young, this daughter took the name of Nyakan-jata's mother in a name-inheriting ceremony—among other things rein-forcing Nyakanjata's own matrilineage. We begin to see more threads of emotional linkage and power manipulation in the village. Kahona himself, a man of good repute, was known as a hunter and above all a chiyanga, an Ihamba doctor, one who could control the wandering tooth. It was he, along with Benwa (linked to Nyakanjata affinally and also through a dis-tant mother's brother—that is, through Nyakanjata's matrilineage), who taught his son Singleton the craft of healing, again validating Singleton's lineage position. Of the others in the chiyanga tutelary succession men-tioned above, Kamawu and Koshita were linked through Kahona, and Chisanji through Nyakanjata. Now, not a soul remains in Kahona Village of Kahona's own matrilineage; Nyakanjata's has grown to fill the place, illustrating a situation that Turner described in 1957 of "powerful slave lineages which, like cuckoos in the nest, ultimately ousted free lineages from the headmanship of villages" (190). However three spirits in the tutelary succession still derive from Kahona's matrilineage, Kahona himself (C5), Kamawu (D13), and Koshita (E5), and it is notable that there is no hint of conflict between them and the Nyakanjata group of spirits.

In the rest of Nyakanjata's personal ritual history, the names of her afflicting spirits and doctors were all taken from her own matrilineage. Through her very afflictions her power was growing. Her afflictions had come in the mode of the Wubwangu, Nkula, and Isoma spirits, all bringing miscarriages. She underwent a Kanenga antiwitchcraft ritual to cure ma-laria, Kayongu, to cure the affliction of a shaking body as in Ihamba, and Chihamba, to greet the demigod way back in 1927 when she was first married. Because it was her classificatory father from Shika who took her to the ritual, we know that even after fourteen years of concubinage her previous Shika affiliation was strong. In her illnesses she was looking back into the past, where the spirits that afflicted her were classificatory mothers and mother's brothers. At the same time that her rituals were mounting up, her family was growing until there were forty-one grandchildren. Even when Kahona died around 1982, she did not move back to Shika, though she was free to do so. She had created the matrilineage around her from her own body; its members did not arise from the headman's matrikin in accordance with the normal pattern in a village.

And now something had gone wrong: the terrible pain described by Benwa had gotten into her. There was no apparent reason for anything to go awry but out of the blue came this barb, not from guilt exactly but from a flash of pure malice. It is possible to see the explanation from this point of view—not that the survivors were sick because they felt guilty, a psychological explanation and not the Ndembu's own, but rather that Sakutoha *was* angry.

It was odd having remembered Sakutoha. If Sakutoha could have seen his own widow Nyanjita in 1985, sitting in Mukanza Village, talking to me, and looking at his old photo, herself hale and cheerful, surrounded by many grandchildren who were also Sakutoha's own, would he have been satisfied and relented from his attack on Nyakanjata, or was the old claim of a Ndembu brother to his sister's allegiance still something so vital? Evidently it was. That ascendancy of a brother over a sister was, except for hunting, all that men possessed under a matrilineal system. Without matriliny there would have been none of the anchoring to the mother, so necessary to enable the generations to survive in those forests where the fathers were often absent. Matriliny would have dissolved into a situation of weak patriliny. And those patrilines would have been full of gaps. The men wanted their independence, and they also wanted their mothers and sisters around at home—not so much their wives, who could not be relied upon under conditions of frequent divorce. Here again, I am following emotional threads, showing how anomalous was the case of Nyakanjata, where her earlier helplessness changed into an updraft of power derived from her own matrilineage—brother or no brother. We do not know how old Kahona, referred to by Singleton as Sambumba, took this usurpation of his previous generation. His work of teaching the healing skills to his wife's kinsman Benwa and his remarkable son Singleton showed at least a positive regard for the Nyakanjata lineage. Sakutoha's tooth flew into Seti in 1974, as well it might, knowing Seti's character. It was Benwa, Kahona's student, who extracted the tooth. Earlier, in 1960, Bakston (D9), as we have seen, had an ihamba in his ear, which was full of pus, giving him headaches. On that occasion it was Chisanji's (C3) task to heal him (Chisanji was the student of Kahona). The steps from Kamawu (D13) to Koshita (E5) to Kahona Sambumba (C5) to Chisanji (C3) to Benwa (B1) to Singleton (D7) are being continued to Fideli (E2), to Vesa, Snodia's husband (D12), and to Snodia's son Luka (E4), a total of nine in succession.

Healing and Hunters

Patterns of healing with dynasties of tutelary spirits are becoming stronger among the Ndembu (see Appendix 1). Among contemporary Ndembu, healers do not invoke the help of the *patient's* ancestor spirits as in the past, because missionaries have taught the people to regard such spirits as demons and idols, and indeed, they are so translated in the *Lunda-Ndembu Dictionary* (Fisher 1984) and in local Christian literature. The doctors, though, seek the help of their own tutelary spirits and sometimes of God—here the succession of healers in our Ihamba case resembles a series of patron saints in that they may return with mystic powers or, as we have seen, an apostolic succession of priests consecrated in an unbroken chain. Here each living "priest" is, as it were, a miracle-working saint and is informed by past holy souls.

During his long apprenticeship, each Ndembu healer drinks leaf medicine at every Ihamba, a privilege not for everyone; this drinking can be seen as a very physical act. Possession of the tooth as an amulet confers another material advantage—it gives good luck to the hunter, and the tooth, if kept carefully and fed (see Chapter 6), may be passed down from a hunter to a younger hunter relative. It is carried by the hunter in his wallet along with *mpelu,* "magical substances," shells for firearms, and in the old days, flint and tinder for making fire (Turner 1968, 175–76). The tooth—a wild object when uncaptured—usually enters in its mysterious way into the bodies of individuals linked to it by matrilineal kinship (see Turner 1968, 304–6, 309–11), necessitating a lengthy ceremony—the Ihamba ritual—to recapture and reharness its efficacy. Its volatility is like the hunter role itself.

Hunter's skills are not automatically available to all; the gift of good huntsmanship appears to be randomly distributed and basically belongs to the individual hunter himself—huntsmanship becomes his vocation. In earlier times, the hunter, owing to his volatility, would be accompanied in parallel fashion by the presence of hunter spirits or demigods such as Mukaala who at first encounter were the essence of wildness, threatening beings, who when obeyed and fed would help the hunter. The following passage about Mukaala would equally well describe the entity called ihamba:

> He cannot be pinned down, he is capricious, arbitrary . . . dangerous. He is a master-symbol of the accidents, perils, and disappointments of the hunter's life. Yet at the same time he can be propitiated, even to some extent controlled, by performance of the proper rites. And if you get him on your side, he can be a source of great blessings—he can help you to slay many animals. What he seems to require is something like a total commitment to the hunter's way of living; a hunter must identify with him . . . become as fluid, mobile, and unattached as he is. If the hunter can't beat him, he must join him. (Turner 1975b, 69)

It was that same wild male hunter in Sakutoha that attacked Nyakanjata, the woman who had become the settled head of a matrilineage.

During the last part of October, Bill and I and Singleton and Fideli used to meet to unravel the exegesis of Ihamba. The house Bill and I inhabited was dark inside; Bill's room was about seven feet by ten, containing his bed, two chairs, a tiny stool for me, and a narrow table on which stood the tape recorder. Fideli translated for Singleton while we went through the medicines and action of the ritual. I was listening carefully to Singleton and caught most of what he was saying, and I was able to comment on some of his phrases directly. Bill sat on his own bed, listening seriously, his fair skin a contrast in that dark place. His sympathetic manner drew much of the explanations of the Africans toward himself.

It was by these means that we began to understand the incessant flood of coming-out significations through all the materials used and all the actions performed. Singleton sat erect, his long legs relaxed, his head alert—beginning to realize himself that I was not trying to denigrate what he did as superstition, but rather I was motivated by an excited love of the coherence and power with which all the elements of the ritual had climaxed. Later, back in America, I strung the exegesis together, showing how the elements combined to form a battery of signification, meaning to "come out."

At the time of the discussions, these powers did their work on my own consciousness; Bill and I would say to each other, "Come out with it!" when either was at a loss as to how to put something; we also used the *mazu* ("words") method of clearing the air, Bill speaking in his gentle voice like his American grandfather the water-diviner. "Get it off your chest" was another phrase we used that applied to Ihamba: our own culture is familiar with the benefits of this kind of "psychorevelation" (a term that combines the ideas of the Ndembu and those of Vic Turner).

Mazu ("Words")

Vic Turner saw Ihamba "less as curing an individual patient than as remedying the ills of a corporate group" (1967, 392)—"sociorevelation" in fact. Turner goes on: "The sickness of a patient is mainly a sign that 'something is rotten' in the corporate body. The patient will not get better until all the tensions and aggressions in the group's interrelations have been brought to light and exposed to ritual treatment." And Turner also reported: "The patient's kin are obliged to confess their private grudges against him; if they do not confess, the doctor will be unable to effect a cure" (1975a, 143–44).

This kind of confession may be compared with that described by Monica Wilson (1959, 134–41) for the Nyakyusa and Mary Douglas (1970) for the Lele. Both concern the hiddenness of witchcraft and the benefits of opening up and confessing. The doctor Muchona said that revelation medicine had the meaning of "speaking private matters in public" (58), and Turner showed that "hidden grudges are brought to light by adepts and candidates in an endeavor to locate the cause of a spirit's anger" (1975a, 58). Here we have the notion of private grudges, matters deep and personal. Thus *words* are also the revelation of individual psyches, from deep within their psyches or souls, from which we might create the word "psychorevelation." The idea of the benefit of revelation is also shown with respect to the afflicting spirit: if the afflicting spirit is "mentioned and hence remembered by many people, it will cease to afflict but will benefit its victim, who becomes a sort of living memorial to it" (Turner 1975a, 212). Effective revelation, then, opens a beneficial path from the corporate group to the private concerns of the individual to the very afflicting spirit within the sick person, that is, the collective, personal, and spiritual dimensions. Furthermore, the common African theme of discovering the actual name of the afflictor is akin to the notion of *words*: "The main processual theme of Ndembu ritual is to make known what has been hidden, partly by naming the afflicting spirit, so that 'it is remembered by many people'" (Turner 1975a, 58). Thus *consciousness* of action at all levels is required, each kind of knowledge being revealed in a mode appropriate to it—*words* for the collective and personal, the divinatory proposition for the name of the spirit, and the awareness of the tooth's emergence for the spirit itself. Fresh material about that awareness, given in Chapter 6, takes us a step further.

The method of *mazu* was also the best way for myself as an anthropologist to lay out the forces within the ritual, that is, to treat the events intimately as they felt to me in the course of experiencing them. "As for this morning," I wrote in my diary that night, "a lot came out."

Childbirth Medicines in Ihamba

I realized that what had not been openly expressed to us in the Ihamba of the 1950s were the childbirth references, the stronger presence of the feminine. Earlier, the concern of Ihamba more strongly concerned the blood of huntsmanship and its danger, rather than the danger from the development of coming-out powers as such in the ritual. In the early version of the ritual, no one except the owner might look inside a receptacle containing an ihamba,

> on pain of bleeding to death when next cut. Women are forbidden to approach closely to a katunda [ihamba hut]. . . . Should they do so inadvertently, they are believed to develop menstrual disorders or to bleed to death after giving birth. . . . When a hunter's wife is about to give birth, he must remove all his hunting gear from his hut and its vicinity, lest it lose its efficacy. . . . Behind this principle lies the notion . . . that hunters shed blood and make it flow. Again, women give life, hunters take it. (Turner 1968, 179)

Clearly, by the 1980s there had been a change. The concepts had swung around, and references to childbirth and femaleness were now multiplied, starting with the concept of the greeting tree, mufungu, as the mother; Singleton said, "You don't cut your mother." This mufungu had greeted us and started us out on our way. We gave her beer, talked through her to the tutelary ancestors, presented the beer to them, putting red clay onto the bark for them and her. Again, there were strong childbirth connections in the mukandachina placenta-expelling medicine that Singleton secretly gathered. It was a dangerous medicine taken from a tree found on anthills and was also a cure for madness. Singleton's warning shout of "Pregnant women, go away!" is a reminder of how overmastering was the induced command to the psyche (spirit, not quite the same as the unconscious) to expel something from the body. Mutungulu medicine was another powerful expellant; it could even kill the inner-born children of the ihamba, the very possibility of whose birth implied the female sex of the ihamba itself—a bizarre notion compared with the concept of the super-male hunter in the earlier analyses. A hunter was said to be "a veritable witchdoctor of copulation."

One might include in the childbirth imagery the elephant tusk nerve, nsomu, hidden inside the tusk, a potent symbol of the open display of what is alive inside an organ; and conversely a symbol of impotence, that which has been forced out, a passive male object *within* a giant tooth.

Another childbirth element was, for me, the slow, long buildup of the ritual toward climax, and the great relief and joy afterward. Nyakanjata was in pain when she was first brought to the ritual, as if brought to bed. The ritual consisted of a series of episodes, or "starts," *kutachika,* in each of which her body made involuntary movement, just as the contractions of childbirth are episodic and involuntary. Toward the end she was totally shaken out of herself, and so weary that it seemed that nothing was going to happen—and that is when it did. One can talk of dissociation, of reaching lower levels by means of an ordeal. Such processes occur all the time in childbirth and are little mentioned in the literature because the main preoccupation of Westerners regarding childbirth has been the prevention of pain, not that something fundamental has changed one's physical and psychic condition. Men have often gone through Ihamba as well—Bakston and Seti, for example—and it would have been interesting to determine whether there was any difference of emphasis in their cases. In the cases that Victor Turner and I witnessed in the 1950s, some involved men patients, notably Kamahasanyi. In these cases, as Vic Turner explained, the blood of huntsmanship prevailed as a theme. However, during the same era women patients were also so treated, notably Nyasapatu, and here the same blood of huntsmanship prevailed. Thus it would seem that the change has been concerned with Ihamba itself, not the sex of the patient.

The evident change of emphasis appears to be paralleled by the newly admitted importance of women in contemporary Zambia. Since the decline of the copper industry, men have found it hard to find work, yet except in the case of traditional plowing cultures such as the Ngoni, they have not taken up agriculture to any extent. Their traditional role used to be hunting, which was replaced in times of economic prosperity by work in the mines, also a male occupation. Now there is widespread alcoholism—Morie's case is not an isolated one. And the work of women in agriculture has grown with the increased size of the family. In effect, the women are the center of existence in modern Zambia. It is their efforts that keep the country from true famine, and this is known by all.

In the country and in town, at every economic level, when a child is born into a family, the neighbors eagerly asks the sex. If the answer is a girl, there is great joy. If it is a boy, there is a grimace of disappointment, a sigh predicting a future burden. Fathers and mothers alike have the same reaction.

Because of this positive evaluation, "childbirth" medicines have become crucial in the battery of ritual forces arrayed in the "coming out" category.

The Ambiguities in Ihamba

The "thing" that was to come out was itself complex, as Victor Turner (1968) noted:

> The nature of an *ihamba* is ambiguously conceived by Ndembu. It has some of
> the qualities of an object of contagious magic (*mpelu*), in that it contains the
> power to kill and "stab" (*ku-tapa*) possessed by the hunter from which it was
> taken or from whose corpse it comes. At other times it is identified with the
> hunter's "shade" (*mukishi*), and seems to be regarded as a special manifestation
> of that shade. When it is "flying," moving about in the body, or "wandering"
> in the air seeking its victim, it seems to be thought of in the latter sense. When
> it is placed in a container, either a hunter's wallet, a *mukata* pouch, or a small
> calabash—when, in Ndembu idiom, it is "quiet" (*ku-fomoka*), it has something
> of the character of a charm or a talisman, helpful to the interests of its possessor
> and, indirectly, of his kin. (182)

The ambiguity of the ihamba, comfortably lived with in the 1950s, has
broadened even further and is peculiarly relished. The interval—the time
span of thirty-one years that I was able to bridge—gave me a vivid awareness of the breadth of the ambiguity. In the West the logicality of of-
ficialdom and its law of noncontradiction has ridden roughshod over many
delicate intuitions and modes of thought that hinted that ambiguous definitions *were* possible. To Africans we must sometimes look like "the man who
mistook his wife for a hat" (Sacks 1970). This patient of Oliver Sack's had
suffered right hemisphere brain damage and could only think abstractly; he
could not actually recognize anything except by the categories of logic.

For some time now, anthropologists have been investigating other
kinds of logic and reason (Wilson 1970, Overing 1985, Boddy 1989) and
discussing aspects of the sense of ambiguity and the greater feeling of fitness
often associated with it.

To begin with, as one reviews the ambiguities in Ihamba, there were
two persons, Nyakanjata and Sakutoha—and even a third, Matunka, when
one includes the first part of the treatment—present in one physical individual. It can be seen how many times Singleton and the others, when
addressing a command to the figure on the antelope skin, changed from
Nyakanjata to Matunka in the same breath. Was it to Matunka that they
said, "If you are annoyed that your children do not love you, shake,"
followed by "you are the grandfather of us all"? There is an intractable
ambiguity about it.[2] Wordsworth has a passage in *The Prelude* describing
ambiguity or different levels in the image of water:

As one who hangs down-bending from the side
Of a slow-moving boat, upon the breast
Of a still water, solacing himself
With such discoveries as his eye can make

Beneath him in the bottom of the deep,
Grots, pebbles, roots of trees, and fancies more,
Yet often is perplexed, and cannot part
The shadow from the substance, rocks and sky,
Mountains and clouds, reflected in the depth
Of the clear flood, from things which there abide
In their true dwelling; now is crossed by gleam
Of his own image, by a sunbeam now,
And wavering motions sent he knows not whence,
Impediments.
(Book IV, lines 256–69)

There are several levels at which one may *see* in Ihamba. The Ihamba doctors were able to communicate at will with the woman in trance, with the spirit of the dead connected with her, or with the tooth of the dead that was concretely troubling her. Bill and I often had the sense that they were calling through Nyakanjata's skin to the thing within. There was a further ambiguity about the doctors themselves. Their actions were pragmatic, even when they were dealing with spirits. And at the same time they had several styles of speech, several levels at which they operated. In everyday circumstances Singleton and Fideli existed as two African village elders who had their secular plans and troubles. Singleton came around to my house on one occasion asking for Western medicine for his child who was coughing, and I was glad to supply it. Matters like these were quite different from the Ihamba medicine collection trip, where it was only those who were accepted into the cult who might participate. The talk while on the medicine quest was quiet and intent, pragmatic in tone except for the invocations, which were spoken in a fierce rapid tone of command—a tone intended to awaken the spirit, as Vic Turner and I had learned in the 1950s.

In the ritual proceedings at Kahona there was plenty of everyday language. It ebbed and flowed with a greater freedom for argument than usual, a greater sensitiveness to being slighted. The affair of the tooth really mattered to them, and they came out with their feelings in these circumstances and "showed their liver," that is, in our parlance, they did not mind wearing their hearts on their sleeve. The addresses, the *words,* and the divinatory propositions were all in a strong mode, the *words* being delivered in a raised tone of complaint, rapid and with a sense of being "uttered." The *words* came out in gouts, like blood, as one might say. In a style hallowed by long familiarity, these modes came into action when the time was ripe, as the reader can follow in the account above. Very often the *words* began like this: "*I say* so and so," in the style of indirect speech. In Chindembu the form is "*Nami* . . ." ("I say . . .") followed by speech in the first person. Frequently, an important relative would speak the *words* on behalf of the patient, using the form "*Nindi* . . ." ("she says . . ."), also followed by the first person.

It is interesting to compare these words with the way evidence is given in a Ndembu village court of law. There is the same firmness of style, there is the same public statement that has to be seriously taken into account. In Ihamba, however, the statement is not given as evidence but constitutes a direct communication between the different psychic levels involved—ordinary human, tranced person, tooth, and spirit person. The difficulty to be overcome, the disease, the reason for having the ritual, is that the inward tooth is stoppered up by the stopping up of words—constituting a theory of words as connected with the physical formation of an illness. This is similar to but not the same as the theory proposed by some anthropologists about the symbolic formation of illness. Among the Ndembu the stopping-up is actual, not symbolic, and has actual effects inside the body. If *words* were just suggestions or representations, they would have little effect. In our proverb we have the line, "Words will hurt me never." But here there is something like a concrete connection between the release of *words* and the release of the ihamba.

In the Ihamba ritual the emotional focus of the grudge is incarnated in the tooth. "You seem to be aggrieved when you shake. You shake as if you were not a gunhunter." Singleton is patently addressing Sakutoha. Sakutoha the tooth has as its origin a revered aggressive figure, a gunhunter, a meat eater. It is a privilege for the patient to be forced to harbor such a one, for it will eventually, by coming out, and by the coming out of all the patient's grievances, have the effect of purifying her. When you are truly one with the spirit and it is the spirit that is shaking you, you are living as a real genuine Ndembu, who is by definition an ambiguous being, both spirit and matter. The moment of interface between the approach of the ihamba to the surface of the skin and its eruption is for patients and adepts one of the most beautiful experiences of their lives.

It can be traced how since the 1950s the concept of the ihamba tooth itself has changed; the ihamba is not only animated, it has consciousness. At the very start of the medicine collection when red clay is put on the greeting tree, ihamba *knows* it has to come out. We *call* it out by various means, with the gentle sound of the rasp, with the tree of revelation, musoli, by the cock's crow, by the elephant's trumpeting, by the deafening clinking of the ax heads, by blowing across the finger horn to make a whistling sound, and by drawing the small horn along the patient's back. You can indeed *persuade* it to come out. It can *smell* castor oil leaves and mukosu soap tree bark, and it *doesn't like* them and *fears* them; it *wants* to be fed on blood; it tends to fly away, and therefore, the doctors take trouble to make it *honest* (its way-wardness makes it the very embodiment of the uncertainty principle); it *permits* us to catch it; it *obeys;* you can fool it into *believing* that assistants who are not fully initiated are great hunters by marking them with red clay and giving them the medicine draft, and you can do the same for ignorant interlopers by making them take the draft. Because the ihamba is so aware, adepts are very sensitive about allowing nonadepts to touch the sacred fire, or about such matters as letting the potent mukosu bark fall to earth.

Then there is the curious nature of the ihamba, so small that it can hide under the fingernails; it travels in the bloodstream, flies out, and enters other people. You can hear it biting, and see it move in your veins. The trouble that it brings is different from other illnesses: what you feel when it is in you is not just ordinary pain. Obviously, there are certain states that Africans recognize which are hard to explain but are nonetheless real and nonetheless curable. The ihamba is also a spirit, and it is to be noted that, according to Victor Turner's recording of an Ndembu text: "We do not usually see a ghost. To see one you must have already drunk pounded-leaf medicines of the dead, of the ghost. The ghost is a person dead already. When he died, if he drank the medicines of the ghost, he will rise again . . . and go into the villages" (1968, 289). Singleton, on the other hand, empha-sized that drinking the medicine protects the person against the intrusion of an ihamba—in this case, the necessary privilege of a small ritual community that needs to be protected.

People handling an ihamba use heavily patented safeguards—the rare small right horn from antelope killed by predators, the rare elephant's nerve, both difficult to find. Because the ihamba's behavior is almost un-tamable, the most concentrated powers must be used. We have seen how the participants at the ritual were in the midst of a tugging maelstrom of passion, with the obstinate ravenous ihamba tooth at the center. How does the ihamba come to emerge? In the course of the ritual, the patient and the participants are exposed to the battery of coming-out influences—forces that reach down deep into the thing that is inside the patient. The *words*—verbal disclosures of grievances—are deliberately elicited; the doctors know that these are necessary for the cure. Singleton said to Nyakanjata,

"We are happy at what you said," although what Nyakanjata said was a bitter complaint. A psychoanalyst may tell the patient he is happy when she reveals her troubles—but a psychoanalyst is not aiming to let some *thing* out of her body when the channels are open. For the Ndembu it would not be enough to merely hold a confession session, as if simply opening the channels would be enough for the cure.

Psychoanalysis may not be a palpable experience, but there is a Western experience that is. The experience of religious conversion for the born-again Christian is an opening of the channels when there is often the palpable feeling that a concrete burden had been lifted from the back. We shall see in Chapter 6 signs that this *feeling* was present but also something even more.

Singleton was happy that communication with the inmost Nyakanjata was open *because* the aim of the ritual was to let this actual thing, the tooth, fly through. This sense that openness is curative is also found in the *zar* possession cults of the Sudan.

> The *zar* emphasizes the importance of openness. . . . Focus in the *zar* is on openings and doorways that lead into an alternate reality: one opens the incense tin to discover which spirits plague [the patient]; coins and incense given the diviner are "keys of dreams" that enable her to unlock the door between the human world and the parallel world of *zayran*. (Boddy 1989, 342)

In Ihamba, at a blink the envisioning of the tooth turns into the feeling that it is a spirit, a person, wild and dangerous, that must be domesticated. In quite another culture, among the Northwest coast American Indians, a similar feature was found. At the Kwakiutl Hamatsa cannibal rites, a "wild man" bites small fragments of flesh out of one of the ritual participants. Then he can gradually be tamed, and along with him the human species can be brought into harmony with the whole array of living beings (Walens 1981, 138–48). Similarly, as a fed, satisfied, and cared-for being, the ihamba tooth/spirit becomes a talisman and provides his provider with meat. Now its ravenous quality is harnessed. As I saw the tooth, that small object was not the Sakutoha I knew—the big benevolent elder who prayed to the greeting tree in Chihamba (Turner 1975a, 51) and gave wise interpretations of ritual to Vic in many sessions. Here our doctors called the tooth Sakutoha, knowing it did not resemble him. An ihamba has its own personality, like that of a different species—wild, unpredictable, grotesque, and dangerous.

Thus there exists a doubling of images, an interesting phenomenon with which Africans and many non-Western peoples are quite familiar. The phenomenon does not necessitate the attention of psychopathologists, for the African practitioners have everything under control. To be willing to view reality as double does not imply a pathological view of life. For example, Philip Kabwita was a Ndembu ghost doctor who dressed in one kind of costume for his rituals and yet went everywhere in a state of unity with his tutelary spirit Casto, who had a different appearance. Philip, the man we knew, was quiet-spoken, sensitive around the eyes, and slender. He wore a grass skirt, rattles on his legs, a tortoise amulet on his breast, and a tall genet skin "hat of invisibility" on his head, and in one hand he held a skin bag and in the other a rattle. But his tutelary spirit was quite different. He was a British Roman Catholic priest, well-built, dressed in long white vestments, with a rosary and wooden cross on his breast and a white skull cap on his head. These two figures coalesced, and it was Casto who enabled Philip to perform his healings. Philip was aware what Casto was like because he, like Singleton, had drunk leaf medicine, and Casto gave him the power to change consciousness at will, which Philip effected by means of his spirit telephone—a conch shell with a cord leading down into his doctor's black bag. Putting the shell to his ear he could hear the voice of the spirit or of far-off friends (E. Turner 1986b, 12–35).

The different nature of the spirit entity may actually be depicted. Many African masks depict grotesqueness and distortion in startling contrast to the everyday human form. The Aztecs of Mexico also drew many forms portraying their gods, forms grotesque in the extreme, poles apart from any figure of everyday life. The bizarre spirit was set against the style of the mundane. These contrasts would evoke recognition and give pleasure because—in the contexts of archaic and more vital religions that had not yet been "purified" from their dynamic quality and thus denatured—such doubling was the materialization of, and corresponded to, this same universal ambiguity that switches across the levels of consciousness. It also told of what cannot be expressed because knowledge of it is nonverbal in its very nature. Moreover an actual community of ritual performers, such as the Ihamba group, is able to experience the nonverbal together.

Roy Wagner (1983, 1–7) has developed certain insights about Western and non-Western consciousness of the double. He tells us that neither part of the double is more real than the other. One's consciousness is not in both places at once, though Western consciousness carefully glues both together, largely ignoring the grotesque spirit consciousness. Freud, once the great guru of the West, insisted that the ego, the rational consciousness, should be ruler. However, an awareness of the different forms of consciousness, an ability to choose on which side to venture, is fundamental to the faculty of clairvoyance, as we shall see later. Thus Philip Kabwita was an adept in clairvoyance at a distance and Singleton was a master of the multiple forms of the afflicting ihamba.

Doubling further exists in the interplay of miracle and practicality at the "coming-out" of the tooth itself, and the drama of "finding the tooth" in the receiving can. My use of quotes here demonstrates my own doubts. Yet—I am asked by the church to believe that a factory-made wafer is the body of Christ, and I do understand that miracle enough to be a Catholic. It is an immensely complex matter on which some controversial things have been written, including the shocking "Credo quia absurdum est," "I believe *because* it is absurd." Singleton can look at me with his cunning delighted smile, and I myself feel the same rebellion against "the shades of the prisonhouse" (as Wordsworth called it) of positivism and am determined to be equally cunning in my true presentation of the ritual.

The Sequences and Processes Involved in Extraction

Earlier, I speculated as to how the ihamba tooth comes out—a key question. Getting the ihamba out is like generating enough speed to take a kite off the ground or developing the understanding to catch a fish. The pressure of all the effects rises slowly by means of a process known as the effect of the impeded form. The Russian formalist Victor Shklovsky described how modern artists sought heightened awareness, sensing the necessity of a kind of delaying tactic that allows frustration to build up, resulting in a strong final energy of denouement or understanding. The Russian formalists referred to a "defamiliarization" process in literature involving the deautomization of perception and habitual ways of thinking. Ann Shukman (1977) quotes Shklovsky:

> And so it is in order to restore the feeling of life, to be aware of things, in order to make the stone stony, that there exists a thing called art. The aim of art is to give the feeling of a thing as something *seen* [my italics], and not as something recognized. The device of art is the device of making things strange, and the device of impeded form increases the difficulty and duration of perception since the process of perception in art is an end in itself and must be prolonged. (41–42)

The impeding of the form in ritual gives time for the extremes of resentment and tension, and their opposite, relaxation, to develop to maturity in the patient; time for the powers of the participants to focus more and more accurately, in an intimate involvement with the cause of the trouble, with the patient's feelings, and with all aspects of the ritual; time, in fact, for all the hidden alleyways of the body and mind of the patient to be explored. The frustration involved, the disappointment as time after time no tooth emerges, builds this involvement and creates a potential for the appearance of the tooth and for health on the negative side, by default, so that the tooth and health spring into existence by a slingshot effect, by sheer necessity. (This was not possible with hopelessly ill patients such as Fwaila in 1952, who died of tuberculosis soon after her unsuccessful Ihamba [Turner 1968, 294–96].)

Deautomization is also an effect of impeded form. Nothing can be taken for granted any longer. "The psychological structures that organize, limit, select, and interpret perceptual stimuli," as Deikman (1975, 204) puts it, have been undone by the process of "reinvesting actions and percepts with attention" (205). In Ihamba every tremor counts, every word is significant. Deautomization, according to Deikman, results in a shift from automatic motor behavior, learnt through habit, to a mode that is "(a) relatively more vivid and sensuous, (b) syncretic, (c) physiognomic and animated, (d) dedifferentiated with respect to the distinctions between self and object and between objects, and (e) characterized by a dedifferentiation and fusion of sense" (206). It is marked by clarity of vision, a heightening of physical perception, and a "cleansing of the doors of perception," to borrow Blake's phrase; it is, in fact, the mystical experience itself, as Deikman describes it (207–8).

Furthermore, the idea of perception in ritual as an end in itself (compare Shklovsky's phrase quoted above: "the process of perception in *art* is an end in itself"—an accepted dictum) is, of course, slightly different in its implications from Shklovsky's idea. Perception in ritual as an end in itself was not considered an issue in anthropology until the explorations of Wagner (1983 and 1986) and others in the field of perception. In my essay on neurobiology (1986a, 225), I proposed that there are levels of human action that go beyond the functional toward action at a level that becomes an end in itself. Is Ihamba one of these? The multitudinous exercises in jumping between levels and facets and modes, the laughter and pleasure, the complex music, the more than psychological level of the ritual, the excitement of the climax, transcend the function of the healing of the body or even of the society. They are most economically explained as the desire of the spirit to manifest itself.

Concerning the particular application of the process of impeded form to Ihamba, one can trace the combination of the impeded proceedings and an accumulating crescendo of coming-out effects that in the end could not be resisted. Let us scan our account to produce a version that highlights these two processes.

The medicine collection is strongly concerned with accumulating and focusing coming-out power. Singleton walks along playing his gentle rasp, calling ihamba to come. Nyakanjata is not near, but his calling wakens the wayward spirit. At the greeting tree he rubs red clay onto the bark, and at this, ihamba knows "I'm soon going to be out of the patient." Singleton will catch the spirit with many medicines, the chikwata thorn tree for one; the mukombukombu broom will sweep those bad things out of the blood; the acid mutungulu will cleanse the womb—which is Nyakanjata's entire body—of ihamba afterbirths and ihamba children; the musoli will in a flash reveal the ihamba where it lies hidden, making visible what is concealed. The use of mukosu bark will let us catch the ihamba once it emerges, just as we catch the bark in our basket, and its washing quality will wash those bad things out of the body. Kapepi wood for the shrine pole that has the sharpened tines is bitter enough to make the teeth drop out. The ihamba will drop helpless before that guardian pole. Muhotuhotu, which casts its leaves off suddenly, will make the ihamba suddenly cast itself out. And the little mole plant, mutuhu, the "no-special-reason" tree, which comes unexpectedly out of the ground, will do the same. The dreaded mukandachina that expels afterbirths will be chewed and its juice put into the cupping horn, right at the slit through which the ihamba comes. Singleton's medicines encompass the universe, as he said, "Medicines for the below and the above, for the inside; every medicine to make ihamba come out."

These, all fresh and pounded together with, as it were, their very names pounded together—for the names too give them power—provide the liquid medium for washing the patient, for drawing out and carrying away the ihamba. There is a whole mortar full of what will give continuity throughout the broken episodes of the ritual. The very rite of pounding on one side of the mortar and the other is calculated to call. Nyakanjata's body is sprinkled continually with the cool tea-like liquid; eventually, there will be few places where ihamba can hide. Her direction, facing east, is right into the sunrise, head on into the epitome of emergence, the epiphany of the sun. The drums for calling began with the ax heads' deafening command. The blood of the rooster with his call is in the medicine, the trumpeting call of the elephant in the tusk nerve is contained in the finger horn. This horn itself sends out its whistle to call ihamba out.

Now the divinatory propositions begin, with the alternative commands, "If you are annoyed because your children don't love you, ihamba come out! If you are not, don't shake." A process of divination thus guides the doctors into the heart of the resentments of Nyakanjata and, indeed, of the family. They say quite explicitly that the ihamba will only come out when the bad *words* are out. The spirit is impeding the action continually, resulting in failure after failure to extract the tooth, to the point of great weariness. As Victor Turner described an attempt to draw out an ihamba in 1951:

> Ihembi went on his knees, and, like a hunter stalking his prey, closed in on Kamahasanyi, holding two purses in his right hand. He shook his head and withdrew, saying that "*Ihamba* has moved away." . . . But the people sang louder than ever. . . . The singing died down. Ihembi said, "It has gone away." (1968, 170)

Singleton too is feeling his way into the condition and the whereabouts of the ihamba, listening for it. This time, at each strong urge of the drums and the singing, I too lean forward singing, my camera jogging as I clap, ready to seize the camera and snap but carried on in the frantic advance, only to fall back myself exhausted at each disappointment. (It is clear that I was operating on two levels—and at the first Ihamba it often had to be on the analytic level.) Would I like to be the organizing doctor myself? I know what it is to be involved in a long endeavor that may or may not be successful. That involvement of Singleton and Fideli locks them in to a long task, and I knew how one could get locked in, as Singleton says when the failure of Ihamba or its relocation in Shika Village is threatened: "Then we are going to have to get Sakutoha out." People *can* go forward and fulfill their aims even in complex situations such as these. Nyakanjata is weary after twenty-two episodes as Bill has counted them. Her very weariness dissociates her, makes her quit her superficial efforts—whatever her upper mind feels those are—and lets the deep effect, impelled by the accumulative power of the medicines and the communications with the spirit, take place. The Sakutoha tooth slips quietly out into the horn, and is safely held by Singleton.

5. Background to the Second Ihamba

About a month later Singleton and Fideli announced that they were going to treat another woman for an ihamba tooth. By this time Bill and I were in good training for Ihamba, that is, well primed with facts and interpretations. I was also getting the feel of the ritual.

For the reader to understand what happened in the second Ihamba, it is necessary to give a wider view of our social surroundings.

The Kawiko Vicinage

One may term the wider circumstances "social field," as Vic Turner did, while the inner events themselves, taking place in what might be called a paratheatrical mode with elements of the social drama, occurred in what Turner (1974, 17) called the "arena"—the scene of action itself, including the immediate social dramatis personae. The general social field of the first Ihamba was constituted by the workings of Ndembu-Lunda society itself and the state of the vicinage surrounding Kahona, as well as the events of the distant past for the family—the murder of Kalubinji, the compensation, Nyakanjata's resistance to leaving Kahona, and her growing grievance against her children—all centering on the present social situation in Kahona and the ritual scene as we saw it in the middle of the village. This sandy area in the plaza was, then, literally if you take the Spanish connotation of the world, the arena. In the second Ihamba a different section of the Kahona family was involved, but the ritual retained most of the same social field, the same doctors, and the same general circumstances as the first. The arena was a new ritual scene in Mulandu Farm, a small group of five houses that had hived off from Kahona and were built along a straight bush track (see Map 2 in Appendix 10).

Map 1 shows some of the villages where the two thousand inhabitants of the Kawiko vicinage had their homes. In the 1950s, the inhabitants numbered about six or seven hundred, so that the population must have

tripled during the intervening thirty-one years, whereas the district population generally had increased from about 30,000 to 69,000. In our area the
increase was caused only minimally by the settlement of refugees from
Angola; the cause was clearly a vast rise in the number of children being
born and surviving. The contrast with the past is remarkable. The actual
birth rate in the 1950s for the northwestern province of Zambia was considered by Western demographers to be unusually low, and they were at a loss
to explain it. From the vantage point of the present, it seems that a good
natural balance had been achieved in an area of poor laterite soils which
cannot survive deforestation. The Westerners' implication that something
was wrong with the birth rate may have influenced Zambian public policy
on population, causing them to take up their present attitude that a bigger
population is better. But this policy has turned out to be a tragic mistake.

In 1985 the two dirt roads that ran through the vicinage were bordered
by sixty-seven tiny villages and farms, occupying an area of about eight by
six miles. In the 1950s, population density in the "built-up" area was about
twelve persons per square mile, and generally in the district about two to
five. In the 1980s, the built-up area showed about forty-four persons per
square mile. The government school was rebuilt at the center of the
vicinage, to which streams of children dressed in bright blue uniform
frocks—the same for both girls and boys—converged every morning at
seven. Headman Kasonda was the head of the school board and was also
the judge of the vicinage court, assisted by his old colleague Nswanakudya
for whom the school was named. The primary group of houses in Kasonda
Village was reduced to seven in number, compared with fifteen in the same
village in the 1950s. Westernized Africans were building more in the pattern
of modern individual farm homesteads than in the old collective kin-based
circle. Under government edict the houses were all made of sun-dried mud
brick instead of temporary wattle and daub, so that a periodic uprooting
from one area and rebuilding in another with more fertile soil—the old
rotation system—was impossible. Even Kasonda, who was relatively well-
to-do, had to buy meal in the off-season, or else he was hungry. Those who
had no money did go hungry.

Our own hut was built of burnt brick, as opposed to sun-dried brick,
and constituted a symbol of political change. It was built as a store by a
nongovernment trader not long after my earlier departure in the 1950s and
served the vicinage around with cigarettes, trade cloth, soap, and other
small items. It boasted a thin concrete floor and plastered walls. In the era
of high copper prices, the independent socialist government nationalized

the distributive industry and established centrally run national and cooperative stores in all district and subdistrict centers, at the same time discouraging small private trading centers, including this one, which was forced to close down. The school was rebuilt at the hub of the community, and a clinic was built close behind the disused store. Mangaleshi, Kasonda's wife, took over the tiny building as a living space for herself and many of her grandchildren.

By the time we arrived and were granted the use of the hut, many years of economic crisis had struck the Ndembu and all of Zambia. These years were reflected in the building. The plaster walls and concrete floor had long since cracked and broken. Bill and I paid Daudson to repair the gappy thatch, a process that sent showers of decayed grass down upon us inside. Gradually the sky patches closed together and we felt more secure. In the two dark rooms we wrote our notes by the light of a small Vaseline bottle with a pierced lid through which a scrap of cloth emerged as a wick for the kerosene. Thus we felt somewhat closed-in during write-up hours. Otherwise, we were out talking or walking to villages along red laterite paths crossed with ant trails, skirting beside abandoned fields, or along the road with its sociable foot travelers.

As the quantity of field material grew and Bill accumulated tapes of both rituals and discussions, we employed our assistant Morie and other young educated helpers to transcribe the tapes, first in their original Chindembu and then into English—a laborious process. Morie and Jennifer, who was my own assistant, sat in Bill's room working at this task at such times when no translator was needed to help us in the villages.

There came a time when Morie began to fail to show up for work. How shall I describe Morie? He was the epitome of ambiguity, sweet natured and unpleasantly severe, efficient and unreliable, open-hearted and jealous, full of information and yet often silent (I begged him to tell me the local gossip but he would not do it), an integrated member of the community and yet not belonging at all, a non-Christian and yet not a traditionalist, a playmate of my own children in the old days and now a man divorced several times. I think he inherited strains from his father, who was both affectionate and jealous (see Turner 1967, 131–33, 148), as well as from his maternal great-uncle Mukanza, a kindly but passionately partisan man, from my old comrade Manyosa with her longing for fun, perhaps from his jealous grandfather, the murderer, and from the great Sandombu the sorcerer—that is, where his drinking was concerned (see Turner 1957). I record these impressions of mine for they constitute a real part of the field and concern human elements that add to the understanding of the events of the second Ihamba.

Quarrels in the Past

Victor Turner's 1954 field notes include a story that casts a light on the past relationship of the Kasonda family with the Kahona family and that partly explains Kasonda's drift away from those "pauper villages," as he labeled the Kahona group, toward a more respectable Christianity. (References to characters in this story, also maps and genealogies, are available in *Schism and Continuity*, 1957.) The field typescript was dated January 30, 1954, and was headed as follows:

> *A Scapegrace from the Copperbelt and His Reception in Mwinilunga*
>
> Today there was a tremendous row in Mukanza early in the morning. When I went into the village to investigate I found the village arranged into groups. The scene outside Sakazao's hut was dramatic. Sakazao and Chikasa [elders] sat on either side of Sakazao's doorway on the ground. Along the trees and pineapple plants that fringed the path to Sakutoha Farm stood a group of people from Kasayi Village [where Kahona was living]. By Nyaluwema's kitchen were gathered a group of interested women spectators. Kasonda stood in the middle of these groups. Bit by bit I pieced out what the trouble was and the long history behind it. Best to begin at the beginning.
>
> The case concerned a young man called Seti who was standing with the Kasayi group playing a guitar. He is the son of the still-living mother's brother [Kahona] of the headman of Kasayi. His mother is the sister of Sakutoha who is living at Kasayi. He has relatives on the father's side in Kamawu Farm, which is about 100 yards from Mukanza. [Kamawu (D13) was the Ihamba doctor who passed on his knowledge to Koshita.] He has spent most of his adult life either in the Congo urban area or on the Copperbelt. He is a notorious thief "from Europeans" and had done time on several occasions. The last time he was in prison—in Kitwe [a Copperbelt town]—he sent his wife back to her village of Kamawu, and wrote a letter to his mother's brother Sakutoha saying that he had given her much of his loot, short and long trousers and blazers, etc. Sakutoha, when the woman returned, as written in the Diary for September, kept on pressing her to disgorge these clothes but she said in a tone that carried conviction that she had none of them, only some skirts and dresses he had given her. At the time Sakutoha did not believe her and continued to nag her about them, until at last she said if Sakutoha came any more she would swear at him. When Kinisa, Sakutoha's daughter, heard this she became very angry and went to Seti's wife with her mother to tell her that why should she, a mere woman, threaten to behave so rudely to a man and

an elder, one moreover that she called *muku,* or in-law of an adjacent generation? Seti's wife spoke to her angrily and Sakutoha came along to pour oil on the flames. Seti's wife in the course of the argument flew up at Sakutoha and attacked him, whereupon Kinisa and Sakutoha's wife started to beat her up. When peace was restored Kamawu called Mukanza, Kasonda, Chisanji [the latter was to be another of Singleton's tutelary spirits (C3)], and others to judge the case. It was decided to leave it over until Seti returned. When Seti came back it soon became clear that he had lied about the clothes he had promised to Sakutoha. Both Sakutoha and Seti's wife were rebuked for their behavior but the main culprit was regarded to be Seti. Sakazao had also been sent to *ku-hakula,* mediate. Sakutoha said he did not want Seti at his village and Kamawu also was not anxious to have him. Seti then proceeded to his father's village, Kasayi, and alleged there that Sakazao had said that it was no use for him to go to his father's village since when his father died the others would chase him away from it. Some of his relatives there were indignant at this statement. They accompanied him to Sakazao and said this morning that they wanted to make a case of slander against Sakazao. Sakazao protested that Seti had lied and called a number of witnesses to attest to the fact that he had made no such statement. Among these were Mboyunga and Kasonda. Seti on his side could produce no witnesses. In addition Sakazao said that he had only been called by his headman Mukanza to attend and speak, not to judge. Kasonda put in that it was well-known that Sakazao "had no brain for speaking well" and it would be most unlikely if he made a judgment that Seti must not go to his father's village but must go to his uncle's farm. Next, Kasonda brought in a lot of evidence about Seti's behavior before and since his arrival at Kamawu to show that he was a liar and could not be trusted. For instance, he had said that he had left many goods with David Shika, with whom he was employed at the Chingola market [on the Copperbelt], to be sent back by the latter. When David was written to, it turned out that he had left one pound in cash only with him. Again when Seti's older brother, according to a letter he had sent to relatives in the neighborhood, had given Seti five articles of clothing to distribute among them, Seti had given only one, a blazer, to a young lad, and had kept the rest himself. On another occasion he had borrowed a bicycle from Chief Nyamwana Funyina, promising him his uncle Sakutoha's beer in return, and had then claimed that the bicycle was his own and had not given the chief any beer. Nyamwana made good his claim to his own bicycle and Seti had run off to the bush in great confusion since he had boasted that it was his own bicycle. Altogether he was a bad lot. Kilisha, the younger brother of headman Kasayi, and crosscousin of Seti, took the same view, as did Kasayi himself. But Seti's brothers, father, and mother supported him. It is, however, unlikely that he will be allowed to stay there in view of the opposition of the majority. Seti's wife is actually the sister's daughter of headman Kamawu and the sister's daughter's daughter of Biscuit of that village. Seti is staying temporarily at Kamawu until his destiny is finally settled. It is probable that he will go back to the Copperbelt since neither his mother's brother's village nor his father's village is willing to have him.

Victor Turner's field notes of the same date carry the Kalubinji murder, including the story of Kahona's acceptance of the gun to free his wife, and the matter of the nonfulfillment of his promise. Kasonda had been so stirred up by the Seti quarrel that immediately afterward he related to Victor Turner the Kalubinji murder story as background material for the Seti case—thereby arguing that Kahona (the father of Seti, Singleton, and the whole Nyakanjata family) was a cheat and a thief. In the Seti law case, Kasonda as lawman put forward as part of his case the argument that Seti was a thief because his father had also been a thief. Victor Turner's notes continue:

> Kasonda also told how Kilisha, full younger brother of headman Kasayi, set a snare and Kahona found a waterbuck in it. He did not tell Kilisha and divided the meat among most Kasayi men but not Kilisha. This probably accounts for Kilisha's opposition to Kahona's son Seti coming to Kasayi Village to live.
> February 26, 1954. Seti has now returned to the Copperbelt to find work.

The cleavage between Kasonda and Kahona was clear. In Kasonda's account Sakutoha himself did not show up as a particularly peaceful man, "pouring oil on the flames." Nephew or no nephew he is shown as not wanting Seti in his village. Concerning Kasonda in 1985, it must have taken all of his Christianity not to have tried to make me believe that Singleton— also Kahona's son—was a liar and a thief, as he had earlier tried to discredit Muchona the Hornet, Vic's main ritual expert. Kasonda labeled our woodman, Smart, Kahona's daughter's son, as an improvident pauper. Standing under our tree one day, inspecting our almost exhausted woodpile, Kasonda gestured to the sparsely green country beyond the anthills and dirt road and remarked that all the people in the non-Christian villages were sinners. Certain later actions of Kasonda demonstrated his disapproval of me too, which I felt was the result both of my choice of consultants and his senior wife's disapproval of drumming.

The Hunters' Conference: The Significance of the Hunter

I will now backtrack to a major event that took place on October 19, 1985, before the first Ihamba, an event that was first instrumental in getting us into touch with Ihamba doctors. A hunters' gathering was organized by Bill Blodgett. The material that came out of this occasion revived for both me and the villagers the ancient world of hunting and turned out to be a useful background to the ritual of the hunter's tooth. We also perceived something of the people's uncertainty about their culture, and Kasonda's ambivalence about it too. During the conference a cross section of the wider field of the later events at Kahona was exposed.

Bill was interested in collecting memories of obsolete hunting techniques and rituals and planned to create a dialogue between the hunters of old and the hunters of today. He took the initiative of convening this conference which was to include all the hunters in the Kawiku area, having obtained a list of them from Kasonda. Kasonda himself had always been passionately interested in hunting and still was. You merely had to show Kasonda's dog Spot a bow and arrow for the animal to go frantic with delight. Bill sent out his invitations and preparations began.

Formerly, hunting was the star activity of the Ndembu, its work of genius, so to speak. It is true that the women's cassava growing enabled the tribe to actually survive—it was the basic activity without which nobody ate, the bottom line of existence. Cassava, therefore, had major ritual aspects, while hunting in the past was ritualized as cassava's other pole, a masculine one. Formerly, puberty and reproduction had also possessed vital religious significance to the Ndembu, but these rituals were dying owing to the association with sex, a topic that was tabooed under the new Christianity. Healing rituals always possessed a strong value for their own sake; the prime example of the genre, Chihamba—now obsolete—had been known to older Ndembu as the greatest event in Ndembu life.

Hunting and the bringing home of an antelope, which provided the most favored Ndembu food, used to be celebrated by hunters' guilds organized in complex grades; these guilds emphasized the comity of males in a matrilineal society. "In the idiom of Ndembu ritual, hunting and masculinity or virility are symbolically equivalent, and the symbols and gear of huntsmanship are reckoned to be mystically dangerous to female fertility and reproductive processes" (Turner 1957, 27).

Traditionally, a hunter's mystical career developed in the following way. A young man after experiencing bad luck in hunting would receive a call in dreams from a spirit hunter, a relative. Through consultation with a diviner he learned that the spirit wished him to become a great hunter, and he was instructed to join the hunters' cult of Wuyanga. On performing the first ritual of Washing, using medicines, the young man would succeed in catching game. The next cycle was preceded by a return of bad luck, followed by dreams and the same divination, ending with further successes and the ritual of Naming, in which he took a hunter's name. The third cycle was at the culmination of a series of great kills and ended with the Cooking ritual, in which the internal organs of the animals were offered to the spirit and all feasted on cooked meat and cassava porridge. The fourth, *Mwima* (literally, "standing-up," "outstanding," or "ripeness"), was the highest honor a hunter could reach. He erected his trophy skulls on a framework of posts like a hut and sat beneath them beside a shrine pole planted atop the simulacrum of a grave. Beads were hung from the trophy skulls above, trailing right down to the ground. Benwa Muhelwa had won this degree of huntsmanship, having started at the age of eighteen by killing a blue duiker antelope with his father's muzzle-loading gun. It was his father who gave him the Washing ritual afterward. In the Naming ritual he took the name Kusukula, "the one who knows the direction of the wind." The Cooking and Ripeness rituals followed. Benwa was an old man with a refined intelligent expression, a small neat head, and thin body; he was just a little tottery on his legs.

All was ready for the hunters' conference. We dragged out of our hut the tiny table, the two chairs and the stools, and most of the grass mats so that the people would have something to sit on. We grouped all these in a democratic half-circle under a shade tree, then the drums were brought up beside the table. Bill set up his tape recorder to capture the drumming and the discussions.

Men and women quickly gathered along with their children who peeped from their mothers' sides. Among the mixed group of fifteen young and old men present there were Benwa, Kasonda, the Christian teacher Windson Kashinakaji (who used to be Victor Turner's translator and was now a benign and open-eyed sage), Johnny from Shika, Zakariya who was Kasonda's crosscousin, and the drunken Mindolu, all of whom were old. There were also Fideli and Kapepi, who were middle-aged, and Morie, Manuel, Amon the repair man, Kamerosa (who had been asked to bring an antelope but didn't and who arrived instead dressed to the nines in jacket, tie, and sunglasses), and Oliver, all of whom who were young. The bearded Manuel was the best drummer present. A pleasant day stretched before us under the green tree, with sunshine, a broad stretch of red African sand underfoot, and thatched huts here and there. The people disposed themselves in comfort and spoke freely.

Conversation ran easily from the very beginning. Kasonda told Kapepi, "Play the drums to learn how," and added ironically, "and also you might learn how to shoot." At this Kapepi took up the position on the second drum.

Young Manuel was trying something on the first drum. "This Wu-yanga drum rhythm's too difficult," he complained. He proceeded to whack out the rhythm that went with the Ndembus' popular songs, arguing that this was only the warm-up stage of the meeting.

"My hands are hurting," said Kapepi after drumming for a while.

Zakariya, who was a true hunter, told him, "Listen, they're asking for the hunter's rhythm. Come on, play it."

Manuel said, "Aren't the hunters going to sing? Or are they just going to sit around?" No one replied to the young man.

Fideli was searching the past in his mind, "Nobody wears the genet cat skin at all these days," he said, thinking of Ndembu history.

Over the other side the old teacher Windson heard him as he sat with the elders. "There's a difference between the old hunters and the new," he said in the singsong expository tone of a Ndembu elder addressing his gray-headed colleagues. "You can tell them by their symbols, their 'trail blazes.' People will say about somebody, 'See him, he's a hunter.' But they won't find any shrine pole by his house, they won't find any animal skulls hanging on it. In the old days you'd see the jawbones of animals hung on the shrine pole."

"But that was long ago," said Kasonda, his elbows sticking out. "They never missed a shot in those days; we were the same, we didn't miss either. Come on, it would be good to see a hunter dance the Wuyanga."

"Nobody prepared us for the old *mukoke-mukoki,*" said Zakariya, sulking.

Old Johnny said, "If these here are hunters they should at least have bows and arrows." Evidently, the hunters had not been told to bring their guns.

"They're just sitting around with their hands in their pockets," said Manuel. Everyone was grumbling about everyone else.

"They're no good at hunting these days because they drink too much beer," said Benwa. "If the hunter doesn't drink he's quite able to go into the bush for three days and bring back an animal."

They began to dispute about the unreliability of hunters.

"But you can use a flashlight. That makes hunting more certain," said one. He was right. The animals are attracted by the light and come close to the unseen hunter.

"No amount of night-time hunting with flashlights will qualify a man to dance Wuyanga," said another, and he added, "If the best Wuyanga hunters were here they'd dance all right."

Young Oliver put in darkly, "Those Wuyanga characters are the ones who kill people's children."

Kasonda said quickly, "We're not counting those." (Everyone knew Oliver meant witches.)

Benwa had some words to say in tones of oratory. We turned to him and listened. It was the story of hunting in the old days. "Long ago, if a hunter decided to go into the bush, he would first tell the women, 'Pound some meal for me to take along.' When the women had done the pounding, they put the meal into convenient sacks for the hunter to carry, and then the hunter sent for the boys who were going to carry the game home for him. Off they went. Out in the bush he would kill a roan antelope or a sable antelope, then they divided the meat into pieces and carried home the honored[1] internal organs and the lungs and intestines; these were for the hunter, because he was going to dance the Wuyanga when they arrived home with the meat. Then they called together the old men of the village like Nswanakudya who stayed behind.

"An uncircumcised boy wasn't allowed to eat the meat of honor, nor was a girl that hadn't yet gone through Nkanga initiation. The meat would be taken to a sacred enclosure. But today nothing's sacred, anyone eats the internal organs. In those days when a hunter killed an animal, the hunter himself ate the lungs and intestines, and he even ate the head. The traditions have been lost because those who practiced them have all died, and the people who are still around don't do a thing except bring in European customs."

At this Fideli smiled at him and said proudly, "I still have my father Benwa with me, and I'll not forget the old ways."

"Ha," said Manuel sticking out his beard. "Your father's already begun to lose his memory." He grinned triumphantly. Manuel was something of a cynic.

"No he hasn't. Wait till I go to Ihamba. I'll get him to remind me of everything."

They were drinking fresh sweetened pineapple juice because there was no orange juice or sodas available at Mwinilunga and because Kasonda would not allow Bill and me to order beer. Nevertheless, a little beer found its way to the gathering via Morie, the cost of which we gladly defrayed. To be sure, this was not much like the old days when Mangaleshi was a skokiaan gin queen on the Copperbelt and ritual gatherings regularly consumed six or ten calabashes of millet beer.

Kasonda had told us that he often thought about the old circumcision rituals called Mukanda, during which he had once been Vic's instructor (Turner 1967, 151–279).

Now from his ambivalent position he said, "We neglect so much of those old traditions—even old men like us neglect them."

"Yes," said Manuel. "Who remembers the traditions? Hey, what about the people who practice Ihamba? They remember them, don't they?" Clearly many of the young didn't know much about it.

Young Amon confessed, "I've not had the Washing ritual; I only know how to shoot."

"You're the son of a Wuyanga," said Kapepi. "Your father Machayi had the Washing. Why don't you try for it?" Amon was silent.

"Zakariya's the only one who's had the Washing," Kasonda told them.

Windson said with a tolerant twinkle, "I can see that in the end they'll thank those who had the Washing." He turned to Oliver. "What about you?"

"No sir, I've not had it."

The talk about Wuyanga made them want to perform the real thing, so Manuel and some of the hunters went off to find a chishinga shrine pole and a termite tower to be used as a spirit house. They decided to enact a single cycle of huntsmanship, consisting of a preliminary ritual, the hunt, and its final ritual. Meanwhile, we brought out Victor Turner's books for the others, and they looked at the pictures of Wuyanga.

Kamerosa took the book and turned the pages, "See. Bwana Turner and his wife, this one here"—Kamerosa pointed at me as I peered over his shoulder—"They were at Samuwika's Wuyanga. Look, there's Samuwika. He's dead now. He was a relative of mine!"

Kasonda took over the book. "He's here in these books. Just look inside; you'll find him." Kasonda had been present himself at the Cooking ritual long ago. "I remember that one," I said, fumbling the pages excitedly. I pointed to a singing hunter in the picture (Turner 1957, 29).

Kamerosa chanted, "Samuwika underground put his wallet around his waist and his gun on his shoulder, and danced on the plain." This was a version of the ancient hunter's song. Samuwika, though dead and underground, was dancing like a hunter.

(Here was the true coeval meeting. Wuyanga was not merely a "custom" in the sense that "the Ndembu perform a ritual called Wuyanga" in the impersonal present tense, but it was a case of "Kasonda and I were actually present at Samuwika's Wuyanga," personally, in the past tense. Their past was my past; we had all, in a way that was sometimes painfully real, passed through the vicissitudes of time. Equally for us all, the presence of Vic Turner's book brought back the past and emphasized that the

Africans and myself were coeval, that is, now sharing the same present. I was not distanced from them and could not regard them as some kind of specimen in a timeless box.)

The hunters soon returned with a forked pole.

"That's no good," said Windson. "Why didn't you bring a musoli pole?"

"It's got to be musoli," Benwa confirmed.

"Well, sir, we'll have to make do with it. It'll show the sort of thing," said Manuel.

Kasonda grumbled away. "Musoli. Only musoli will do."

"That's all right but where can you get musoli around here?" There was an enormous musoli tree outside the school by the soccer field but no one was allowed to touch it.

Zakariya said, "No problem. We'll pass it off as musoli."

I was watching but happened to lose the sense of the words for a time. Only when the tapes were translated later did the proper sense emerge. At the time I was looking disgustedly at the bit of wood they brought. It had only one fork; it was stubby, not fine and long; it didn't look right. And they hadn't peeled the bark off. "You should sharpen the ends," I said.

Kasonda immediately warned the others, "If you try to cheat her, she'll know."

Windson repeated, "She knows all about it."

I understood that bit and nodded sagely.

"Carve it then," said Windson and they did so. "Plant it," and they planted it.

When they were ready the performance began. Zakariya ran to his house and brought out his muzzle-loading gun which he presented to Benwa, for Benwa knew the rites. Benwa leaned the gun up against the shrine pole. He crouched down, then drew imaginary white clay dots beside his eyes, and an imaginary white line on the ground outward from the shrine. He then addressed the shrine in the peremptory voice of ritual:

"Come to us. We've given you white clay. We're going into the bush, you my ihamba, and you my mukongu. Let's go together and kill animals. Maheza!"

"Maheza!" replied the others. "Ngambu!" said Benwa. "Yafwa!" they replied. (This was the first time for thirty-one years that I had heard that chant; at this time, I had not yet gone to the first Ihamba reported above. I grinned with pleasure.)

They sang the "Iyaji-nayin wo-o," the hunter's song that Vic always loved and performed. It went,

> Put on your wallet,
> take your gun and your ax,
> the animals are running.

The song rang out in long plangent lament with quick running speech within it. Tears started in my eyes.

The onlookers began to direct old Benwa who stood before them ready for the hunt, with his gun on his shoulder and his wallet on his back, and an ax stuck in his belt.

"Start walking slowly. Stalk the game."

"Don't crouch yet."

"Not till you reach those small trees."

"Start by testing the direction of the wind. Kneel down and test it." Benwa knelt and picked up dust, which he threw, watching it blow. After all, his very name, his Ndembu name Muhelwa, meant, "He who knows which way the wind blows."

"Move out from there and go to the hill. Yes, that's right, hide behind the tree."

"The animal's about to run."

"Ha-ha! Kill it!" This was Manuel.

"Creep up on it! Creep!" Benwa lay down, crawled forward, then pretended to fire, "Paya!" He at once started up and rushed to the imaginary animal, giving it a coup de grace with his ax.

Windson said, "There's your hunter eating meat." They were all laughing with pleasure.

Manuel ran to the spot and brought the imaginary carcass home on his shoulders to help the old man, for Benwa's legs hurt; he was at least eighty years old. Nevertheless, Benwa started to dance before the shrine, while the drums beat:

> Welcome the dead beast, hunters,
> The dead beast who makes the sun set and brings trouble.
> Maheza! Maheza! Ngambu! Yafwa!

After that every hunter present performed his own dance. The proceedings were marked by keen competition for the honor of dancing in the

Figure 22. Zakariya and Edie dance with the gun.

center with the gun. When Zakariya took his turn I went into the center
with him myself and did what I had learned in the northern Ndembu capital
of Kapenda, where the hunter's wife used to dance with the hunter using
the gun as a bridge between the shoulders of the pair—just as Vic and I had
demonstrated in many anthropology departments since we first learned it
in 1951 (Figure 22). So Zakariya and I danced with the gun between us.
Then drunken old Mindolu danced. He attempted to put on the hunter's
belt, but failed to get it even halfway around his pot belly. Everyone howled
with laughter. He danced just the same, tall and majestic, his face tilted
toward the heavens in a myopic stare.

Afterward they discussed what they had done. Benwa recounted his
actions and prayer at the forked shrine, though this time he spoke in an
ordinary voice. Some of the company noticed that certain observances in
the ritual had been left out. There was no washing, no collective stirring of
the cooking pot. Tradition disappeared a long time ago, they commented.

"These here are Christians," said Zakariya.

Manuel argued, "It's difficult when you are trying to begin afresh."

"The tradition's now left behind as history," said Zakariya.

"He's the one who had the Washing ritual," said Windson indicating

Zakariya. "That's why he can remember tradition. We weren't washed, and we can't remember it at all."

Fideli told them, "What we're saying is this: the elders are passing away, so for that very reason we must try to keep the traditional customs. In the days to come, if they ask, 'Tell us what your ancestors did?' who'll be able to answer? Nobody, because we're all believers of some kind." To believe, hear, or understand (*kutiya*) now means "to be a Christian," or "to have a faith."

Fideli looked into *The Drums of Affliction,* which he had on his lap. "I think I know that man, I know his family from the old days. These pictures are pictures of Ihamba, aren't they? I'm so thankful. Between this book and me, I'm going to tell you the facts properly and quietly. In the Ihamba they performed long ago they used different medicines." He later expanded this. "You can regard Ihamba scientifically, using time. In the 1950s they used twenty medicines; in 1974 it was down to only one; and now in 1985 we use fifteen."[2]

The conversation turned to the hunters' demigod, Mukaala, the hunters' spirit manifestation in the form of a trickster, who might deceive you, on the one hand, and help you to hunt, on the other. As Victor Turner (1975b, 68–69) put it, Mukaala

> stands for the now-vanished autochthones who once owned the land as a hunting resource and not in its cultivable capacity. As such, he does not represent any specific segment of traditional Ndembu society, whether conceived in terms of political, kinship, or territorial organization. He stands for the air men breathe, for the open and high land, for the caves that penetrate the earth itself. He stands for the broad intertribal hunters' domain, and within that domain, mostly for the open country, for the plains on which herds of antelope are found, for the swamps into which men may fall, for the rocky outcrops and hills. . . . He stands for the unrestricted component of existence . . . someone from outside *ordered* Ndembu society, yet playing a key role in Ndembu *culture.* He is a troglodyte, before and below Ndembu society, and simultaneously an outsider to it.

Windson took up this very theme. "Mr. Benwa," he asked. "Do you remember about Mukaala of the tall termite hill?"

"Ah-h-h. Now that I'm a Christian I don't remember him."

"I mean, when you were hunting in the old days."

"Yes, I remember how it was when I was with him."

"You may remember him but do not trust him," instructed Windson, who had been a mission teacher. "Did you ever hear him whistling?" (This was repeating a query of my own.)

"In those days he used to find me when I was walking along in the bush, and he'd call 'Wo-o-o,' and I used to answer, 'Wo-o-o'; if he found you there, you were gone."

"You were gone? What did he want to do to you?"

"He wanted you to get lost in the forest."

The conversation wandered to other things and then again fastened on the possible causes of the disappearance of Wuyanga. Even the famous dancer Kapupuleti who was present confessed he didn't know the Wuyanga dance. Kamerosa in his fine clothes came in for censure.

"You're useless," they told him. "Your father's a hunter, and we're ashamed of you."

"Even putting on a tie."

"Take off those goggles."

Meanwhile, young Amon was complaining to Windson, "All this time you've only taught us about the good things European culture does."

"You tell me, what does it do that's bad?"

"It's the reason why Wuyanga died out, for one."

Benwa and Fideli were busy for a moment tracing the date of its disappearance at somewhere between 1959 and 1963. Meanwhile, the singers were chanting these lines:

The animal moves steadily, ey-ey-ey,
The sable walks steadily.
The waterbuck walks steadily.
The sable walks steadily, ey-iyayi.

Windson listened and said, "Now you're asking me as an old and experienced hunter: 'Why did that Wuyanga hunting song die on you?' It's true. Christianity and the Europeans caused it."

"OK. You've said it. Tell us more about the hardships we went through," said Amon. "We're Europeans ourselves now, aren't we?"

"You are for sure," said Benwa. "You're the one that followed them, son-in-law."

Windson finally identified the date of the abandonment of the gun-hunting ritual as 1963 or 1964. He was aware that it coincided with the date of the struggle for African independence. During the local takeover Windson had opposed the triumphant revolutionary party with its radical policy.

"Wuyanga has really gone downhill now," said Fideli. "The elders' explanation is that there aren't enough animals to be found. But the real reason why it's been forgotten is because of schools and education."

Windson and Zakariya questioned this.

"Listen," continued Fideli. "When a person like my friend Kamerosa here gets education, we discover he hasn't been initiated even by the time he finishes school. How is he ever going to be initiated? When a person gets an education, he doesn't like to have such things as the gun-hunting ritual embodied in him. In short, educated people find these customs outdated."

"So that's your explanation?" said Windson. He turned to Zakariya. "What's yours, sir?"

"It was independence that caused it. In the old days there were fewer hunters, but now the animals are diminishing because anyone can get a license. People these days regard the ritual as useless because almost anyone can shoot."

Kamerosa broke in, "I say it's because of Christianity."

"How?" asked Amon. "Isn't Western culture the same as Christianity? And if they're different, which of them is the cause?"

Benwa said, "It's because the elders who started this ritual are dead or tired. They are tired because the young refuse to be initiated."

Zakariya agreed that Western culture was the cause. "In the old days we had headmen who ruled and instructed us in our homes. But since we've moved into townships and schools have been built, people acquire whatever custom they can copy. There are no more elders to teach us, and as a result our customs are slowly dying."

"Yes," they all concurred. "That's true."

Soon after this we slaughtered a goat and divided it for the company. At this point Kasonda went to sit in the kitchen by himself. He was heard to say to his grandchild, "Your father's going a different way. Just you keep quiet."

"Why is he sitting over there?" asked Zakariya, and Morie told him that the conversation was for hunters only. Mangaleshi, Kasonda's wife, also kept in the background, partly in and partly out of the conversation. I left at this point to stir some porridge and cook the meat for the guests.

All through this account the swirling currents of ambivalence may be traced—the troubles that assail hunting being ascribed to drinking, to European ways, to modern education, to Christianity. The discussion kept returning to the issue of Christianity and the old customs. Windson said with an amused smile, "Christianity has destroyed the customs," and he truly did not seem to mind, he seemed to be very satisfied; he could be objective. Kasonda was partly drawn in by the fascination of hunting—and partly was aloof from it all. The young men, Amon, Manuel, and Kamerosa, tended to be shamefaced and bitter about the loss of the hunting culture. Morie went along with the majority on this occasion, although he was busy with the tape recorder most of the time. He enjoyed the trickle of beer, that is, about two "plastics" full—a "plastic" being a half-gallon plastic bottle. The women in the singing circle complained bitterly about the small quantity of beer as they were not getting any.

My own feelings of ambivalence about the past were expressed at this meeting. When we discussed the dreams that a young hunter formerly experienced at the beginning of his ritual career, Benwa admitted that he had had no such dreams himself.

"I had three bad dreams last night," I told them. "They were due to a headache. First, I was in a plastic hospital building trying to find my way upstairs. It had plastic walls like modern bathtub units, and all it showed inside was the inverse pattern of stairs. I found my way outside this wall, and there were the stairs, but with no balustrade. I was holding my daughter Rene by the hand; she was two or three years old and was wearing a red woolen dress (such as I myself used to wear at three years old). Though maybe it was Rene's daughter Rose. No, it was Rene. At the top of the stairs some people jostled us and Rene fell off. When I went to pick her up, her head was bent back (like the children 'hypnotized' at the Zaireans' magic show at Nswanakudya School, or like a certain congenitally crippled Ndembu child with only one eye that was brought to me for treatment). I blamed the hospital for having no balustrade. Then I woke up. In the next dream I was on the ground floor of a large building which might have been my old home at Ely, now dilapidated. On the floor of the kitchen was a flood of thick pumpkin puree, yards long. I had to sweep it up. People said to me, 'Use dustpans.' Again I awoke. The third dream was on the next floor up in the same building, in a room where a litter of garbage, sticks, and dust strewed the floor. Somehow I knew it was my grandmother's house. It was a hard job trying to sweep up the garbage, having to pass the broom around chairs and everywhere."

Mangaleshi who had been listening from the side said, "Your sweeping was the sweeping of demons from your heart."

Benwa said, "Pumpkin means meat, and the dreams are caused by *chisaku*, evil medicine, which has the effect of killing a relative of yours; you may know nothing about it." I had heard the traditional doctor Chipeshi explain chisaku, which is the motiveless malignancy of a witch. This was rather frightening: were my children safe, so far away? In my notes that night I wrote:

I have to throw my personal fate into this fieldwork if I am to substantiate my ideas about dialogic anthropology. Even to start a process of interinvolvement will set one off into total involvement, that is, it's all or nothing. To touch it at all is to participate totally with no holding back—which is incidentally quite the reverse of the way Western nurses are trained. They have to distance themselves emotionally from their patients, the argument being that distancing is necessary for efficiency. Anthropologists have to be their own guinea pigs, for better or for worse. How else would fieldwork have any substance at all, seeing that we have human personality anyway, whether we like it or not?

As I write at 4.30 A.M. I half dream of somebody's hands constructing a little paper bird, which begins to flutter. The person is going to let it fly away. Now there is hard rain, and leaks are coming down on my bed. . . . I got up to shift the food away from the drips and knocked over the lantern, breaking the glass. 5.30 A.M., signs of returning dysentery. Rain again at 7 A.M., and bed bugs.

To me the yellow pumpkin puree represented a dread of disintegration, or the flood of field material for which a broom was a futile instrument. The hunters' conference the following day proved to be such an unexpected flood, a flood of talk about disintegrating values, and a picture of a decayed house of fundamentalist Christianity, which indeed my own grandmother's house actually used to be. The nightmare experience of the stairs showed myself holding *myself* by the hand, alone outside the hospital—a building that expelled me and had nothing for me except reverses, the inverse pattern of stairs, like an Escher drawing. It echoed my bad experience with Vic's heart attack. And even on the outside normal stairs I failed to protect my alter ego. Such are the echoing and re-echoing despairs that attack those who are sick, as the Ndembu well know. And they know more, about real witchcraft, real healing.

Nevertheless, there was a paper bird that flew away, and that was good.

Now in the daytime the hunters' discussion kept coming round to Christianity. I said, "All the peoples of the world have their religions, and that includes the Africans before the missionaries came. Their religion was true. And Christianity is true: you get great human beings like Jesus Christ, in whom is gathered the unity, the love, the happiness of all things." I went on: "Your old religion wasn't bad. Why do the missionaries translate the spirits of your ancestors as 'demons'? When you feel the need for unity with their spirits, it's not very nice to have to call them demons, *nkishi.*"

One participant sitting next to Windson and Benwa said to me, "Which do you choose, Christ or the old ways, Satana?" I muttered to myself, "That's my old enemy exclusivism." And I answered, "We should join the traditions together with Christianity; there's no need to turn against your ancestors; they knew what was good like people do everywhere. There's Chipeshi the healer, he uses traditional medicines and is guided by God. And he has a natural healing gift." Everyone agreed; they respected Chipeshi, whom I witnessed healing a seriously sick man. I described healers in various cultures, Korea, Bali, Ceylon, Brazil, and the United States. I told them how people fall down in the spirit in these societies, just as in their own Ihamba ritual.

But swiftly the barb came back: "Jesus said, 'Thou shalt have no other Gods but Me.'"

"That's the Old Testament," I said. "What Jesus said was that the whole law and the prophets was summed up in, 'Love the Lord thy God with thy whole strength, and thy neighbor as thyself.'" Then I asked myself which of us was the devil quoting scriptures? Can love be a law anyway? Love? Law? Any more of these binary discriminations and bliss will fly away.

Luckily, the conversation turned to the merits and demerits of using dogs on the hunt. Then Benwa showed us his dark brown genet fur apron, with two medicated cowries fastened to its upper back along with a wooden peg and tiny horns filled with medicine. He explained that you wear it as an apron with the tail hanging down between your legs when you are going to war. When you flap it from side to side under fire no bullet will hit you, for you are invisible. The skin has no kindness or mercy to others. In order to test the invisibility medicine kept inside the cowries, you should try breaking into someone's house and steal their meal. If the medicine is working you will not be caught.

"I was once coming back carrying meat from the hunt with my friend Fanuel Nganji," said Benwa. "Suddenly, I saw something behind a tall termite hill. It was an elephant with many young ones around her, preparing to attack us. They charged, but Fanuel said, 'Stay quite still, don't run. I'm wearing my genet skin apron of invisibility. Just touch me.' I did that and we stood there touching. The elephants went by as close as this house (twelve feet away) and did us no harm."

The genet cat is known for its "sex" smell, and with its long phallus-like tail and its connotation of semen, it is the very essence of masculine power: a curious animal, so savage that it is hard to face. Other animals were discussed during the afternoon; the hunters' knowledge of nature was excellent, and I discovered that their system of classification of animals' footprints had not changed since the 1950s.

All through this wandering discourse and during the somewhat unorganized events, an atmosphere of pleasure reigned, along with curiosity about fellow hunters, a mixture of doubt and chagrin at forgetting, and much dialogue between old and young—one could follow the minds of the old flickering back and forth in time and the young taxing them with questions. The conversation showed strong consciousness and concern and intellectual interest in discussion for its own sake. This small community enjoyed viewing itself for what it was, the participants being stimulated by the unusual occasion and the presence of microphones, a tape recorder, and cameras. Such equipment will develop reflexivity really fast.

The obvious enjoyment of the debate on the causes of the demise of the hunters' Wuyanga was related to certain gifts shared throughout the continent of Africa—those of jurisprudence and public speaking. I heard constant reference to *mulonga*, "cause," or "because"; it also means "law case." Cause and effect, and the recognition of these, was a brain exercise in itself; this proceeded alongside the emotional content, that of pride or regret, and the puzzlement which showed up in Amon's words. (Amon was a clever electronics and watch repair man; he fixed my pocket tape recorder for me.) Windson and Benwa were in their element—in this case, Windson as the teacher and philosopher and Benwa as the storyteller and the repository of old lore. Fideli was intellectually excited, showing pride in his own culture, attacked and battered as it was by Christianity and Westernization. It was he who came around to Bill and me afterward and asked us to come to an Ihamba ritual in his village. "We do many of them, many," he said. I hadn't realized. At once I felt that a living connection had reappeared between me and the Ndembu and between their own past and present existence. The reader will have already seen how the link became concrete in the process of the Ihamba related.

On this occasion of the hunters' gathering, Benwa, Manuel, and the others reenacted their culture, just as Americans reenact their culture in "living history" exhibits such as Colonial Williamsburg and in historical movies. When Benwa was praying at the shrine, imperfect as the rough-hewn pole was, there was a magic moment when we wondered if his ihamba and mukongu really were listening to him. Also, few present would forget the stirring and pathetic sight of the wizened old man lying on his belly and shooting. Time had folded over backward, and the experience excited many mixed feelings in the onlookers, opening up questions of who was responsible for the loss of their culture, also opening up in me some strong reactions against missionizing Christianity. The hot plaza sand of that impoverished village was the scene of much thought.

My own presence as a link to the past, along with Vic's books containing pictures, Ndembu texts, and lists of medicines, was an even more concrete sounding board for the play of memories back and forth in everyone's mind. My volume of *The Drums of Affliction* disappeared at this gathering, as if it were the general property of the Ndembu, which of course, it was. I needed it though; the anthropologist's métier is words, and large parts of Ndembu culture were bound up in those pages. The book reappeared later in the house of Rosa Matooka, the mother of the high commissioner to Zimbabwe, who lived in a tin-roofed house on the way to Kahona.

There we were, teetering on the brink of trouble on account of the drumming (Mangaleshi had forbidden us to drum three days earlier), risking our welcome, infringing on a past that was labeled outmoded, disputing with the doctors of Christian law, simulating a spirit ritual, provoking debate, and throwing our weight by means of the artifice of a social gathering into the balance on the side of tradition. The elders in their dignity, led by Windson, overrode any possibility of trouble at the gathering. Kasonda expressed his ambivalence by changing his spatial position halfway through the proceedings. It should be noted that he later assisted Bill wholeheartedly in his study of drum-making and in the making of a mask. At the gathering the atmosphere was warm, glowing with pride as well as spiced with argument, also tinged with sadness, and there were hints of secret hopefulness from those like Fideli who knew that healing rituals worked.

Trouble with Morie

The troubles that we risked at this meeting began to widen as our involvement with Kahona grew. An earlier event also contributed to its sparking. At noon on September 27, 1985, as I was walking back from a girl's initiation ritual, I found myself accompanied by a buoyant little woman of mature skill and youthful beauty, Zinia of Kahona, wife of Bakston, already mentioned in connection with the Kahona family genealogy. As we walked along the road Zinia taught me the botany of the roadside plants, much as Muchona had done for Vic thirty-two years previously (Turner 1967, 131–32). Zinia and I ended up full of laughter for some reason, and my tiny notebook ended up full of medicines. She was the one with whom I had danced at the girl's initiation song fest at Kahona, when she sported a face fascinatingly polka-dotted with tiny white discs, topped by her black hair done up in sprigs. One could not help having fun dancing at these song fests; besides, there was Nyakanjata too, wearing no top at all, blissfully treading out the sexy dances.

During our subsequent conversations I asked Zinia if anyone remembered the old initiation breast dance, which used to be performed naked down to the waist. In this dance the actions of the body were a skilled matter of double timing, a combination of swift vibration and slow swaying. Zinia gave me much information on the fading girl's initiation for which I rewarded her. At length in the privacy of our hut, she consented to perform the dance naked-breasted, contriving in the authentic manner to shake her long breasts up and down—breasts that had fed six children.

Later that day after she had gone—this was October 14—trouble descended on the house. In the narrow passage between the rooms appeared Morie, balanced and haughty. He had a ploy that feigned to save my face and yet would enable him to accuse Zinia and me.

"D'you know what they're saying?"

"Who? What?" I asked.

"I don't know who." He wasn't saying who. "They say you're snapping her naked and you've put something up her 'what.' It's her, she herself has been going around blabbing to everybody about what you did."

"Tell me who told you this," I asked again, fascinated and yet shaking with shock. Her "what"? I got out a pen and wrote wildly. This was gossip indeed—but it was against me. "Was it the Christians?" They would think the dancing indecent, for sure.

"It's the old people, not the Christians. If you call her in she'll tell you the story. It wasn't about today, it was the first time, when you paid her four dollars."

Lord. Did they think Zinia and I were lesbians? Or was she on drugs or something?

"No, the clinic man's on drugs, but not Zinia. No, she doesn't have a girl friend or anything. She drinks sometimes. You put a plastic thing in her."

Oho, birth control. Now I knew the meaning of his phrase "up her 'what.'" I was laughing inside and also very angry and trembling. Morie frightened me. As if I had actually done it and was guilty.

"No, it's not true, of course," I said.

Morie had already shot out a card. It certified that he was a member of the Zambian police force. "I will arrest them," he said nastily. "I'm here to protect you, and I'll arrest them."

The whole gamut of consequences rose up in my mind—Kahona

people in the toils of the law—I myself used by Morie, put on a pedestal as the protected one, and thus by implication the smeared one, actually in the dock—finding no privacy anywhere for the noble old initiation dance—and much worse than anything else, that police card, in the hands of one who didn't turn up for work, who was offensive in his liquor, who sneered at our traditionalists—a *policeman* in my employ, to "protect" me? I was sick. It's hard to describe my reactions to the word "police." The police stood for the authority system, the capitalists against the workers, the respectables against the fun people, structure against communitas, against the spirit of human fellowship. The police!

"Put that thing away," I yelled. I tried to grab it and put it into his pocket. He struggled and held it up higher. "Just put the damn thing out of my sight. I tell you I can't look at it." I was growing more and more sick. I had vowed never to lose my temper here. Dammit, I loved these people. "Put it away! I'll go away and never come back."

The hideous blue card was there no more. Suddenly, Morie started quivering. "Oh I'm sorry, I'm sorry, forgive me"—he was squatting on the floor at my feet like a slave; I was still standing upright. I immediately squatted on the floor too. He lay down in the narrow passage. "Forgive me!" he shrieked from down there. By this time the shouting attracted old Johnny to the spot, hovering behind with a concerned face ready to defend—whom? He was confused. By now I was lying on the floor too, half giggling to myself, half angry, and altogether embarrassed, but I was *not* going to be the superior one. "Who am I to forgive anything?" I sneered, against myself. This could not go on; after a moment both Morie and I scrambled to our feet and fled in different directions under the gaze of an assembly of onlookers.

"Didn't you know that Morie was totally smashed?" said Bill afterward. The sick feeling of adrenalin was still in my body.

"Oh, I suppose he was." God I could be stupid sometimes, and indiscreet.

Morie never used that police card after all. Life went on somehow, but the incident had such an effect on me that I was afraid to talk to Zinia again.

The situation with Morie developed like this. His continual absences from work made it necessary to put him on an hourly schedule, a schedule he didn't seem to comprehend; he only knew that we owed him his full salary—and this difference of opinion started eating into our life. Morie's son, young Morie, age sixteen, came into the picture at this point; he was a highly intelligent English-speaking lad who had got thrown out of the school for thieving. He was bright enough to work the recording equipment and could work for several hours at a time, so we employed him in recording and translating. But he also coveted our American batteries, which we needed to keep the tape recorder working properly.

It was in this era, after the first Ihamba, that our best conversations with Singleton and Fideli took place, easy flowing expositions in an atmosphere of "we know that you already know a good deal of what we know, and it's almost like family." The tail end of the apostolic succession of chiyanga doctors in one sense took in Bill and me, as well as young Luka. It was a responsibility that meant much to me and was a good reason for my writing this account on behalf of that succession.

We were getting closer and closer to how Singleton and Fideli understood their ritual to be. We could not analyze the medicines biochemically, but we were there in the center of the sea of significations along with them and buoyed up in this sea. One thing after another began to make sense, above all the way the separate threads of the different elements reinforced one another, the force of which we ourselves started to feel.

Now Fideli reminded us there was going to be an Ihamba for Meru, the sister's daughter of Nyakanjata. We promised to be there.

6. The Second Ihamba: The Performance for Meru

The second ritual in the Kahona family was scheduled for Thursday or Friday, November 28 or 29, 1985, but the day was changed at the last minute because of a conflicting and indeed overriding event. On Thursday morning everyone was at the Mwinilunga airstrip, two miles past the school up the dirt road, to watch the arrival of an astonishingly white plane bearing none other than Princess Anne, the daughter of the Queen of England. Anne had decided to visit Mwinilunga in the course of a world survey of needy children on behalf of the Save the Children Fund, having been informed that Mwinilunga District, Zambia was—after parts of Ethiopia—the most backward district in the most economically distressed country in Africa, which was the poorest continent in the world. Anne had not been allowed a visa for Ethiopia, so here she was.

Unfortunately, the scheduling of this event on that Thursday interfered with Singleton's arrangement to take an ihamba tooth out of the body of Meru, Nyakanjata's niece. Fideli sent us word that the ritual would be held a day earlier. If I had not been keeping a careful diary, I would not now be able to include the information about the princess's visit, because after leaving Africa I forgot all about it.

Ihamba was at the forefront of our minds. We came as arranged on the Wednesday, arriving in Kahona Village at 7.00 A.M. for medicine collection. We would not visit the same trees as "you do not cut a tree twice." This time we would take from Singleton's special tract of forest which he was preserving as a kind of herb garden. Vesa met us and led us out of the village to collect Fideli, then we went down a red eroded path to a crossing of the ways, then to the left past a girl's seclusion hut until we reached Singleton's house, outside of which Vesa called and called until Singleton came growling out, all shaggy with sleepiness. Then together we went down past Benwa's to the string of huts of Mulandu's (D3) settlement (see Map 2 in Appendix 10). We stopped for a moment beyond the open kitchen that belonged to Meru's small two-roomed brick house in order to equip ourselves with the same medicine-collecting materials as before, then we set off directly behind Meru's house into the low reviving forest, walking along a single-file path, and making the way musical with the song:

Mukongu, katukatu-ey—
Mukongu, katukatu-ey—

Up, hunter, and go
Up, hunter, and go

We sang the second line a note below the first, in falling tones, with Fideli's light baritone continually sounding a fourth below and Singleton's rasp softly sizzling. So we started this next Ihamba with the walk through the trees, all the time repeating the plaintive song. We were tuning, repeating, focusing, and collecting medicines as we went. All of us together, Singleton, Fideli, Vesa, Bill, and me, by now a mutually agreeable group, acted as one. We soon found ourselves at a mufungu, our greeting tree, which we spotted near the path. We heard Singleton's loud "Twaya, Come!" addressed to the spirits that handed down their skills to him, and saw his classic hunkered-down position at the tree and saw him bless the spirit with red clay and connect his ancestors to himself with red lines. We took medicine from another mufungu, then from the musengu blessing tree using the east and west sides of the trunk, cutting into bark that had never been cut before—as always. We took the mukosu bark lid, the leaves from the mucha to create a gathering, both from the east and west of it, then to a small mututambulolu, also "for a gathering."

As before we took the entire roots, bright orange-yellow ones, cutting down the small tree completely and leaving the tree replanted and the hole filled up. We took from the muhotuhotu some of its long sensitive leaves set in opposite order, leaves that fall off like the disease; and musesi this time, which we had not gathered before.[1] It was a very strong tree with hard wood and could take even chisaku witchcraft away. We cut a kapepi forked shrine pole, and then took a network of mutungulu roots, digging out all the roots of one plant while they emanated their lemony scent. Off we went again, singing, "Mukongu, katukatu-ey," walking contented, mesmerized by the sizzling of the wooden rasp in front. Then we came out onto a dry swamp and crossed its white infertile clay by a path through dying reeds, aiming for the low trees beyond. Once among the trees we hunted for a long time and eventually found the rare musoli, and took bark and leaves from the east side of it, the side of sunrise and revelation.

We went wandering through the higher woods and across an old site of Mukanza Village, looking for a small termite tower. I searched too, but Singleton saw one first, bulging out of the ground among the trees. Vesa sheared it off; we saw the termites flooding the broken bowl beneath, each grabbing an egg which it bore off to safety. Vesa trimmed the domed top away from the cylinder and selected a section below it which he squared off and added to his basket. Then he carefully replaced the domed top on the broken termite home; and we proceeded. We took a prickly branch from a chikwata beside a giant termitary and dug up some of its roots to catch the ihamba.

After the greeting tree the medicines were collected in the order in which they were encountered, except that the shrine pole and the firewood were left to the end. We found the "no reason" mutuhu by the side of the path, it was a plant barely four inches high, so we took it all, exposing its startling black roots, ones that showed so brilliantly white inside. This with the flaming yellow-orange mututambulolu, and the chikwata root, rosy red inside, and the mutungulu network, sweet and fruity smelling, and the prickles of the chikwata, made a telling collection. There was more in this collection, though, than color, scent, or prickles. There was the effect of drinking the mixture whose exact properties were unknown to me—and there was the cure.

Finally, we found ironwood for the fire, which I offered to carry because Etina, the ritual carrier woman, was not there. This small task gave me a role in the ritual and helped to establish me as a chiyanga in the healers' guild.

We returned to the Mulandu Farm at about nine o'clock, finding all deserted. Singleton called out for a mortar, a cup, and a knife. They first took an antelope skin from the kitchen and laid it down in the shade under a tree they called the Ihamba tree. They set the medicine basket down carefully on the antelope skin so that it did not touch the ground. Then Singleton and Vesa went off to give word and fetch materials.

A white cup was brought, and a flat pan. Singleton set to work to peel the inside of the mukosu bark lid to get rid of the inner wood still left on it. A mortar and pounding pole was brought, and Singleton, Fideli, and Vesa started fixing the medicines. They handled the chikwata branch carefully, picking off the leaves and throwing away the thorny stalk, while saving the chikwata roots, red inside. The big orange mututambulolu root was cut up by Fideli with his ax, and some of it was put in the white cup, along with the black mutuhu, painstakingly peeled down to the white. Fideli removed the ax from its handle and used the iron ax head to crush the acid mutungulu roots; he was careful this time to carry out the whole prescription correctly and in the right order. Fragments of white peeled mutuhu and selections from the other medicines were heaped in the center of the basket. Fideli turned around and identified the Ihamba tree under which we were seated as a munjimba, which is medicine for Ihamba and for hunters. It makes the animal "forget"—*jimbala*—to keep a careful watch for the hunter. One may use the leaves and roots, and eat the fruit.

The castor oil leaf was ready on the receiving can, with the bark lid on top. Etina was now present and pounded the leaves in the mortar. While I watched, the familiar setting came into being where at first there was nothing but a patch of waste ground: the chishinga pole was set up with its sharp horn-like spears, with the spirit house at its foot; the antelope skin in front lay ready for the patient, the mortar beside it containing the pounded leaf solution, the flat basket nearby holding leaf cups. Fideli showed Bill how to make a leaf cup out of a milk leaf by curling it around and poking the stalk through the side of the leaf. The basket also contained the white cup of orange mututambulolu roots and a cup for serving leaf medicine. The hardwood fire was already burning, with the pan of fragrant roots waiting to be put on it; while the small receiving can was prepared for the most important item, the tooth. This receptacle now contained a nest of root fragments, water, and blood from a rooster's claw, topped with a large castor oil leaf and the bark lid from the mukosu tree. We needed drums, so Bill went all the way back to fetch them.

Fideli told me that hunters undergo an Ihamba ritual even though they are not sick, in order to qualify for the hunters' cult. It reminded me of the training analysis that an aspiring psychotherapist has to undergo in our culture. One has to be clear and clean in oneself to be able to see well as a hunter.

A boy brought water in a calabash, and they poured some on the ground to the east of the pan and some to the west, then into the pan, then into the mortar and into the white cup. A razor blade was obtained. Around us in the windy sunlight, people were gathering, Nyakanjata, who was now reasonably well, Luka, and a few children.

Singleton began to medicate his chiyanga doctors. Each drank a cupful of the leaf medicine; a cup was handed to me and I drank the liquid, which tasted pleasantly of fresh leaves. Immediately, my head fired up and swam. The drink contained no alcohol, but I felt the same recognizably loosening effect as before. Nevertheless I went on writing my field notes with no change in legibility.

Singleton and Fideli were consulting about the orientation of the ritual mise-en-scène. The patient's antelope skin and the utensils had all been placed to the west of the shrine pole where the shade happened to fall in the morning. They should have been facing east," said Fideli. "It's a mistake. But it doesn't matter." But it did matter, as we shall see.

I myself was sitting on a stool a little northwest of the pole and facing it, with the water calabash on my right. As I turned back the page of my reporter's notebook, I saw out of the corner of my eye something rolling to and fro. I looked, and there was the calabash rolling by itself. Though my brain swam I looked at the calabash carefully and saw the shadow of wind-moved leaves passing back and forth on its surface. The movement was an illusion caused by the moving shadow. Then I saw the calabash rolling by itself again, then it was still. Quick as thought there entered my mind the word "marvelous." I wrote it down. "Remember Rudyard Kipling's *Kim*," I said to myself, "when the hypnotist makes Kim see the broken pot reassemble itself, then Kim sees through the illusion?" I was interested in this now-you-see-it-now-you-don't effect.

Meanwhile, the doctors' practical work was going ahead. Singleton chose some leaves and made leaf cups. He chewed some more raw leaves— he at least was used to the medicinal effects—then stuffed the chewed wad into a cupping horn to smear it with juice, then removed it. They put the flat medicine pan containing the mutungulu roots on the fire to warm. I began thinking about the tiny antelope horn which has to be taken from an animal killed by a predator. It so happened that Singleton and I were both thinking about strange horns. He indicated a new cupping horn, one with long spiral projections. "This one isn't from an antelope but from a stag," he said. "An ikuma, with several points on its antlers. They're like the forks of a chishinga pole." I nodded and wrote it down.

One of the few deer of Africa, I was thinking. The rarity requirement again; the doctor Philip Kabwita uses a horn from a one-horned goat—a unicorn.

There was wax on the end of the strange horn. Fideli told us later, "That wax is what we use to seal the hole in the end of the horn. It's special wax, *chilundi*, it's very hard stuff from a small insect. It's an insect that makes its nest in the ground. It has honey and doesn't sting." I wondered what could that be.

"It's a kind of bee," Singleton told us.

Now they took the hot medicine off the fire, and all was ready. A small procession was approaching the shrine, it was Vesa leading Meru by the hand. Meru was the woman who had turned up at Nyakanjata's Ihamba, her "daughter"; to us, her sister's daughter (D2; see genealogy in Appendix 11). She had a look of her old aunt Nyakanjata. She was fifty-five but seemed over sixty on this occasion, obviously very tired and not at all well. She had an ihamba in her, but where it came from nobody yet knew. All the night before she had worn red clay on her wrists as a method of divination: if she slept well with the red clay on her it was a sign that there was an ihamba inside. The red clay was also a protection for us; the ihamba must not be allowed to escape into any of us—Singleton said it could even find its way overseas to America. Vesa brought the sick woman forward and carefully set her down on the antelope skin with her back to the chishinga pole, where she sat and lit up a home-rolled cigarette. I could see a graze on her knee that had been painted with gentian violet by the clinic assistant. Meru pulled faces at the sight of the medicines around her—this was a miserable suffering woman, but proud and haughty.

Vesa set to work. He plunged his hand into the mortar and seized a mass of leaves that had settled to the bottom. Using the mass as a sponge, he proceeded to rub medicine on the exposed parts of Meru's body—above the cloth tied around her breasts, also on her arms and legs.

"Her head as well," instructed Singleton, and Vesa rubbed her head. Vesa took red clay out of the mongoose skin pouch and made a red line down Meru's forehead and nose, then down each temple and cheekbone. The ritualization of the scene and the people had begun, and at this point, all of us doctors shared a "plastic" of honey beer. Still for Meru herself the ritualization was not complete: she kept fussing and directing the assistants where to place the stools for the participants. They gave Meru leaf medicine to drink. Now Singleton and the others stood over her with castor oil leaves; they licked their hands, put the leaves on their fists, and slowly went "Shw-shw," waving their fists here and there over her. Suddenly, "Paya!"— they clapped down on their fists, and the leaves fell over Meru in blessing.

"Maheza!" Singleton exclaimed.

"Maheza!" we shouted.

"Ngambu!" said Singleton, and we shouted, "Yafwa!" The drums began with their rapid threefold beat. They called for ax heads and soon the deafening clink compelled our hands to clap, starting an effect like strobe lights in my brain. They sang in plangent woodland harmony:

Welcome, great hunter, brother hunter,
After you've killed.

When you became a hunter you bred up a familiar,
You had a human-headed snake to do your killing.
Sing for my child and my relatives in this village.

Singleton came close and shouted "Twaya! Come out!" directing his call into Meru's body. Did the tooth that was wandering inside and troubling her come from her grandfather Nkomba? They were beginning to seek its name.

"Shake, shake, if it's you, Nkomba," they commanded her—or commanded the spirit inside her body. She twitched one shoulder, then the other; her body rocked in time to the music as she sat with her palms turned up.

"Maheza!"

"Maheza!" we all shouted in unison.

"Ngambu!" returned Singleton, and we replied, "Yafwa!"

"Is it Kadochi? Shake if it is. Quick now!" Singleton danced the antelope mating dance before her. Already the group had increased to a crowd of about thirty persons, at least half of whom were children. A young woman with an armful of school books passed behind the crowd, saw what was going on, and gave a sniggering laugh. She went right on walking. Anger rose within me. Snob! I thought.

The doctors were saying, "Maybe it's Kashinakaji's tooth. If it's Kashinakaji, shake. Come quick!" Singleton drove off the crowding children to make room for his dance; he sped back and forth bent forward with his arms stretched in front like forelegs, growling his song, then he danced all around the assembly in a clockwise direction, holding the people together and sacralizing them. Now Nyakanjata danced forward and put two pennies into the basket. Meru was shaking well, but Singleton ended the episode by pressing down on her head with his mongoose skin bag, which quieted her. As often as he beat down her tendency to shake, it came up again all the more strongly.

"If you want the cupping horns, shake," he told the spirit. Meru shook. Now Fideli got to work; he dipped the horn in hot medicine, then unwrapped the razor blade. Meru looked sourly at it: she was afraid of the pain.

Singleton assured her, "We'll only make one cut." Accordingly, Fideli gave one tiny stab at her back, and as the blood ran down her black skin, he set the horn over it. He sucked hard and blocked up the end with the solid wax made by the miniature bees.

"Twaya!" barked Singleton.

They had acquired two other horns which they sucked on lower down on her back, pulling on them really hard so that they stood up. Using three horns was more like the old days when they used four. Then Vesa held out a leaf cup of medicine over the wound on Meru's back and let the liquid drip down upon it, also on the lower horns, and on her finger- and toenails. Here my writing showed some sleepiness, for I noted, "stridulator with the cat," but can't remember what I meant.

Meru suddenly said her first *words.* "I don't agree. I've got something on my liver.[2] It's my children; all my children are dead." Then she told us outright, "I just want to die because there's nobody to look after me." The people heard her frankness and were pleased, and they sang:

The hunter doctor will come with a stranger.

But support for the song faded. "What's happened to the drumming?" asked Fideli.

"No one's drumming, no one's singing, nothing."

Singleton frowned. He noticed that a cupping horn had dropped off Meru's back. "Bring that cupping horn to me, Fideli. Don't you do the cupping this time."

"OK, you do it."

"You play the drum. I'll sing and do the cupping."

"These boys don't know how to sing," grumbled Etina, so they tried different songs:

As the cow goes by she makes a path.
Who went by? It was a cow.
Ihamba's coming out today, ye wo-wo-wo.
Ihamba doesn't want to come out.
Are you ihamba or a disease?
Ihamba's a tooth, ye wo-wo-wo.

Luka, the only one playing a drum at that moment, peered around. "You're not singing," he said to Nyakanjata. "Why don't you join in the chorus?"

"See what I'm doing?" she asked. She was dancing.

Singleton was watching Meru. He said in a matter-of-fact voice, "There's a difficulty here. You said your *words,* just a few of them, and now you seem to be aggrieved when you shake. You quiver as if you're not a gun hunter at all. What's worrying you when you quiver like that? What's up? I told you your brother Mulandu and I can help you with your worries. You spoke the truth when you said you might just as well have died because all your children are dead. You said, how can you stay the same and walk about when your children are dead? Sure you had worries, and we were happy when you came out with them. But I haven't seen you shake happily yet. You did when we began, but now you're stiff with worries. What's the matter? There must be something else."

They applied the horns again and resumed. There was something recalcitrant inside her body that did not want to be dragged out. Meru herself was not helping at all.

Derek Mulandu (D3), Meru's brother and the head of the farm, a man with an elderly face and concerned look, addressed his sister's body: "Maybe you're annoyed because none of the relatives on your father's side are here. Do you want them to come? If that's what you want, shake, but if it's something different, don't shake. Maheza!"

"Maheza!"

"Ngambu!"

"Yafwa!" they echoed as Meru shook.

"Beat the drum! Sing everyone. Where's Luka?"

"Here, all on my lonesome. How do you expect me to sing? I'm drumming."

"Don't you have friends who can help you sing?"

Nyakanjata said, "A merciful person would rally around and help a friend."

Irritation was growing, and uncertainty. And the weather was hot. They took it out by beating a child who was making a nuisance of himself.

"You should fear your elders," they said to him, and Fideli added, "Aren't you the one who washes my trousers?" He laughed dryly.

Now they tried this song:

Kambowa was my father's slave.
Let me torment him, father. Maheza!

It seemed in keeping with the mood.

"Look," said Mulandu. "You can see she's not shaking for that one."

Old Nyakanjata came forward nodding. The people noticed she had something she wanted to say (Figure 23).

Mulandu saw it too. "Yes, there's something on her body."

Figure 23. Nyakanjata says her *words* at Meru's Ihamba.

Mulandu said the *words* for her instead. "You're annoyed about money," he said to Meru. She listened, her head drooping to the left. Then he announced, "It was all because of her younger sister Liza: they had a bad quarrel about money. Meru brewed a calabash of millet beer, and Liza took it away to sell it. Afterward Meru—she's the older of the two—said, 'Where's the money?' The younger sister answered, 'Liya bought it and hasn't given me the money.' Actually, Liza had the dollar in her pocket all the time. Liza said to herself, 'I'll see if my older sister will make a fuss.' Of course, the older sister began to get annoyed, real angry. I was sitting there at the time. She and her younger sister started shouting at each other. Then the younger sister said, 'No, older sister, I've been deceiving you. Here's your eighty cents,' and she handed her eighty cents, just eighty cents. The older sister refused the money. 'I'm not going to take it because you're cheating me. I made the beer. Why should you cheat me? I say no, bring the full amount here. And quit being so quarrelsome, Liza.' Later Liza told me, 'That's right. I did it just to see what she'd do.' There you have it."

Now Mulandu addressed Meru's body. "If you're aggrieved because your sister cheated you, shake, and if not keep still."

Most of this sounded like a legal deposition. It was neither that nor psychoanalytic case material, but it was related to the inward tooth, again

Figure 24. The ritual scene of Meru's Ihamba.

stoppered up by the stopping up of words or grudges. The flow of human relationship was the concern; we ourselves might envisage it as the traffic flow of human communication, either flowing smoothly the way the system intends, or snarled and dangerous. To cope with the snarl Africans do not use psychological terms, such as psychosis, which are imponderables, explaining individuals' behavior, but they see something concrete amiss in the physical body, something that can even concretely affect the group. Nevertheless, they see that "something" as also spiritual.

The weather was growing so hot that the people cut tree branches and set them up over Meru and the doctors, for shade. Once again the doctors attached the horns to Meru and continued. There were now four additional men in the group and seven women. By now a kayanda drum, a monfusa, and a small musenki drum were in full rhythm. Etina were pounding in an empty mortar to increase the sound. She paused for a moment to adjust Meru's waist cloth over her legs for her, while Fideli turned Meru's hands palms upward, and they went on (Figure 24).

After eight weary episodes Luka turned around and said, "It's so difficult to make ihamba come out if the people don't sing."

"It must be Kashinakaji," said Singleton who had been musing awhile.

Kashinakaji the elder (C1), as distinct from his son, the teacher Wind-son Kashinakaji (see also Turner 1968, 133), was called by Meru *mandumi*, "mother's brother," and was probably the classificatory brother of Saku-toha (C2). Now, in his form as a dead hunter like Sakutoha, he had come back to afflict Meru. It is likely that the affliction by Kashinakaji had the same general cause as the anger of Matunka and Sakutoha toward Meru's aunt Nyakanjata, the revenge of neglected males on women that head lineages.

Meru's family was so badly wrecked that she called them "dead." Her grown-up daughter had died, and it had hit Meru sorely. Also the daugh-ter's large family of children had been taken away by their father and was dead to her. Why? Had some of Nyakanjata's previous slave status attached to Meru, through Nyamaleji, Nyakanjata's sister? Hints show that Ny-amaleji herself had been a slave.

As I have experienced it myself, even if a person possesses a large family the death of one seems like the death of all. The old Nyamukola of the 1950s, now deceased, suffered something similar. She was heartbroken that her daughter Zuliyana was childless, and she was sick with an ihamba because of it (Turner 1968, 296). In fact, Zuliyana later gave birth to two fine boys. Like Nyamukola before and like Nyakanjata, Meru seemed to feel that she had too few children to help her.

No hint of any conflict came out in the ritual about Kashinakaji, who was the father of our former helper Windson and a respected councillor in the court of Chief Mukangala. The main focus was always on present grievances. The past was shadowy, taking expression in present woes.

Now Mulandu, Meru's brother, addressed the spirit: "If you're an-noyed because Paulos the elder isn't around, shake hard; if not and it's something else, stop shaking."

I was thinking, for some reason, of a Ouija board, then generally of the connection between the foreign body inside Meru, that ghostly entity the spirit, and one's emotional state in relation to the social group. The power and character of the ihamba tooth—from which sprang the effort to get it out—spread to us all, while the anti-ihamba power of the medicines domi-nated the physical vicinity (thus we see the danger of miscarriage to any pregnant woman nearby). Singleton was tracing the effect of ritual, tracing its delicate tuning, in those sensitive psyches who being kin knew one another very well. The importance of tuning was seen in the simple state-ment, "It's difficult for ihamba to come out if the people don't sing"—and its inverse, "It is easy when they do"—as we shall see at the climax.

I looked up and saw Mulandu's face concentrating urgently upon the swaying form of Meru. I wrote at that moment, "Here we are now—it is the *Now*." Here I was, in a real if exotic situation, with my friends involved and working in a central role, and I myself in it too.

Singleton gave Meru more leaf medicine from the white cup containing the orange mututambulolu root chips. "She'll be dizzy," I thought.

Singleton dripped medicine onto her head from a leaf cup. We all began to sing, and she shook. Singleton took off the horn, then picked up his mongoose skin pouch and held it in front of her face, afterward brushing her back with it.

They began a heated discussion on the subject of Paulos. The confusion occasioned by the rescheduling of the ritual had upset everyone. Mulandu said, "Paulos came yesterday and found nothing going on. Next he heard Ihamba was to be on Thursday, and said he'd come then. Today's Wednesday." Because everyone was expecting him to say Wednesday, *Hachisatu*, he said it in the Zambian schoolmaster's manner, prompting his hearers in a kind of guessing game, "*Ha—*" and they completed the word triumphantly, "Ha-chisatu!"

Mulandu was irritated because Paulos was not there. He had given the original message to Paulos, "Ihamba on Thursday," but Paulos had received no second message about the change of the day to Wednesday.

"That's why he's not here," concluded Mulandu.

On hearing this, Meru looked grim—resigned, but still grim. The drums sounded, and she began to shake; at least some major misunderstandings had been aired. They put a divinatory proposition to the ihamba: if you want Paulos to come, shake. She did shake, so they sent Vesa on the long trip to Paulos with a message asking him to come as soon as he could. Meru's face relaxed. We all took a break, and I slipped away for some coffee to wake myself up.

I saw the whole sequence as a lesson in opening up, the disinhibition of the psyche. This appeared to have grown even more central to the ritual over the years.

When I returned and sat waiting, a small woman by my side greeted me. She told me she was Nyamuwanga. This was an old woman I had known in the 1950s, who was noted as a witch. She still possessed the little pointy breasts of adolescence and the perky chin I knew, looking no older than before (Turner 1957, 148–54). She made a barbed remark just as in the old days—about my forgetting who she was; then she stroked my English sunburnt arm and said, "Nice."

"Your arm is nice too," I said. I pointed to the veins on both our hands, perfectly similar. "We're just the same." We shook hands in the Ndembu soul-sister fashion. I always liked Nyamuwanga, which was tricky, because nobody else did.

"Don't give any beer to the old women," commanded Singleton. Nyamuwanga looked disappointed. Benwa's sister, old Elesi, happened to be playing the drum. Elesi looked around anxiously. Singleton's disapproving voice reminded her of the low estate of women; she also knew that drumming was a man's job but liked to do it just the same.

"If my husband comes along and finds me drumming I'm going to run," she said. At this point Luka handed beer to me, and beer to Elesi, and I gave half of mine to Nyamuwanga. So that was all right, we old women did get some. Morie was given a drink too.

By now there were about a dozen men and a dozen women present and many children; Bill also returned from his break. To his horror he found that Morie's son Morie Junior had flipped the tape cassette wrongly, turning it back to the already recorded side, thus erasing it. "Look what you've done," said Bill angrily. "You've ruined it." The crowd became silent. This bit of quarreling was true Ihamba material.

"Tell Bill to say some *words*," said a woman.

Bill subsided and closed his mouth.

"How could he?" said Fideli. "He doesn't know the language."

"Perhaps those two foreigners are closing up ihamba."

"They're doctors, why would they do that?" said Fideli.

"Both of them ought to add their grudges," she persisted. And her friend said, "Yes, Edie's the one who was here a long time ago."

"The Europeans were the people who killed Jesus. They clothed him with only a loincloth."

"You heard about the loincloth?"

"Yes, and it's the Europeans who were found guilty. We don't know the whole story of the killing of Jesus. They were the ones who told it to us."

Here Fideli announced: "Let me also give a few *words*. This is the truth. Ihamba, I can see you shaking and shaking, as if you're genuinely grieving inside. You say, 'Although there are many people in this village, I haven't seen one of my relatives here. When they have a ceremony, I always attend theirs. How come they don't attend mine?' It's true, you're sulking; you say, 'Why are the doctors quitting nowadays? They complain it's a hard obligation, and leave off. These days our people don't tread the old ways.'"

Then Fideli invoked: "If the spirit's really annoying you, rise up quickly with healing skill from the ground. If not, be quiet, *nzo-o!*"

Meru, with her back stuck with two horns, said her *words* in a raised voice. The words poured out: "I say as soon as someone brings me honey to make beer and I've just managed to get it brewed, a certain somebody takes the beer away from me. Then the ihamba comes. But I say no, no, no. If you don't sing for me, I'll die. I'm old, and all I have left is hardship, with my little children dying. And see what happens? I brew honey to make beer to sell, and then what happens? My younger sister sells it. It's my understanding that right up to today I'm still the elder and a certain someone's still the junior. As for me, all I want is to die, but I don't die. As you say, I've struggled in vain against my sister, and it's a sad thing. The way things are I'll die."

Singleton was still for a moment, attentive. He said, "I've seen it. It's the ihamba, so he's got to come out of her. Mr. Mulandu has put on his *words* and the things he said have also come out in *words;* he said things that revealed the bad spirit. It's come. We are now happy, we may say we're very happy. This is it, we're saying *words* and it's coming. The ihamba will soon find you've fallen down, and we've given money for it to come out. See, here's the money. And another thing—listen, Fideli—*you're* not happy. When my mother had that thing taken out, you weren't particularly happy when Johnny came and touched you on your leg and hand. There's another person here doing the same thing, and that's why you're not happy." He looked around accusingly. Then to the body of the patient: "If that's not true, keep quiet and don't shake; if that's the way it really is, let the bad spirit come out. Our forefathers in the grave have heard my *words.*"

"Don't you realize your parents were sinners?" broke in a woman onlooker in a voice of reproach. "You're no Christian."

"There's a Christian here named Snodia," answered Singleton. Snodia, or Synodia, was a Christian name derived from the church word "synod."

Singleton continued addressing the mingling of a spirit and the living Meru: "I'm now saying, forgive us, grandfather ihamba. You're the father that produced me and the others. Don't let these people upset you. Just believe in the path your father followed. I'm yours, and I'll have to take you from the body of my sister so that I can keep you with me, grandfather. Believe in me alone, there's nobody else. Don't imagine you have to take notice of these women. No. Who are these women? They haven't got anything, they can't do anything. What can they give you? Just you pay attention to us. The man who's turning up any minute is your brother, your brother you wanted. He meant to come on Thursday, now at last he's arrived. He's coming here right now and will find us."

He ended, "Maheza!" "Maheza!" we answered.

"Ngambu!"

"Yafwa!" we replied. Paulos, indeed, arrived creating quite a stir. Paulos, the revered headman wearing a hat, was welcomed by many. He went to the medicine basket and put down the biggest village contribution yet, twenty cents. He had his own complaints.

"When I was living with my wife at Luanshya on the Copperbelt, people treated us with respect and didn't let us down by changing the date of an Ihamba without telling us. Why wasn't I told?"

"It's all because the airplane of the queen's daughter is expected tomorrow," explained Singleton, and he patiently sorted out the misunderstanding. Having heard him out, Paulos went to stand to the west of the crowd amid a little knot of clients, including Morie.

Now an assistant attended to the graze on Meru's leg which was attracting flies. A patch was put over it. Then as the drums began again Singleton savagely addressed the horns on Meru's back, "Twaya! Fuma! Get out!" as if he were shouting at a thieving dog. Meru raised her voice again in a chant of complaint: "Etina never helped with the medicine collection. Why was that? My relatives don't love me." Etina (F1) was Meru's classificatory granddaughter.

Singleton indicated Etina busy pounding in the empty mortar to increase the percussion. "Don't worry about that," he said. "She's here now."

Meru was mollified. Singleton chanted the slogan, "Maheza!" and they responded.

Etina put on her own *words*. Everybody chanted the slogan and was pleased. But now the ihamba was refusing to come out because Meru wasn't annoyed. Maybe she was pleased because Paulos had arrived, but after a time it turned out that there were still further matters hidden inside her.

Fideli was anxious to say some more *words*. "Don't be worried, even though my liver isn't happy because ignorant people touched me last time." He sang:

Can I go with you, orphan boy?
Yes—an orphan—an orphan too.
Oh yes, father, oh yes, mother,
I haven't any father, can you sing for me?
I'm not happy, I don't feel good.

He was referring to Benwa, his father, who had not put in an appearance all day. Benwa's absence was another symptom of the breakdown of the unity of the neighborhood which was being revealed to us in the course of the Ihamba ritual. Furthermore, Singleton himself had money interests.

"Pay, pay for Ihamba," he called to the people.

"Pay? You must be joking."

"Do it. I keep telling you, and you don't." Then to Meru: "When five snakes bite you, you'll never get up again. You wanted this ritual."

They sang:

Father, we've found a witchcraft creature.
Who feels like having a woman?

And they all shrilled and sang:

Let's go, ihamba.
Ihamba, like smoking marijuana.
Don't touch him.

The assistants bent over Meru to suck on the cupping horns. "Don't touch her so much," snapped Singleton. Now the heat was drawing up black clouds above us; Meru fell shaking in the midst of the singing, in the dim light under the shade branches, just as Singleton was saying, "What trouble it's giving us!" Voices broke in, "Look at that. She's down! She's in trance. That's just what you want. Look at that. Witchcraft dancing in her. At last you can see it." There was a gabble of voices. I leaned over too. The doctors indeed wanted this thing to show itself so that they could bring it out. Singleton worked on the horn but when he took it off it was empty: another disappointment. Meru sat up and the horns were reset.

Singleton said, "She wanted all her relatives to come around, but they're away. How many men are here? How many women?" He looked around disgustedly.

Meru spoke from her ritual position: "I feel resentment."

Singleton poked the finger horn up into her hair above her brow. The drums began anew. He danced savagely backward, hopping on one foot. "Keep singing," he gasped. The sweat was running down his face.

Now a woman pushed forward through the crowd with some bitter words to say. It was Snodia herself, maternal cousin to Meru. "A certain woman was too busy brewing beer to come when her mother-aunt was having her ihamba taken out." It was true, Meru only put in the briefest appearance at Nyakanjata's Ihamba the month before.

Meru burst out, "I'm supposed to die, then, and the maggots will crawl on my body. I'm supposed to go to the village law court and confess, 'Yes, a certain woman was brewing beer.' Remember all the children I produced; they went somewhere or other and don't know I'm their mother. *She* is the mother who brought me up." She indicated Nyakanjata. "When I was suffering from an ihamba Elesi and my grandfather could see how it was, but they just kept to themselves, among the men, not me. Not even my brother came to my help. Before that again my daughter brought me to this village, but there was fighting when they saw me come, and they chased her away. You say you're Christians and that God will do his work. You're doing nothing."

"We've seen the ihamba," said Fideli. "And you have put on your *words*."

Meru's pain got to us all; we stood with bitter expressions, gazing at her. Fideli took a leaf poke and dripped medicine on Meru's head. Singleton held his skin bag in front of her face, then brushed her face with it. But Meru would not shake.

Singleton again addressed the horns. By now his voice was harsh toward the ihamba. "If you're annoyed because Benwa isn't around, shake; if not stay quiet. If there's a problem on the mother's side, shake, but if not, stay quiet! Nzo!" She shook. "If there's a problem on the father's side, shake!" She sat quietly. So it was on the mother's side.

Daudson was on the drum now, once more defying his Catholic wife. Smart and Zakariya joined the crowd too. While the percussion thundered they sang keeningly:

Where does Wuyanga come from?
Where does the elephant come from?
From the place of Wuyanga?
Just you wait and see.
The chief has come.

In the midst of the heady rhythm Meru keeled over in trance, her body twitching in the dust.

"She's fallen!"

"Twaya, come out!" shouted Singleton as he bent over her body and worked on her back with his horn and bag. "We'll show them chiyanga," and the song took up the refrain:

Wuyanga, Wuyanga, Wuyanga, Wuyanga, Wuyanga, Wuyanga—

hypnotically, endlessly, in which I also joined:

Wuyanga, Wuyanga—

shaking my head with pleasure as I sang, ending with them in the "Maheza!" "Maheza!" "Ngambu!" "Yafwa!"

Singleton exclaimed: "The cause of it all is this. You're here in the village of your mother. You left your father's place a long time ago. This is what I'm saying. If you are not Kashinakaji, you must give us another medicine to quiet the trouble. But if it's on the side of your mother, something bad on that side, then it must come out. Maheza!"

The status of Meru's mother Nyamaleji was here questioned as if she had also been a slave. By the rules of slavery it was now clear that Nyamaleji was indeed a slave. If Nyakanjata had had problems, clearly Meru had had worse, being deprived of her grandchildren.

They sang:

Walking in the low trees, in the bush,
We're afraid of the place where ihamba comes out.
We believe your words, mother, brother, cousin, uncle.

Singleton called on the spirit: "Kashinakaji, if you really are in there trying to eat this person, come out!" Then he begged and bludgeoned the spirit: "I'm following exactly what Paulos said, I've said all my *words*. You need only listen to what I've been saying. Haven't I shouted loud enough? We want this thing to come out; let's beat the drums, let the drums touch the earth. You've been refusing, I tell you. Now! We want this thing to come out! Just that. If there's somebody there, come out! Kashinakaji, you're dead, you must keep quiet. But if you're alive come out! We're not happy. Maheza!"

"Maheza!"
"Ngambu!"
"Yafwa! He's dead!"
"We'll sing the Wuyanga song":

You've killed my child, my brothers, and my kin,
You've killed my son and my friends,

Witch creature. Ye-ye-ye.
Touch him, touch him, touch him in a certain place.
It's always "touch him,"
Even my wives, you and me,
They've taken Wuyanga away.
Where to, witch creature?
I am chiyanga, I am a hunter.

"Maheza!" Singleton was straddling in his dance beside Meru, bending over her and shouting into her body. Her long face looked straight ahead with an inner fury. She was shaking sporadically, sometimes with jerks, sometimes falling over, dropping bloody but useless horns; the sun burned hot and frustration was high. Something was wrong, yet at this point many things began to change and jell, and now there was a matter which hurt me too.

It so happened that as midday approached and our ritual site became very hot I sought shade on the opposite side of the circle. This brought me near Paulos where Morie was also standing saying something to Bill. Now, while I watched Meru's shaking, I became conscious of Morie's harsh voice in my ear.

"Paulos complains that you never came to his house last Saturday with Anthony Pritchett,[3] so Paulos waited all day for nothing." I sat rigid, feeling guilty as I often did with Morie. Why did he have to interrupt the fascinating process before my eyes?

I muttered, "Our calendar must have got mixed up." Morie promptly translated this to Paulos as "She forgot! *Wunajimbiri.*" I was furious with Morie for making me out to be rude, but it was true. I had forgotten.

I started around, now remembering that on Saturday we had to go to the funeral of Line, the old Mukanza carpenter whom I knew in the 1950s who had long been senile. How could I have gone to Paulos's village that day? But was it auspicious to mention death and burial at an Ihamba ritual? Everyone around me quieted, and I felt they were reading my mind. The silence grew total: why, they were waiting for me to say my *words.* The matter of the conflict with Morie was involved, and, what made it difficult, it would mean shame for Kasonda if I came out with it. Deeply embarrassed, I looked down and gestured that it didn't matter, then rose to get away from Morie and went off around the men to where Bill stood. They had wanted me to come out with my *words:* it was part of Ihamba. My heart was full of rage against Morie. What could I do? He was my old friend's son—what was even trickier, my landlady's son. I sat trying to resolve my mind about Morie and Paulos. After a second I again rose and went back around to Paulos, and there I grasped him by the hand and told him about the Saturday burial; he seemed to understand. I arranged to visit him on Monday morning instead—but where did he live, I asked?

"Morie will bring you," said Paulos.

Morie was still standing nearby. I shrugged and said, "Possibly," then returned to Bill and stood clapping to the drums which were playing the next round. I felt miserable.

In front of me I heard Nyakanjata herself breaking in, "Her children don't look after her, that's the trouble." Her feelings were laid together with Meru's in sympathy. And Snodia immediately put on the *words,* "It's from the mother's side." Singleton added, "The mother's side."

This sent Meru right back to the primary cause, Liza's deception over the beer. "Liza cheated me. She's not even here at the Ihamba. I'm annoyed: Liza, my younger sister."

It was stalemate.

What followed happened quicker than I could write it. Into Singleton's mind came the memory of the mistake they had made in orienting the ritual scene at the beginning: Meru had been put facing west, and she still was. His intention became clear to me as I was pushed back to make room for the drums. We all moved back, and a lot of shifting took place. Meru was raised, and the antelope skin moved, then they seated her on the other side of the chishinga pole. Spirit house, basket, pans, mortar, and receiving can were moved, Singleton also took up his new station so that, at last, Meru was relocated in the right position, east of the chishinga pole, facing the dawning direction of the sun, where it first comes out. Now the scene was exactly the same only in reverse.

"E-eyo!" said Mulandu with great satisfaction. "That's right." Meru looked outward, her face very serious; this was the position of frankness and revelation. I was gazing Southwest across the shrine; Marie was sitting south of it. The sky had grown dark and a wind came up. "This is about Morie and me," I realized, "at least as much as about Njesi and Zinia in the last Ihamba." My thoughts pained me again, while beyond, the drums thundered and Singleton hopped rapidly, foot after foot, in front of Meru.

"They *wanted* my *words.* They're to do with me and Morie. I'm 'annoyed' about Morie, and must bring it out. But I can't confess publicly as it involves Kasonda, a Christian, who's jealous, yet a friend—and then his drunken son. But how I want to participate, right here, and can't because of loyalty!—And these great people, waiting for my *words.*" So I accepted the impossibility, and accepting it, tears came to my eyes. The tears "came out," and I felt the stab of their pain.

"OK, OK, OK. So it *is*. And its woe. That's it."

And just then, through my tears, the central figure swayed deeply: all leaned forward, this was indeed going to be it. I realized along with them that the barriers were breaking—just as I let go in tears. Something that wanted to be born was now going to be born. Then a certain palpable social integument broke and something *calved* along with me. I felt the spiritual motion, a tangible feeling of breakthrough going through the whole group. Then Meru fell—the spirit event first and the action afterward. Singleton was very agile amid the bellow of the drums, swooping rhythmically with finger horn and skin bag ready to catch the tooth, Bill beating the side of the mortar in time to the drum, and as for me, I had just found out how to clap. You simply clap along *with* the pounding pole, and clap *hard*.[4] All the rest falls into place. You own body becomes deeply involved in the rhythm, and everyone reaches a unity.

Clap, clap, clap—Mulandu was leaning forward, and all the others were on their feet—this was it. Quite an interval of struggle elapsed while I clapped like one possessed, crouching beside Bill amid a lot of urgent talk, while Singleton pressed Meru's back, guiding and leading out the tooth—Meru's face in a grin of tranced passion, her back quivering rapidly. Suddenly Meru raised her arm, stretched it in liberation, and I *saw* with my own eyes a giant thing emerging out of the flesh of her back. This thing was a large gray blob about six inches across, a deep gray opaque thing emerging as a sphere.[5] I was amazed—delighted. I still laugh with glee at the realization of having seen it, the ihamba, and so big! We were all just one in triumph. The gray thing was actually out there, visible, and you could see Singleton's hands working and scrabbling on the back—and then the thing was there no more. Singleton had it in his pouch, pressing it in with his other hand as well. The receiving can was ready; he transferred whatever it was into the can and capped the castor oil leaf and bark lid over it. It was done.

I sat back breathless. But there was one more task. Everybody knew that they had to go through the last operation, the divining for the afterbirth. Singleton addressed the body: "If ihamba hasn't come out, shake, if it's come out, don't shake but be quiet, nzo-o." Meru was quiet. At once there was a huge flash of lightning—the light of a clap of thunder that exploded simultaneously overhead. Meru sat up panting. The longed-for rain poured down, and we all rushed into the kitchen shelter.

"Go to the house you two," said Fideli, and Bill and I rushed on through the curtain of rain to the house door. Bill stumbled before he entered, fell into the mud, and then came in out of breath. Singleton entered with his blue shirt dark with water, carrying the receiving can which he set down on the floor. I had a big smile.

He held up his hands to us. "See, I have nothing in them," then squatted down and dredged a long time in the bloody mixture. At length he drew out an old tooth, a molar, natural size, ordinary and concrete, with a dark root and one side sheared off as if by an ax. It was the ihamba.

On December 3 Morie's son Morie, aged 16, came to our hut with his grandfather the judge and sued us because he said he, young Morie, ought to be paid as much as his father Morie. Kasonda advised us to "Give a fly what he wants." Very irritated, we paid young Morie at the rate of a school graduate and resolved to leave the field earlier than we had intended.

On the evening of the same day, December 3, Singleton and Fideli visited our hut to explain what was coming next in Ihamba and discuss Meru's ritual. Bill and I were extremely pleased to see them. The first thing that Singleton said was, literally, "The thing we saw, we were five." This was his statement that the doctors too had seen a "thing." Singleton was counting the five doctors, of which I was one.

We settled down to talk, and I respectfully described what I saw, but Singleton made no comment. He did not give any details about what he actually saw. I was in no mood to become analytical so did not push the matter further. When the keystone of the bridge is put into position and everything holds, you tend to just look on with your mouth hanging open. This is what happened to me. If I had become analytical at that moment I would have had to be a different person from the one that saw the spirit form. The climax as I have recorded it gives every indication that all the doctors saw something and that their reaction was not notably different from mine, that is, great satisfaction at having seen it. I was there, and it was obvious.

The conversation in the hut went like this. Fideli translated Singleton's words, with Singleton interrupting to carry on what he wanted to say even before Fideli was finished translating his previous sentence. Singleton understood a good deal of the English, and I understood a good deal of the Chindembu. Fideli was in his element, knowing we were sharing an important treasure. His voice was rich and generous, while Singleton's was urgent and precise. A rapid swinging flow developed in the conversation and as it went on it became deeply personal and interconnected.

Singleton began, then Fideli said: "I have to explain what his words are."

"Yes?" I said.

This was on practical matters. "We have two cartridges. We'll go into the bush, and if we kill an antelope we'll bring it for all the five doctors. Then we'll take out the liver for those who saw Ihamba with his or her eyes. We'll cut a hole in the middle of a little piece of liver, put the ihamba into the hole, and put it in a bottle which has maize meal in it, as you know. We'll explain it to the actual people—our own friends who went into the bush with us—so that they know what Wuyanga is and we can be compared with many others. It's something that's very important. We've got a right to tell you so that we can be seen as different—because now's the time while you're living in Africa, and we should tell you these things exactly. This is your first moment of knowing what Wuyanga is, not from someone who thinks in lies but from me, Muhelwa,[6] who was given the medicine of Ihamba from Sangunja."[7] He ended with a gesture of respect to Singleton.

At this everybody clapped in honor of the statement murmuring, "Mwani, mwani, mwani."

Fideli said, "Bill, would you like to get some more beer?" After Bill had done so and we were settled down again Bill said, "I want to ask something."

"Yes," said Fideli with great tenderness, "You can ask me, Billy, anything you want. Even if you have to break the night and go on till morning, I'll do it."

Bill asked, "When the patient sits there, she sits with her legs sticking out. Why?"

"She stretches her legs out because the ihamba has a strange problem," Fideli answered. "Ihamba always runs like an air. Get me?"

Bill said, "Yes, it's an air, it can fly."

"Yes, it's always flying about. The medicine we collect in the bush prevents ihamba from getting into her legs. See?"

"And the dripping-medicine?"

"Ah." Both of the doctors grew excited.

"On her toes?" asked Bill.

"Yes, I'll tell you, Bill. Write the things I'm telling you, don't write on your own, just write what I'm telling you. It comes from him"—indicating Singleton—"and it comes from my father. We get the dripping-medicine from a bush called mutuhu. It stops the ihamba coming out at the wrong place. And that's also why the patient sits with her legs stretched out. Every medicine is for that, so ihamba won't run away. It's a passing air, get me?"

Bill went on, "So it's the same thing with the small antelope horn you put in here?" He pointed to the front of his hair.

"A good explanation," said Fideli. "It's to stop ihamba coming out of her body and going into someone standing around. We have to catch it in the can."

I broke in, "It's like a cork in a bottle."

"Yes, you know what it's about. I'll give you a good example. Ihamba can touch you when you don't know it—touch you, exactly that. So you give the patient a horn tucked into the front of her hair, and also between her toes. It makes ihamba stay inside the body so you can catch it in the cupping horn."

The talk turned to the red clay that had been put on Meru the night before the ritual, to "test" (*makunyi*) whether she really had an ihamba.

"A test," I said. "Yes, that's what you're saying: *makunyi,* a test." This word also meant the divinatory proposition. I said to Singleton, "I saw you make the makunyi again and again. And I was going to ask you questions about that. It's a test, isn't it, to see if your question is right or not?"

Fideli interrupted me very solemnly. "Mrs. Turner, let me explain that. Mrs. Turner, here you are with Billy, and I'm here with Mr. Singleton Kahona. We're different from you, Mr. Kahona and me. You know everything. See, you're like my father Benwa, and my uncle Mr. Kahona is like Bill. Bill has accompanied you and learns from you now that you're here on this trip. Like Mr. Benwa and Mr. Singleton. Get me?" This was comparing myself and Bill to Benwa and Singleton in a similar teacher and pupil capacity. (In fact Bill later received an A grade from me in this field school course as from Evergreen College.)

"Well," I admitted. "I know some stuff from the old times—a lot."

Fideli went on, speaking as Singleton, "My father handed down to me the responsibility of the red clay marking. Now I possess the right to cure someone and not fail in it. Get me, Billy? On my honor, it's true, before God and my father and my uncle, because the thing is from my father. How can I fail to cure a person? I know things from my father. I can't fail with my cures. There's no question about it—things from your husband, Edie, your late husband Mr. Turner—he told you things. You came and gave us things. Have you failed? Have I failed?"

"No way," I assured him.

"How can I fail? How could my in-law Benwa fail to cure my mother, how could I? She is my mother and I couldn't disobey her."

I said, "I know exactly what you mean. Your father was the one who taught you the skills."

"Sure," said Fideli.

This was Ndembu wisdom Singleton was talking about; he obtained Ndembu wisdom from his father, I obtained Ndembu wisdom from my husband. Cultural background made no difference here. The inheritance of Ihamba skills was what mattered.

I went back to the topic of the test, the divinatory proposition. "So you're divining all the time, aren't you? At every stage you're saying—the ihamba itself is telling you what to do. Like—inside her it's telling her to shake, to answer the question. 'If it is so-and-so, shake. If it isn't, don't. So you're learning from the ihamba inside."

Fideli looked from me to Bill in wonder. "*She* knows, she's on to something. Yes. I think, Mrs. Turner, we've come to the end." And Fideli was going to wrap up the evening there and then.

Bill broke in, "Can I ask some more questions? I've loads of questions."

"Yes," said Fideli.

Bill went into the matter of Liza and the beer with the two doctors. Singleton said, "Yes, the two sisters were quarreling about money." Fideli went on, "Liza said some nonsense—"

"About not having the money," I said.

Fideli immediately said, "If she hides the fact that she's got an ihamba, ihamba will not come out."

Singleton was saying in Chindembu, "Meru wanted Liza, that sister of hers, to be at the Ihamba. But it seemed she was somewhere else. She sure was somewhere else. Before we took the ihamba out of Meru—that's the very ihamba that bit Meru—it heard the sisters and said to itself, 'Ooh, the older and younger sisters are quarreling.' So we gave them the test, remember?" Fideli translated most of this.

He added, "The ihamba came while they were backbiting. It was listening to them."

Bill said, "Why doesn't ihamba want to come out when there are quarrels? Why won't it come until everyone's heart is at peace?"

"Right," said Fideli, again translating for Singleton. "That's a thing I'll have to explain. Ihamba is an air person. Even if you're in England ihamba can hear your words. You'll turn back to call me—I'm telling you my words—you'll turn back and call me, 'Kahona! Come and see me in London.' . . . Remember this, Billy," Fideli impressed upon him, and indeed, on Bill's return he became seriously ill, in London in fact, at the St. Pancras Hospital for Tropical Diseases, stricken with malaria and trichinosis from which he recovered even thinner than before.

The two doctors became so emphatic that they were often speaking at once. "You'll be the only chimbanda[8] doctor in England, and you'll be like us Africans there. If you sent a message to me we'd do exactly this. We'd send a message to England that Bill should come here. We'd hear, 'Bill spoke something.' You should do exactly that. You should come. In Ihamba you should come. No hesitation."

I said, "Yes, absolutely."

Fideli said, "You'd be right to come. Please do it. It's a very important thing. Whatever is needed in Ihamba we have to do."

"Supposing," said Bill, "the Ihamba ritual takes a long, long time and the patient doesn't shake—say for sixteen hours. Do you give up?"

Singleton said, "You mean there's no sign of ihamba? But the ihamba *will* appear. The patient simply has a lot on her liver." Fideli added, "The patient has thoughts inside her body. They may be hard thoughts, or her thoughts are rotten like Meru's about Liza; if she explains the thoughts exactly as they are, the ihamba will in fact come out."

I wanted to explain my own predicament. "Do you know, that time with Meru, I felt myself that I had thoughts in my head." And I told them in furtive tones about Morie (I was afraid that Morie might be listening through the window gap). "I realized what was going on in my head. I couldn't say my *words,* my mazu, but still I thought, if I don't get on well with Morie, still he's a person, and then I began to cry. It was at that very moment that Meru fell down, and after that, the ihamba came out of her. So everybody whose thoughts are closed up, stopping the thoughts coming out, they stop the ihamba coming out."

On hearing this Singleton said: "My mother said, 'my children are away.' She was grieving." He lingered thoughtfully on the word, "grieving." Evidently, he understood something of this other complicated connection with my weeping—my own sorrow. The two men fell to arguing about the translation Fideli was giving Singleton. Singleton found it hard to believe Fideli. "Translate *everything!*" he shouted at Fideli.

Fideli took up the translations again. "The time the ihamba was caught—that's what you want to know, isn't it?—it was, in a manner of speaking, from the time when Paulos arrived."

"Don't tell her lies," put in Singleton.

"There were," said Fideli slowly, "in our family some women slaves, you know. When we were beating the Ihamba drums for Nyakanjata, there were some women around who were Christians. Even if you're a Christian and ihamba comes to you, you're finished—never mind if you're a Christian. That's the very point, that's what I say, and it's the truth. You see, for

Meru's Ihamba there were no Christians around." For some reason he sighed and was sad. "Snodia was there."

"Yes," I said, and I reviewed Snodia's bitter *words* about Meru.

"Go on, that's the truth," said Fideli, encouragingly.

"Maheza, maheza, the animal is dead," said Bill behind there.

"Hu-huh," said Fideli indulgently, with a smile.

"When Snodia came with her *words*, then . . . that was making the ihamba come out, and it came out," I said.

"Yes," said Fideli softly. "That was the exact truth. And ihamba comes! That time we called you into the house to come and see what it was. That was it. It's very important."

I commented on how many people had been coming out with their grudges, such as Njesi and Zinia, "They came out with it—"

"No," said Fideli, and Singleton was disturbed.

"Still, they kept coming out with things all around. Even pregnant women were in danger," I said.

"And that's the truth, exactly, eh?" said Fideli. "Mrs. Turner, you have to know this. Ihamba is another thing, a certain thing, *different* from Chihamba or Punjila, as you know. Like us, you're a chimbanda, you, Mrs. Turner, and Bill, and Mr. Singleton Kahona. I can't add someone. No, how can I? I don't want to add that one, because it's not fitting. This is a very important *chinjikijilu* ['trail blaze'].[9] When it comes to the point I know that."

Singleton did not want nonparticipants brought into the circle. Njesi and Zinia hadn't been putting on their *words*, they had been affected involuntarily, like pregnant women. Singleton didn't like Njesi. We may note that the matter of slavery had come out, if only for an instant. However, Christianity was more of an issue with Singleton. Generally, he was interested in keeping the form of Ihamba intact and controlling who were its practitioners.

Later that evening, Singleton reenacted some of his own divinatory propositions with much feeling, keeping his eyes fixed on the microphone as if it were the ihamba. In his notes Bill described this meeting as "fantastic, great, after an emotionally exhausting day. We drank honey beer, listened to the tapes, and sang and laughed a lot. Throughout the visit Fideli kept exclaiming, 'I'm so happy!' praising God and the Baha'i messiah Baha'ullah, talking about his upcoming Baha'i-sponsored trip to the temple at Haifa in Israel, and trying to get Singleton to say what Ihamba was all about." Singleton stressed again the hunger of the ihamba tooth, its desire for meat, and, practical as usual, how to satisfy it. This was finally done as follows.

On December 6, at 6.00 A.M. nine days after Meru's Ihamba, my assistant Jennifer came to our hut to tell us to go to Mulandu Village, because Singleton had obtained the duiker antelope he wanted in order to finish Ihamba. He was going to feed the tooth with its rightful prey. We went and found Bakston the hunter, Fideli, and Singleton surrounded by a crowd of small children. They were gazing down at a pale brown animal lying on a mat, its long legs ending in tiny neat hooves. Bakston carried the dead animal to Meru's house and around to the chishinga shrine pole beyond. He laid it on a concrete drain fragment at the east side of the pole.

"Maheza!" barked Singleton, and we all joined in, "Maheza!" "Ngambu!" "Yafwa! My friends! The animal is dead!"—following it with the Ihamba song. Then they gathered the dried leaves from the previous shade branches into a bed and laid the carcass upon it. Bakston squatted down and began cutting. He first cut off its penis, then skinned the animal entirely except for the head with the two small horns. Then he carefully cut and removed the penis ligaments; he opened the abdomen and laid out the intestines and stomach. The liver and spleen was put aside in a bowl. "Chiyanga doctors can have those," indicated Fideli. "You," he said to me.

The lungs and heart were for Singleton. Singleton attended to an internal organ still inside. It was a blind-ended tube, the gall bladder. Singleton removed it carefully and emptied a dark fluid from it, then filled it with blood from the body cavity—"to feed ihamba." He knotted the end of the tube, then turned to the liver and cut out a half-inch piece, which he trimmed into a disc, then into a small torus with a hole in the center. He took this disc and the bag of blood into Meru's house, and we followed him.

The winnowing basket lay ready on the dirt floor, with Singleton's mongoose skin pouch on it, along with a clean Vaseline jar with a lid, now half full of maize meal, made from the grain which is hard "like a tooth." Singleton added his liver disc and the sac of blood to the things on the basket. Now he took out of the pouch some red clay which he crushed with the end of his musengu horn and smeared over his fingers, for protection; after which he took up the liver ring and carefully removed from his pouch the ihamba tooth, then chose a tiny piece of red clay; and holding the tooth and clay together he inserted them into the hole in the liver ring. He put the ring containing the ihamba into the Vaseline jar on top of the corn meal, stuffing it in and positioning it with his thumb at the center of the surface of

Figure 25. The contented tooth.

the meal. Then he poured over it the blood from the sac, and screwed on the lid. The bottle was now colored brilliant red above and white below, a union of blood and meal. "Marvelous," I wrote in my notes. Bill wrote later: "Subjectively, I felt very strange. Images flashed through my mind . . . bread and wine; semen and menstrual blood; solid and liquid; ying and yang; a boulder in the stream and the water, time flowing past, life itself." Apparently, we both felt as if a kind of resolution had occurred. Even the reader may sense the effect. Singleton said that when ihamba was fed with blood it was satisfied, and so it appeared to be[10] (Figure 25).

Singleton now found the cupping horns and wiped them out with some of the blood from the sac, so that the blood might call out ihamba next time the horns were used. Bill commented in his notes that the strong inhalation needed to produce the suction in the horns draws the bad spirit out of the patient's body through the incisions. The exhalations that were performed in the process of producing the *words* of the patient and ritual participants are breaths coming out, bad feelings coming out; the doctor inhales, drawing toward him those evils by the power of his medications and of his own inherited spirit and helper; and he stuffs them into his protective skin bag, the bag made from the snake-killing mongoose. The ihamba tooth stays there for a time, rendered passive by the red clay, then is finally fed and given blood in the permanent safety of the Vaseline jar.

Now that the feeding was done, Singleton called Meru into the house. She came running, radiant and smiling all over her middle-aged face. Singleton took the blood sac and marked her on her shoulders and beside her eyes. She was obviously in good fettle, and the blood would keep her that way.[11]

7. Ritual and the Anthropology of Experience

So much for the account. To me the experience was of major importance. I was going to have to research the matter more fully back home. When I did arrive back home I was able to find some parallels in ethnographic literature.

For instance, although I was not in trance as Maya Deren was in her experience of the Haitian Voudoun dance, yet like her I had the knowledge that I had broken through, we all had, we had gotten our heads above water. Deren's trance was triggered by the drummer:

> The drummer . . . can "break" to relieve the tension of the monotonous beat and bodily motion, thus interrupting concentration. By withholding this break he can bring the Loa [god] into the heads of the participants or stop them from coming. He can also use the break in another way by letting the tension build to a point where the break does not release tension, but climaxes it in a galvanizing shock. This enormous blow empties the dancer's head, leaving him without a center around which to stabilize. He is buffeted by the strokes as the drummer "beats the Loa into his head." He cringes at the large beats, clutches for support, recapturing his balance just to be hurtled forward by another great beat of the drum. The drummer . . . persists until the violence suddenly ceases, and the person lifts his head, seeming to gaze into another world. The Loa has arrived. (Deren 1953, 242)

I was interested in this drummer of Deren's. Was the consciousness of the approaching spirit there in him? Compare my own clapping. It took the "calving" event, coming first, to teach me to clap. As for Singleton he had prayed to his ancestor spirit to direct him at each turn of the ritual. He was able to listen for the right time, for the moment of "lifting." We can recognize these effects in the operation of Singleton's Ihambas, and in Victor Turner's account of the earlier Ihambas as well.

The Event as Fact: Subjectivity and Objectivity

I was concerned about the event as fact, bringing in questions of the anthropology of experience. My experience might well be termed a subjective one by those who have never shared anything like it. Even some of those who have had an experience will be uncertain about where such a sense impression comes from: "from out there?" And if not, from where? Most of these latter will nevertheless maintain that what they saw they saw. Their brains did not "make it up." As I wrote in the Introduction, few anthropologists have addressed the problem fully. There is a book that makes the attempt, *Deadly Words: Witchcraft in the Bocage* (Favret-Saada 1980). Here the subject matter is actual witchcraft. The author maintains that in order to understand the experience it is necessary for the ethnographer to undergo it and thus surmount the difficulty in which anthropologists find themselves when dealing with such a strange phenomenon as this. The author did in fact experience witchcraft and learned how to resist it.

> To understand the meaning of this discourse [the "gift" of unwitching, "seeing everything"] there is no other solution but to practice it oneself, to become one's own informant, to penetrate one's own amnesia, and to try and make explicit what one finds unstateable in oneself. (Favret-Saada 1980, 22)

Favret-Saada produced a good ethnography. In this chapter I am grappling with the implications of her and my field material, adding certain other examples.

Generally, anthropology is divided about subjectivity; many historical tides of influence have gone toward creating that division. Deep questions about objectivity and subjectivity are involved here. I do not wish to increase a rift, rather to mend it, always mindful of the marvels of empathy shown by any anthropologist when speaking of his field people.

But I ask, what exactly is objectivity?

Ralph Burhoe[1] (1974) in an article entitled "The Phenomenon of Religion Seen Scientifically" discusses objectivity and what it is generally supposed to be. First, he quotes Ashby to show the intractability of science:

> If consciousness is the most fundamental fact of all, why is it not used [by scientists]? The answer, in my opinion, is that Science deals, and can deal, only with what one man can *demonstrate* to another. Vivid though consciousness may be to its possessor, there is as yet no method known by which he can demonstrate his experience to another. And until such a method, or its equivalent, is found, the facts of consciousness cannot be used in scientific method. (Ashby 1960, 11–12)

Burhoe takes Ashby to mean:

> Because science is a part of linguistically transmitted information its communicability requires "objective" language, and private experience is of no use except to the investigator himself. (Burhoe 1974, 25)

Burhoe then compares the argument of the Nobel Laureate physicist P. W. Bridgeman:

> Many are familiar with the fact that the "objectivity" and the "outside" dimension of the world of our experience are established in part by the correlations that we make prior to language. As infants we make correlations between the outcomes of two or more separate routes to experiencing a ball. We experience it by seeing a round blob of color, but we also experience it by the tactual and kinesthetic feeling in our hands and arms. By such multiple correlations of experiences from many perspectives, certain preverbal patterns or symbols in our experiences become "objective realities" out there in the world (Bridgeman 1959, 45ff).
>
> A physicist [says Burhoe], develops objectivity in the same general way. When he wishes to assert that something is real, true, or objective, all he really needs to say is that several independent experiences have confirmed that some relationship or correlation among events remains unchanged. Bridgeman has called this process one of finding "different routes to the same terminus." He and others do not stop with their own private experience, however. The term "objective" is enhanced when it is found that others performing the same or similar operations report essentially equivalent results, at least insofar as words or other cultural symbols can communicate "equivalent" experiences from one individual to another (Bridgeman 1959, 52). Another physicist who has carefully examined the problem of knowing and of physical science, Margenau (1960), has provided a very helpful analysis of how scientific conceptual systems that portray the objective world are built up from the private "plane of perceptual experiences," which are the data or the givens of subjective experience. (Burhoe 1974, 25–26)

What I am attempting, then, is to "portray the objective world . . . built up from the private 'plane of perceptual experiences' " of all those who hooted with praise at the emergence of Sakutoha's ihamba, of the five doctors in Meru's Ihamba, and also the experiences of many other Africans and, indeed, as far as one can estimate, of many ritual performers throughout humankind. It will be remembered that I did not see what the crowd saw at "Sakutoha's" emergence but the hooting was totally spontaneous—and it was not in praise of a small ivory human tooth, which was only found later. It was clear they shared a common perception. The four other doctors besides me in Meru's Ihamba actually saw something, according to Singleton. I could not ascertain if what they saw looked exactly like what I saw but can asseverate that the fact of their seeing at that particular time and under those particular conditions was highly significant to them and to me.

Fabian (1983) has some interesting words to say that are relevant to the problem:

> I want language and communication to be understood as a kind of praxis in which the Knower cannot claim ascendency over the Known (nor, for that matter, one Knower over another). As I see it . . . the anthropologist and his interlocutors only "know" when they meet each other in one and the same contemporality. (164)

This is put straight and to the point. Knowledge is a living thing that may decay when out of touch with its origins. Social science is no ordinary science. Might one suggest that if a fieldworker had some strange experience related to that of the field people this might actually be part of the common coeval condition of the two of them? It would put them in the same framework, in the same "era." One might also adduce the arguments of anti-ethnocentrists such as Vincent Crapanzano, Kevin Dwyer, James Clifford, and Stephen Tyler, who support the subject peoples' political rights and ethnographic authority, and even encourage the ethnographer to be frank about his or her presence during the events recorded in the write-up.

There are other instances. In a remarkable essay entitled "Word, Eye, and Mind in Anthropology," Paul Stoller (1984) relates his own apprenticeship among the Songhay of Niger and his experiences of sorcery—which led him to evolve a different attitude toward the philosophy behind anthropology.

> Once the anthropological writer has experienced "the inside" or "the place where logic bites its own tail," the discourse of ethnographic realism is no longer completely adequate. When I confronted first hand the powers of Dunguri [a priestess] in Wanzerbe and acted like a Songhay healer, all of my assumptions about the world were uprooted from their foundation on the plain of Western metaphysics. Nothing that I had learned or could learn within the parameters of anthropological theory could have prepared me for Dunguri. Having crossed the threshold into the Songhay world of magic, and having felt the texture of fear and the exaltation of repelling the force of a sorcerer, my view of Songhay culture could no longer be one of a structuralist, a symbolist, or a Marxist. Given my intense experience—and all field experiences are intense whether they involve trance, sorcery or kinship—I will need

in future works to seek a different mode of expression, a mode in which the event becomes the author of the text and the writer becomes the interpreter of the event who serves as an intermediary between the event (author) and the readers. . . . Anthropological writers should allow the events of the field—be they extraordinary or mundane—to penetrate them. In this way the world of the field cries out silently for description and . . . the anthropological writer, using evocative language, brings life to the field and beckons the reader to discover something new. (Stoller 1984, 110)

This is truly allowing the dialogue with the people in the field to assume to the full its potential importance to the ethnographer and his or her readers.

There is a difference between Stoller's account and my own. My experience took place in the midst of a considerable group of people, he was alone in his struggle with Dunguri's powers. But there were similarities. As with Stoller, I knew and was familiar with the relationships of many of the field people with each other; I was using the Victor Turner method of following social dramas, being aware of social process at every turn. Thus we can see that the presence of Nyakanjata at Meru's Ihamba, that of Mulandu, and especially Paulos, affected all of us, myself included. And the climax was for myself strongly associated with what happened after the arrival of Paulos. Existentially, I knew I ought to assist in these people's affairs and thus was not only doing anthropology as an observer but for a time joined in.

What Victor Turner said about ritual in 1955 after he came out of the field takes us to a further stage of understanding: "Ritual is a stylized or formalized activity that has efficacy *in its very form*" (his italics; unpublished ms). What does this mean for Ihamba? I found my experience as factual as childbirth. This is how I see that "efficacy." I have given the circumstances of the ritual—the form in action which carries that efficacy, the score, scenario, script, choreography, careful to nest the event in its social matrix constituted by the pressures and resentments of the kinship group of Kahona at that point in 1985, after generations of trouble, after burgeoning reproduction, along with the development of a corresponding dynasty of healers. Let us glance once again at the score of Meru's Ihamba and deal with it in yet another way (from time to time I deal with the event in the form of "theme and variations") so that we learn intimately the impelling process which leads the participant from ritual frigidity to the orgasm of experience.

Let us remember the medicine collection, when we walked in the fields straight toward the greeting tree, at the foot of which we prayed, thus entering the realm of communitas. All the material bits of tree were trophies of our search, pragmatic yet part of Lévy-Bruhl's "mystical participation." Then, when we were back home where Fideli performed the laborious peeling and chopping up of medicines to produce the leaf tea with its enlivening effects, we were in a kind of kitchen for the psyche, in a place which was also being set up as an earthy home and attractor—what we call a shrine—for a wandering spirit. The proceedings were developing their impetus toward the drum ritual (*ngoma,* that resonant word) until at last rhythmic sound, social assembly, and singing began. What songs to sing, what kind of participation, all became a concern, at the same point at which the patient was drawn in and seated, hopeless and unresponsive. But could drum music be resisted? Soon we all began to sing and clap, and Nyakanjata to dance, Nyakanjata who had been so sick the month before. Then they could get down to opening up Meru's back, now that they had her sacralized: open her back, plug on the horns, get the spirit inside her moving by suction. She would eventually go into trance. How we wanted this! But nothing was going to happen all at once, this was real life. Patience and a carefully developed listening skill had to be deployed.

We could now address the spirit, just a little, by means of the divinatory propositions—speaking to Meru and the spirit in the same breath. The spirit was developing into consciousness inside her—that conscious ihamba. Our songs and battering drum bouts fulminated bravely—we came to a climax. But it was no good, so we tried again. Meru's feelings were sore, the ritual was reaching her soreness until it burst from her. And she spoke, those *words* which were only too true, against her own younger sister. And the stupidity of shifting the date of Ihamba, so that the great Paulos was not there—it was a mighty disappointment. Which was put right.

All the episodes drove on with their weariness, contention, prepartural despair—everybody feeling, "It'll never happen, it can't happen." There was always the breaking into dissension and joining again for another episode, breaking and joining in unison, working up in an extraordinary boosting effect, like the expelling and receiving of breath, but a much bigger matter than that—for all the emotions were involved, all the life stance of each person, parting and coming together, systole and diastole, working in the style of the impeded form which burned us with impatience. The psyches of all were in similar straits, all of us needed to be desperate for the bursting through, the breakthrough; Meru, Singleton, Fideli, Nyakanjata, Snodia, and Edie. Then, when the psychosocial body was ready for some unseen triggering—even perhaps including that of the white stranger's frustration and tears—all of a sudden the soul of the whole group was delivered from its oppression, and the patient's brain, negated by trance, allowed her body to open and provide the outlet for the spirit to escape— that opaque mass of plasma—into the air, to be stuffed into the homey hunting-flavored mongoose skin pouch.

This then was the form that was effective—effective when performed, not read as in this passage, though something of the feeling of the occasion may be empathized by means of verbal description. To pare it down any further would lose all its material weight, and again, it should be emphasized that a verbal description is but a shadow of the reality. This is a truism that has been made continually in culture after culture, age after age, about any spiritual experience.

The Human Tooth

I have been discussing the experience of seeing the thing come out of Meru, an experience in keeping with what the Ndembu say about afflicting spirits. But what of the human concrete tooth that Singleton showed Bill and me in Meru's house after the ritual and later when he fed the ihamba? The dilemmas are many. Which was the disease, the spirit form or the tooth? Did two "things" come out of Meru? Or did Singleton knowingly use sleight of hand to produce the concrete human tooth? In this connection the reader may be reminded of the renowned essay of Lévi-Strauss, "The Sorcerer and His Magic" (1977, 445–53). I will quote the question that Landy asked concerning the Kwakiutl shaman Quesalid discussed by Lévi-Strauss, "Since the sorcerer is aware that he is using sleight of hand how does he retain his own faith in the system?" (1977, 445). Quesalid was originally a cynic who deliberately obtained "shamanic" training in the art of hiding a tuft of down in the cheek, which the practitioner could pretend was the pathological foreign body he had sucked out of the body of the patient. Having learnt and practiced it, Quesalid found to his surprise that he was actually curing his patients by these means. We might suggest that traditional peoples do not make the same precise distinctions about real magic and artifice that we do. Does the truth lie in Lévi-Strauss's claim that the cure demonstrates "the coherence of the psychic universe, itself a projection of the social universe" (446), implying that the cure takes place

in the psychic world, itself emergent from the social world in much the way
Lienhardt described divinity growing out of experience? Lévi-Strauss lists
the many elements of the total situation in a healing ritual

> in which sorcerer, patient, and audience, as well as representations and pro-
> cedures, all play their parts. Furthermore, the public must participate. . . . It is
> this universe of vital effusions which the patient . . . and the sorcerer . . . allow
> the public to glimpse as "fireworks" from a safe distance. In contrast with
> scientific explanation, the problem is to articulate . . . the states, emotions, or
> representations into a whole or system. The system is valid precisely to the
> extent that it allows the coalescence or precipitation of these diffuse states,
> whose discontinuity also makes them painful. To the conscious mind, this last
> phenomenon constitutes an original experience which cannot be grasped from
> without. (452)

Something deep is referred to here which corresponds to the focusing
in Ihamba—in Lévi-Strauss it is "coalescence." Also the Ihamba patient's
social and physical misery corresponds to Lévi-Strauss's anomic "painful"
states, while the Ihamba climax is Lévi-Strauss's "precipitation." It can be
seen that in the 1950s I was unable to grasp the experience because it was
"from without," whereas in Meru's Ihamba I did personally grasp the
experience of the social calving and the sight of the spirit form. Still, in
Mulandu Farm I could not at first figure out what I ought to think about
the *concrete* tooth and its wanderings in the veins. What exactly did happen
in Meru's house after the ritual? Did Singleton use sleight of hand to pick
the tooth out of the receiving can, which was what Victor Turner believed
had been done at the Ihambas of the 1950s? Singleton did not tell us; there
was nothing in the tapes—many of which were recorded in informal and
private circumstances—that hinted of duplicity. And there was always my
own experience of seeing the thing that came out of Meru's back.

Later in my reading I came across a chapter entitled "Extracting
Harmful Intrusions" in *The Way of the Shaman* by Michael Harner (1980,
113–34), one of the few descriptions that does not ascribe an extraction to
trickery:

> Illness due to power intrusion is manifested by such symptoms as localized
> pain or discomfort, often together with an increase in temperature, which
> (from a shamanic point of view) is connected with the energy from the
> harmful power intrusion. . . .
> A shaman would say that it is dangerous not to know about shamanism. In
> ignorance of shamanic principles, people do not know how to shield them-
> selves from hostile energy intrusions through having guardian spirit power [it

was because of this that Singleton warned us that we should drink leaf medicine to shield ourselves from the escaping ihamba]. . . .

The shamanic removal of harmful power intrusions is difficult work, for the shaman sucks them out of a patient physically as well as mentally and emotionally. This technique is widely used in shamanic cultures in such distant areas as Australia, North and South America, and Siberia.

If you ever viewed the film *Sucking Doctor,* which shows the healing work of the famous California Indian shaman Essie Parrish, you saw a shaman pulling out intrusive power. But Western skeptics say that the shaman is just pretending to suck something out of the person, an object that the shaman had already secreted in his mouth. Such skeptics have apparently not taken up shamanism themselves to discover what is happening.

What is happening goes back to the fact that the shaman is aware of two realities. As among the Jivaro, the shaman is pulling out an intrusive power that (in the Shamanic State of Consciousness) has the appearance of a particular creature, such as a spider, and which he also knows is the hidden nature of a particular plant. When a shaman sucks out that power, he captures its spiritual essence in a portion of the same kind of plant that is its ordinary material home. That plant piece is, in other words, a power object. For example, the shaman may store in his mouth two half-inch-long twigs of the plant that he knows is the material "home" of the dangerous power being sucked out. He captures the power in one of those pieces, while using the other one to help. The fact that the shaman may then bring out the plant power object from his mouth and show it to a patient and audience as "Ordinary State of Consciousness" evidence does not negate the nonordinary reality of what is going on for him in the Shamanic State of Consciousness. (115–17)[2]

In this passage the dual nature of the intrusive object is directly addressed: "The shaman is aware of two realities" (116). He captures the spiritual essence of the intrusive object—which in the shamanic state of consciousness among the Jivaro may have the appearance of a spider but at Meru's Ihamba had the appearance of a six-inch spirit form—gathering it into something that is its ordinary material home as seen in ordinary consciousness, that is, half-inch twigs in the case of the Jivaro, and an ivory tooth as we have seen, among the Ndembu. The dual system also appears among the Walbiri of Australia whose doctors found a dingo spirit inside a patient which they extracted in the form of a worm (Cawte 1974, 48). Quesalid may have been successful because he provided a material home, a tuft of down, for the intrusions he drew out. Lévi-Strauss argues that Quesalid was an imposter but became a great shaman, in whom the radical negativism of the free thinker gave way to more moderate feelings until he completely lost sight of "the fallaciousness of the technique which he had so disparaged at the beginning."

The dead hunter's tooth itself becomes more significant looked at in the manner of the Jivaro example above. As Victor Turner saw the tooth, it was the slaying weapon par excellence, the epitome, the personification of the sudden aggressivity needed to bring down a fleeing animal. And he said that the Ndembu saw in the chishinga sharpened pole "the slaughterous power of huntsmanship itself" (1967, 298). I myself regard the tooth and the chishinga as more than symbols. They are powers giving an actual vision. In the tooth is conflated "all the powers inherent in the activities, objects, relationships, and ideas" (298) that we saw focused in the Ihamba ritual. The tooth constitutes one of the poles (as if magnetic) of the two *realities,* between which distinctly recognizable powers jump back and forth, much as I have emphasized in Chapter 4 on ambiguities. The curious thing about the above passage of Victor Turner's is the belief that shines out of it, itself transmuting symbols into reality.

Now when I consider the ihamba tooth, which was the resultant, the trophy, the material prize gained from the long morning of ritual, and wonder about its appearance at the end—after what I saw, and after what Benwa said about its journeys in the body—what then? Was it that the presence of the tooth, brought to the ritual focus, was employed to pull out toward itself the bodily harmful thing I saw, magnet to magnet? Singleton used the same word, ihamba, about the thing that was inside—the one I saw coming out—and the tooth. The doctors could "dissolve" (as in a film) from one to the other. That little hard tooth, bubbled into a big shadowy spirit form invading the veins and arteries, visible, audible, reminds me of a similar report made by Essie Parrish, the Pomo Indian shaman referred to above:

> When that sick man is lying there, I usually see the power. These things seem unbelievable but I, myself, I know, because it is in me. . . . Way inside of the sick person lying there, there is something. It is just like seeing through something—if you put tissue over something, you could see through it. That is just the way I see it inside. I see what happens there and can feel it with my hand—my middle finger is the one with the power.[3] . . . The pain sitting somewhere inside the person feels like it is pulling your hand towards itself— you can't miss it.[4] (Harner 1980, 127–28)

The skill of Benwa appears to correspond to that of Essie Parrish, even though she was an English-speaking highly articulate woman from an entirely different culture. It was Benwa who told us that you could see the ihamba moving through the veins of the body, "I'm telling you the truth"

(Chapter 1). He did not use the "tissue" image; but there are many references in the proceedings to seeing and sensing the ihamba. Singleton said, "I've seen it. It's the ihamba, so he's got to come out of her" (Chapter 6); "With his slender nsomu horn Singleton drew many lines around the cupping horn on Nyakanjata's right shoulder" (Chapter 3); Fideli says, "When ihamba goes into a horn you ought to feel the horn vibrating" (Chapter 3).

To return to the enigma of the double nature of the ihamba, one may see it like this: what is important is the moment when Singleton clutches the "thing" in his skin pouch. This is the moment of translation into the outward world of the ihamba that was within—its exit from Meru's body. He then puts it into the receiving can, and later in the house its form is visible to everyday sight as a tooth somehow deriving from the spirit form. Then it *must* have meat, then the object that is numinous is a hard concrete tooth, and so the occasion of its feeding with blood produces that palpable experience of satisfaction that Bill and I sensed at the feeding in Meru's house. The fact that the doctors allowed the same word, ihamba, to run as it were out from Meru's body, into the bag and receiving can, and later into the Vaseline jar, attests to its processual unity, its unbroken flow of identity. We could put it backward: "that ihamba tooth in the Vaseline jar was the ihamba that was in the receiving can, which was the ihamba that Singleton clutched in his mongoose skin bag, which was the ihamba that came out of Meru, which was the ihamba that had been hurting her with all the agony of a tooth." When operating in the forward sequence of time, in a cause-and-effect pattern, Meru's affliction by a human tooth looks impossible; in the West the only words for such a process are "trickery," "sleight of hand," and the like. But these terms derive from quite a different world from the scene at Mulandu Farm. Looking backward from the outcome of the Ihamba to Meru's sickness, the picture does not seem so impossible. This is because the past is only verified by the future,[5] and in this ihamba's future it was destined for feeding, and thus its past took shape after the event, as a computer shifts everything it has written to adjust to new insertions.

What ihamba itself consists of is the biting inside, that hard spirit which cannot come out without a sudden transformation, effected socially by living people communicating with the spirit, ready for the "coalescence or precipitation of the diffuse states," in Lévi-Strauss's words. It is what it is.

8. Seeing Spirits

Because the seeing of a spirit form is the central episode of this book, I shall discuss what is involved in this kind of seeing and also briefly refer to its incidence in other cultures.

Seeing as direct perception[1] is the prime faculty of the Ndembu spirit healer. Benwa could *see* the ihamba tooth moving in the vein, Singleton could *see* the spirit when he had drunk leaf medicine, and I *saw* the large thing come out of Meru's body. This kind of seeing appears to be necessary in spirit or witchcraft diagnoses.

Consciousness of what the special eye can do is implicit in the words for such specialists: firstly, our own word "seer" (see-er) interestingly retains the psychic characteristic. We do not call those who watch television "seers," only "viewers." The South Pacific Vanuatu people call their spirit healers "*kleva,* or *matalesi,* literally, 'see-eye.' They are seers, supposedly able to 'see' directly the causes of illnesses . . . their therapy is less a matter of trial and error" (Ludvigson 1985, 59). The Navajo called their diagnostic specialists "star*gazers*" (Mindeleff 1898).

There are certain characteristics of such seeing: it is usually necessary for the seer to be in an enhanced state of consciousness, which in its turn is associated with certain circumstances. Trance is commonly present; total attention may be a factor; having been moved by some unexpected event may be another factor. Immediate understanding between people in the same situation may also occur—a kind of collective pentecostal experience associated with communitas. Joy often accompanies the experience.

The condition is rare. Few people are in the enhanced state constantly, and any given person may only experience it once or twice in a lifetime. However, such rare events are often valued in inverse proportion to their frequency.

There are well-recognized levels of seeing: ordinary, in the imagination, and several unusual ones. The first I shall mention is ordinary sight in an everyday context. The second may be connected with developed thought and "seeing the point" of a sophisticated argument, or it may be an intent and thoughtful gaze at a complex object. The third is fantasizing in an idle mood—Wordsworth's "vacant or in pensive mood" which merges into the waking dream. The fourth is the regular dream, often not remembered, arising inside the individual's brain in sleep. The fifth is the "great dream," the kind we feel strongly must have a meaning. It is regarded by all as important, whether in the domain of psychoanalysis or as prophecy or message. This also seems to be a product of the individual who does the dreaming insofar as the person is asleep and not using outward sense organs. However, many religious people, both in the West and East, will claim that some spirit or god comes to them in this way "from out there." Such a message is recognized as coming through the mind and not the waking senses. The sixth, "visualization," describes the technique of allowing and even training the mind to start pictures and events going, then to follow their course. This covers a wide field, from intuition, whether or not ascribed to a spirit, to many healers' techniques, and to the lesser shaman's journey. In the latter example, the shaman does not see with the eyes of his body but those of his spirit. Prophecy, clairvoyance, and healing power may result. In the seventh, there is the seeing of a vision, a ghost, a spirit form, or a prophetic event with the eyes of the body. What is seen is regarded as "out there," and not as projected through the mind. A major example of this is the greater shaman's journey, as in the case of an Eskimo shaman who, Rainey was told, flew from Point Hope to Shishmareff, a far distant place, where he was even seen and recognized by others (Rainey 1947, 277).

This list and the number of its items are by no means absolute or complete. The Catholic church used to recognize three forms of vision, the corporeal, imaginative, and intellectual (Roure 1912, 15:477–78). The corporeal corresponds to my seventh category, the actual sight of a spiritual entity "out there"; the imaginative to my sixth, the vision within the mind, and the intellectual to my second, deep understanding. William Blake in 1802 wrote of four categories:

'Tis fourfold in my supreme delight
And threefold in soft Beulahs night
And twofold Always. May God us keep
From Single vision & Newtons sleep.

Here "fourfold" is something which my seventh, sixth, and second might combine to express, "threefold" might be my third and sixth combined, "twofold" is my second, and "single" is my first. Blake, a born shaman, never wished to see his vision collapse entirely to prosaic levels.

These typologies are taken from the genres of theology and poetry.

Ethnographers on their part have described a variety of seeing events in detail. Richard Katz (1982), working in the ethnography of religion, shows that the !Kung healers of the Kalahari were conscious of "clear seeing." He says:

> Seeing properly allows the healer to locate and diagnose the sickness in a person. Wi, an old experienced healer, speaks of Dau, who is still comparatively young in kia [the state of "boiling energy"]: "What tells me that Dau isn't fully learned is the way he behaves. You see him staggering and running about. His eyes are rolling all over the place. If your eyes are rolling, you can't stare at sickness. You have to be *absolutely steady* to see sickness, steady-eyed, no shivering and shaking. You need a steady gaze. Your thoughts don't whirl, the fire doesn't float above you, when you are seeing properly."
>   Dau acknowledges that he is not a *geiha*, that is, a "completely learned" healer: "A geiha is a person who really helps people. He is someone whose eye-insides are steady. He can see people properly. I heal people, but I can't see them properly." In seeing properly, not only does one see where and what the sickness is, but also, with that "absolutely steady" stare, one starts to treat the sickness. (105)

The consciousness of skill or lack of skill here is obvious; training and experience count for much; they stimulate discrimination and consciousness among practitioners about what they are doing.

Junod (1962) also refers to what he calls "second sight" among the Thonga of Mozambique. "The magicians . . . certainly believe themselves endowed with personal power due to the development of their faculties of second sight, etc., which they attribute to the spirits (ancestor gods) from whom they have inherited their drugs" (517).

Going further afield, a borderline case between *seeing* and feeling, one without the use of drugs, is described by Geertz (1977, 149). He terms it "intuitive insight through meditation" and describes how a Javanese Hinduistic practitioner "meditates, going into a near trance and clearing his mind entirely of any 'pictures' until he gets an abstract and formless feeling which tells him what the disease is and what the cure should be. Despite the lack of mental pictures, however, the diagnosis and cure may be quite concrete."

Lévi-Strauss (1963, 188) refers to the talent of the *nele*, a type of medicine man among the Cuna Indians: the talent is "considered innate, consists of supernatural sight, which instantly discovers the cause of illness—that is, the whereabouts of the vital forces, whether particular or generalized, that have been carried off by evil spirits."

Claire Parsons (1985) describes diagnosis among the Tongans of the tropical Pacific:

> The *faitoʻo* [healer] I observed and spoke with told me that an X-ray of the affected part was unnecessary, as they had sufficient means available for diagnosis. They can "feel" the broken bone or dislocation, just as they can "feel" a muscular condition which no X-ray will reveal. In any event, there was little discussion of the diagnostic process. The healers simply "knew" which type of disorder it was after examining the injured person. (96)

Janice Reid (1983) describes a Yolngu healer in Australia diagnosing a woman's injuries:

> The *marrnggitj* [healer] took two magical stones and placed one between the patient's breasts. The other was placed against her side. He leant down, peering intently so that he appeared to be looking through her body in the line of the two stones. Then he used another stone to treat her internal organs. (67)

This and Harner's description of seeing as if through glass focuses attention on some kind of extra faculty, of which the healers themselves are well aware.

Mindeleff (1898) has described in detail how the Navajo diagnostician known as the "stargazer" *sees* the cause of disease:

> The stargazer chants, then he says, "Everyone must close his eyes. No one must move or speak. Everyone must concentrate on the illness and try to see something." . . . He walks away some distance. . . . When there is no noise, the stargazer places a crystal or stone in his hand. He chants. He prays. . . . Then the stargazer holds out his arm and hand in line with the moon or some star, and gazes unwinking at the crystal. Soon he sees something. He closes his hand upon what he has seen in the crystal. Also there may seem to be a line of light which is "lightning" from the star to the crystal or to the ground around him so that the ground appears light. The stargazer sees the hogan and the sick man, even though his back is turned to it. . . . He sees a man, or a bear, or a coyote, or perhaps the head of a coyote, or perhaps the bear is biting the patient. (quoted by Morgan 1977, 165–66)

William Morgan tells how the Navajo have tenaciously preserved their ritual, and comments:

> When a [Navajo diagnostician] describes trancing it is difficult to distinguish his meaning from Jung's words: "A vision, which by intense concentration, was perceived on the background of consciousness, a technique that is perfected only after long practice." Jung has remarked that "if once the resistance

to free contact with the unconscious can be overcome, and one can develop the power of sticking to the phantasy, there the play of images can be watched, and the creation of myths takes place." This requires the same concentration which [the Navajo diagnostician] describes as being necessary for the diagnosis of sickness. Furthermore Jung's material has called forth the following conclusions: "I have to declare that these facts are psychic facts of indisputable effect. They are not the discoveries of an idle mind, but definite psychic events. They obey absolutely definite laws, and have their own law-determined causes and effects, which accounts for the fact that they can be demonstrated just as well among the most varied peoples and races living today as among those of thousands of years ago. As to what these processes consist in I have no theory to offer." (Jung 1928, 246; Morgan 1977, 167)

I am interested in Jung's postulate that there are absolutely definite laws about psychic events, with cause and effect, with their own set of interrelated ideas and procedures. Direct perception at an enhanced level appears to be a hard-won faculty which has value not only because it aids the healer to cure the sick but because it is felt to be of value in its own right.

The Difficulties of the Healer Mode

Seer-healers have to be able to journey back and forth, to oscillate between realities in these healing tasks. As Boddy puts it, "During possession dramas, two levels of meaning—quotidian and extraordinary—oscillate and nourish one another" (1989, 353). Bridge imagery also expresses the difference between the two different worlds which such healers experience. Eliade (1964) quotes the Altaic shaman as crossing a sea

> by a bridge the breadth of a hair; he sets foot on it, and, to give a striking image of his crossing this dangerous bridge, he totters and almost falls. (202)

In the Ihamba ritual, Fideli maintained that he and the other doctors were in a special state. He did not want to be touched; others were charged extra for entering the ritual sphere unbidden; and only doctors could go on the sacred medicine hunt. He frequently exclaimed at the difficulty of the ritual process, aware as he was of its delicate nature, and he and Singleton warned of its danger.

It has been said that rationality by itself cannot come up with an explanation of these matters. "Belief" is also an unsatisfactory path toward it. Here in the problem of rationality and experience is revealed both the dual nature of the seer's perception and a picture of the slipperiness of the attempt to explain, like the slipperiness of the Eliadean shaman's bridge. We are referring to a type of attunement not ordinarily practiced. I was jogged into it in part by Morie's "shock" behavior, which did more for me than any amount of observation and documentation could have done, and had not in fact done in the Ihambas of the 1950s, either for myself or for Vic Turner. The moving around of the entire Ihamba orientation near the end of the ritual turned out to be also an act of ritual repositioning for all the doctors and the patient. Singleton's skill at this juncture was at its height—he could *see* that the tooth would now come out. His earlier mistake about orientation paralleled the initial mistake somewhere along the road of letting the ihamba tooth escape and get into Meru. Both were mistakes that brought about the repositioning of psyches at a different level. A speculation on Singleton's first mistake in the form of a composite story is given in Appendix 8, where a final variation on the theme of Ihamba is presented.

The following case illustrates the difficulty some anthropologists experience with regard to the healing techniques of non-medical doctors.

The anthropologist James Dow (*The Shaman's Touch,* 1986) found sucking shamans among the Otomi Indians of Mexico. His subtitle, *Otomi Indian Symbolic Healing,* carries the implication that traditional healing is achieved by the psychological power of symbols over the sick individual— meaning "representations"; Dow does not accept that there is any empirical or actual effect or power in what the shaman uses. He has difficulty with the methods of his shaman friend, Don Antonio, which he discusses in a passage worth quoting, along with Don Antonio's own version of his treatments.

> Sucking is the treatment for illness caused by objects implanted in the body by a sorcerer. . . . The patient uncovers the part of the body where pain or discomfort is felt. The shaman massages the area to work the object loose. He may first magically draw up the object from deep inside the body to just below the surface with a crystal. Then he places his mouth on the skin of the patient and sucks against it strongly. He clears his throat forcefully and then spits a substance into a cone of paper. . . .
>
> A natural question to ask is whether or not Don Antonio believes he is really able to suck things out of the body. Obviously the skin is not broken and he doesn't really do it. This is a magical procedure the effect of which is to reduce pain and discomfort by psychological suggestion. I have not asked Don Antonio the question directly, hoping to find the answer in his teaching about the subject. Clearly it is a delicate matter, and I have not received a direct answer. Perhaps this is not a proper question to ask in the first place, because to

imply that he fools people would be to question his power to heal by hypnotic suggestion. He does have this power, so in the mythic world of the healing shaman he does suck objects out of the body. In the scientific world he does not really do that, but he heals symbolically in a way that depends on the patient's belief that he does.

He chews tobacco in his mouth and sucks so hard that there is some blood mixed into the mass of mucus and tobacco shreds that he spits out. The substance he spits out is so loathsome and the retching sounds he makes are so unpleasant that I have seen no patients examine what is in the paper cone when invited. Most are content to take his word about what it is.

And Don Antonio's version:

[He uses three crystals.] Of these crystals, one is for yourself alone, because if you have something in your own body, a pain here or there that can't be alleviated with medicine, if you can't get well, you need this crystal. First sprinkle it with a little white rum and start to pull out the illness. The crystal will pull it up. So one is enough for yourself. You can use it over here if you have a problem in the middle of your back. You can feel the illness moving inside as you pull on it with the crystal. . . . The others are used to cure your patients when the illness is so deep in the body that you can't use your mouth to suck them out. In that case you use a crystal. The crystal will bring it up to right below the surface of the skin. Then you can get it yourself. . . . You place the crystal on the body. So, the crystal begins to dance by itself and begins to pull it up toward the surface. When it's close to the surface, stop using the crystal, put a bit of cigarette in your mouth, and get down to suck it the rest of the way. So then you have got it. . . .

Each time you're going to suck out these bad things, the patient will say, "It hurts me here. It hurts me there, or over there on this side." Right at that spot where it hurts are the bad things in the body. These are always magically induced by sorcery. . . . Evil illness . . . is seen during consultation. . . . To cure this, chew on these cheap cigarettes. Since the tobacco is strong, five or six cigarettes will be enough to cure a person. When one is finished, take another. . . . The tobacco neutralizes the power of the things that you suck out. They can't withstand the shock of encountering the strong tobacco. The stuff that is pulled out is like vermin. The tobacco stuns it. These evil things behave like animals.

When I suck objects I spit them out into a paper cone, because the stuff is so rotten. Sorcerers implant cow meat, pig meat, sardine meat, chicken meat, or whatever meat there is. They implant it, and so these bits of meat are cooked inside the body of their victims by the heat of the blood. So when you're about to suck out this stuff, you won't be able to stand its foulness. So this is why you use cigarettes. . . . At the moment that the illness is about to surface in the body, put a piece of cigarette in your mouth. If a piece of flesh is coming up, its rottenness will not be able to resist. Spit it out. . . . With this you pull it up. Pull it up with a crystal. This you'll have. But, the thing will not pop out on the surface of the skin. It's inside the flesh. It's below the surface, and then it comes up into your mouth. (107–10)

The personal closely detailed nature of this statement is typical of the statements of shamans themselves. In this case, one asks not whether Don Antonio believed he was sucking things out of the body but rather what he sucked out and why it does not pop out on the surface of the skin but is below the surface and then comes into the mouth. It is the same dilemma that faced me; except that I was able to *see* the bad thing come out. Meru's skin showed no huge tear, only the small razor mark. But the thing came out easily. No one was going out of his way to hypnotize me, I simply joined in a collective seeing, as Singleton said afterwards: "We saw." James Dow calls it hypnotism and suggestion. Don Antonio's account contained no hint of hypnotism or suggestion, it was very pragmatic. The young Harner would have agreed with Dow, the later with Don Antonio. I cannot agree with Dow because his explanation does not correspond with my experience.

Throughout these examples there arises a picture of a skilled man listening carefully to something in the body of a sufferer that is physical yet has a spirit component.

Suffice it to say that this faculty of listening is not as yet regarded as a "scientific" one, as Westerners would use the term, but in my experience it does exist.

Coda

I have discussed the social context of the events and the difficulty with the spirit experience and the tooth. I have tried to document what the people really said. Concerning the story of Morie, myself, and Kasonda, I have not analyzed the events structurally or politically—taking it that Morie's dilemma is clear enough, and that the role of Kasonda was one of a reasonably good man trying to save his soul according to his lights. I have shown how I preferred the work with Singleton to working with the churches, and confess that there was little I could do to correct my prejudice. Bill got on well with the church people, and they gave him great comfort when the news of his grandmother's death reached him from America. My own nostalgia for the symbolic riches of the past shows. I did experience that past, and it still saddens me that much of it is well-nigh forgotten.

As for the future I see a laboratory of traditional healing on a continental scale developing still further in this the poorest of continents. It is a laboratory that is kept from being swamped under the domination of science by the very poverty of the continent. For sensitive spirit medicine to work, there has to be some kind of hiatus—a gap between the technological possibilities that the West offers and any hope of their fulfillment. By this I mean that where a life of modern technology fills the viewpoint from horizon to horizon and absorbs all human attention, no gap exists in which other sensitivities can grow. But where this is not so, and technology does not crowd the viewpoint, where the people are not locked into intensive Western medicine, the ideas of the people are still open to odd and elusive causes of disease. These ideas are not fully describable by the word "psychological," but overlap into a world with which the people have become familiar owing to that very hiatus; the spirit world *in* that hiatus, in a liminal space, as Vic Turner would have called it.

This consciousness is illustrated well in one of the best African ethnographies, in a passage describing the expelling of a spirit from a mad woman among the Thonga of Mozambique by Henri Junod (1962 [1912]), a follower of Arnold van Gennep. Thonga ritual is based on the idea that the spirits of deceased people causes disease. During the curative ritual "worship" is addressed to these spirits (479). The Thonga ritual most relevant to the present book is not the removal of a *tooth* from the back as in the case of the rituals I present (nowhere documented except for the Ndembu as far as I can ascertain) but a ritual to cure madness. Divination is performed, the drumming is started, and the people gather and sing passionately. The song "always has the same object in view . . . namely to compel the spiritual being, the mysterious and possessing spirit which is there present, to reveal itself, and declare its name, after which it will be duly overcome" (484–85). At the climax when the patient is cured, he is "born again" (495) and will in the future be protected. Junod comments that the rites "tend to the development of subliminal faculties" (496). He says that among the Thonga "the dead are on all fours with the living . . . the invisible world has more importance than that of sense experience." And he adds admiringly, "They lack the sense that anything is impossible" (1934, 298). It is the kind of positive perception possessed by the Thonga that is the key to the success of African healing to this day—their healing is more like religious enlightenment, in a very concrete way.

It is different in the West. If we have a serious disease, we never stop trying to find a Western cure. Up to the very end we are primarily in the hands of medical doctors and in extreme danger are expected to pray, if at all, to the God of some major religion. No command like "Come out!" is issued to a bad spirit inside. Western medicine treats the body as an object, not a responsive organism, a body that hears, and the doctors don't imagine they can see deeply in the course of some complex curative ritual. On the peripheries, in Africa, Appalachia, in the favela slums of Brazil, among Eskimos, and in countless other out-of-the way spots on the globe, the gap has not been filled up, and the healer is familiar with the forces of the spirit world warring within a person. The healer can feel where the spirit is, what is going on inside the body, he or she can sense the moment when the presence of the spirit "kicks in." This is the ritual process that Victor Turner was striving to touch, he knew it well. It is not commonly known that he revived the stopped heart of a friend in Chicago who suffered a heart attack at a party. A medical doctor was there to witness the event—it was the old technique of laying on of hands.

This book then is in its curious way an attempt to vindicate Vic's general position as against his own psychologism, to vindicate his insight that there is something beyond the social context—though it needs the social for its soil and root system. Thus we may be talking of a world of religion—but of another view of religion, not as morals, not as mental prayer, but in the form of ritual objects effective in their own right, a matter of spirits, and people with knowledge of them operating a ritual process that can actually be sensed.

Appendix 1. African Spirit Healing and Ihamba

The Ndembu group belongs to the major Central African group of the Lunda whose territory overlaps Zambia, Angola, and Zaire. The Lunda are one of many southern savanna and central African peoples who practice traditional healing in the form of rituals to clear spirits from the afflicted person. The material on spirits and their extraction is rich. Virtually all the peoples of tropical Africa possess some of the traits associated with this traditional practice. Common characteristics include the use of "medicine," that is, herbs and other substances for curing, the expertise of a "doctor" or traditional health practitioner, drum music, singing, and sometimes dancing. Often a gathering of neighbors or cult members assist in singing, thus giving power to the process, and the general principle is the coming to terms with and expulsion of the harming spirit. Behind that is sometimes the principle of making the harmful thing "visible" (in the Chindembu language, *kusolola*) and naming it, the better to cast it out. In addition, the doctor may often be helped by a tutelary spirit, and confession is often encouraged to clear the air so that a healing may take place (see Turner 1968, 171–72; Wilson 1959, 134–41). All of these are relevant to the material in this book and also to most of the other Ndembu curative rituals, with minor variations.

Ihamba is thus, in most respects, a typical Ndembu and African ritual. However, except for the Shona (see Appendix 4), the ritual itself is different from the others in an important matter. The extraction is by suction, and something is shown as a result. This particular feature is somewhat different to exorcism as such. Where then is its place in African culture? Owing to the paucity of detailed material on rituals related to this feature of Ihamba, one may do no more than make a sketchy picture of its place among the rituals of neighboring peoples. At least, we can say that it is because of the internal coherence of the former Ndembu hunting cults that Ihamba, the healing version of these cults, has shown such persistence and that this has helped to give strength to the reputation of all Lunda people as great ritualists.

Otherwise, Ihamba still remains a curiosity, a ritual that performs extraction of an object by suction, like many in the shamanic world but like few in Africa. May one speculate that this incidence may be the remains of a fairly universal world skill the arts of which have become overlaid by less concrete forms?

The studies of African spirit affliction are numerous. As we have seen, the more general forms of Ndembu ritual can be seen as nested in a still wider cultural matrix. In order to place Ndembu ritual idiom in its context further afield, to show this nesting, a variety of documented cases are given here.

For instance (reviewing the neighbors of the Ndembu and from there on outward), among the neighboring Lovale we find a more generalized term, *lihamba*. "Spirit possession rituals treat illness for men and women. A spirit and its ritual exorcism or possession are called *lihamba*" and consist of medication and possession dances (McCulloch 1951, 76; see also Spring 1978, 171). Gerhardt Kubik states that *lihamba*, meaning simply a curing ritual, is found in many parts of the Lunda-Chokwe-Ngangela region. Actual tooth rituals are occasionally to be found, in addition to the Ndembu case (personal communication). White (1949), speaking of the Lunda, reported a change in *lihamba* from an affliction by an ancestor to an affliction by a stranger. But as this book shows, the Ndembu type of Ihamba is truly an affliction by an ancestor. The Kaonde pray to their *wakishi* ("ancestor spirits") when ill (Melland 1923, 133). The nearby Luba and Barotse use cupping horns (Burton 1961, 84–85; Reynolds 1963, 63–69). The Lemba drums of affliction in Zaire included "purification with the cupping horn," also in the same general idiom of Bantu Africa (Janzen 1982, 16).

Mediums among the Tonga of Mazabuka continually feel a spirit within them and while dancing fall in a trance, while their own personality is quite in abeyance (Colson 1969, 77, 87). This trait is in keeping with that of the two personalities of the Ihamba patient. The southern Bantu Zulu and Shona also use cupping horns (Krige 1936; Gelfand et al. 1985), while the Thonga of Mozambique perform violent spirit-removing dances, during which they show they are clearly conscious of what a spirit-inhabited person is like (Junod 1962 [1912]). Among the Bushmen: "During trance the half-conscious medicine man removes illnesses from the bodies of his patients, and then leaves his own body and coerces the G//aua devil spirit to take the illnesses away" (Barnard 1979, 72).

Further north, the Fipa of Tanzania make incisions and introduce medicines to cure the sick. They see "sickness as the manifestation of a kind of injurious communication between human beings . . . , the obverse of their perception of the self as emerging from a continuing process of constructive interaction with others" (Willis 1977, 278). The latter, constructive interaction, is also the indispensable condition for healing among the Ndembu. Among the Hehe of Tanzania, sucking out disease is common, and purges and emetics are used (Edgerton 1977, 441, 442). Among the Luo of Kenya, to deal with spirit possession and to destroy evil in the body, cuts are made and medicine powder rubbed in (Whisson 1964, 294); and the Hutu of Ruanda hear a spirit speak through a horn tied to a pole (Christopher Taylor, personal communication).

Further afield, the Nuba of the Sudan may be mentioned. A shaman goes into trance on behalf of a sick person and learns from the spirits how to treat the disease. Among the Sidamo people of Ethiopia, the patient shakes in a violent ritual of possession and spirit voices are heard, after which offerings are made to feed the spirit (Hamer and Hamer 1977, 368–69). Also in Ethiopia is found the Zar cult, a dramatic possession event in which women in trance shake and dance until they fall exhausted. Here the spirit is pacified with fresh blood (Kennedy 1977, 378). Raymond Prince (1964) reports that the Yoruba introduce substances into cuts on a mad patient's body to fight the disease and expel it in the feces and urine (101). Another example is the Temne of Sierra Leone, where Dawson (1964) portrayed the case histories of disturbed patients: "When he falls sick, [the patient's] first task in the new role of patient is often to demonstrate his sickness, e.g., spirit possession" (329), which seems to echo the revelation theme of the Ndembu. In the Indian Ocean near Madagascar, the Mayotte people practice spirit healing too. They work on the body by squeezing and thereby locate and extract a small rotting cloth bag full of evil substances (Lambek 1981, 44). Sheila Walker (1972) has conducted a general analysis of spirit possession in Africa and among African-Americans, relating it to social and cultural change.

Already the themes of spirit possession and exorcism, medication, dancing, trance, the making of incisions and the use of cupping horns, feeding the spirit, revealing and confession, can be seen repeated all over the continent, and testify to the typical African nature of most features of the Ndembu Ihamba.

An interesting modern structural analysis of healing rites is that of Anthony Buckley (1976) among the Yoruba, a study that places emphasis on the inside and the outside of the skin, with reference to the taking out of disease—a truly African concern, for the hidden is dangerous, and what is brought out will do good. "There is a type of infusion (*agbo*) which can be used to drive the *eela* [disease] out on to the surface of the skin, where it can be cured" (406).

In all, we can trace over the continent of Africa how varied—in a kind of patchwork style—are the cults of affliction that are concerned with spirit manifestation. Yet many have characteristics in common. The variations continue to ramify: healers are becoming more individualistic, not less, and their numbers have been increasing, as reported by Charles Piot for the Kabre people of Togo in 1984 (personal communication), Christopher Taylor (1987) for Rwanda, John Janzen (1978) for Zaire, Anita Spring (1980) for Zambia, Wim van Binsbergen (1979) for Zambia, Anthony Pritchett for the Ndembu in 1985 (personal communication), Harrison and Dunlop (n.d.), Imperato for the Bambara of Mali (1974–75, 41–53), Messing (1976), Frankenberg and Leeson (1976) for Lusaka, Zambia, Yoder (1981) for the Chokwe, and others. By 1982 the number of traditional healers in Zambia had increased to 12,000 registered traditional health practitioners and many more that were unregistered (Twumasi 1985).

Appendix 2. Types of Spirit Healers

In order to place the art of an Ihamba doctor like Singleton in the context of other healing arts both in Africa and in the world, I give a typology of healers.

- Seer healers in action. They are helped by spirits who direct their actions and sometimes speak through them while they are in a trance (Africa, African-American peoples, also worldwide). Among Bantu-speaking peoples the term *nganga* is often used for the spirit doctor. The Zulu and Nguni Izangoma diviners are typical examples (Gussler 1973, 88–126; Kohler 1941). A new healer may experience the onset of the gift by being caught by a spirit in a passive involuntary manner, as among the Zulu, Ndembu, and many central and southern African peoples.
- Sucking or cupping healers (a category of active seer healers), who remove harmful intrusions from the body by some form of suction (certain instances in Africa, and many in the Americas and Oceania, see Appendix 6). An Ihamba chiyanga doctor such as Singleton was a cupping healer of a special kind. "Chiyanga" implies some intimate connection with the ihamba tooth, whose good aspect brings successful hunting, and whose bad aspect requires a skilled doctor to extract the tooth and nourish it with blood.
- Passive shamans. These go into a full trance with the help of drumming or song. They fall and lie recumbent, at which time their spirit leaves their body. The shaman aims to find the lost spirit of the sick person and bring it back to his body. The spirit of the shaman flies through the air or travels underground, eventually catching up with the departing spirit which he seizes and brings with him on his return. The spirit is then returned to the patient's body, or blown into it by the shaman. Another task of the shaman while in a trance may be to fight with a spirit sent by a sorcerer to harm a victim (especially in circumpolar regions, Asia, and the Americas).
- Mediums possessed by a spirit, in a trance, recumbent. Helper spirits

use their voices to communicate through them to the healing community (typically, the Nuba *kujur*, see Nadel 1946, 25–37; the Mayotte *Trumba* spirit host, see Lambek 1981; and scattered examples worldwide including cases of speaking with tongues, or glossolalia).

- Active seer healers with divining and diagnostic powers and healing hands (almost universal).
- Active seer healers who use a variety of objects such as medicines or crystals to cure the patient (almost universal).
- Psychic surgeons who perform surgery with minimal or no incisions. Examples include peoples in the Philippines, Japan, and Latin America.
- Herbalists and ethnic surgeons with generalized empirical knowledge of body function. Their diagnostic gifts approach those of the healer with the divining hands; they may use bloodletting techniques for empirical reasons. Healing hands and divination may also occur among nurses and others in the Western medical profession. Healers who use "energy" to heal constitute another large category, too varied to enumerate here.

As regards the psychic state of the patient, it may be classified in a number of ways: the patient may have been invaded by a harmful spirit, attacked by a witch, or penetrated by some harmful sorcery substance. He or she may have also lost his or her helping spirit, become a scapegoat or surrogate victim for the sins of the community, or elected to suffer in order to become a doctor or even to become a cause of edification in others. The variations on these themes are countless and have been exemplified in the collections of Beattie and Middleton for Africa (1969), Landy (1977), Kiev (1964), Kleinman (1980), Loudon (1976), Prince (1968), and Bourguignon (1973), as well as Walker's general disquisition on spirit possession (1972) and many other monographs.

Singleton, the principal doctor in Ihamba, was an active seer healer, informed by his tutelary ancestor spirits, but was not behaving as in a trance. His manner did not change during the ritual as if he had become someone else or was undergoing an out-of-the-body experience; he was practical and in command (although he recognized and protected the spirit quality of the ritual). However, Philip Kabwita, a Ndembu ghost doctor whose work I also studied in 1985, frequently entered a trance state when his tutelary spirit was communicating with him by mystic shell telephone (E. Turner 1986b). The question may be raised whether the term "shaman" may be applied to him, a term which is normally used for Native American and Asian spirit practitioners. Among anthropologists, Herskovits (1948, 371) defined shamanism as ministrations that involve the practitioners' use of "helper" or "familiar" spirits in solving the problem at hand. By this definition Singleton was a shaman. However, I have used the word "doctor" for his role in keeping with the terminology of most Africanists.

Classifications of healers cannot be really neat and mutually exclusive; nevertheless, anthropologists strive to see the phenomena more clearly. As Victor Turner said:

> When anthropologists reflect upon these stubborn and puzzling facts they devise a number of makeshift frames . . . constructed ad hoc with an eye to the nature of the materials they confront. Only after a good deal of experimentation the investigator learns how to make a workable fit between data and frame. [The studies] reveal anthropological diviner[s] in action, at the beginning of a long seance that has by no means been concluded. (1975a, 29–30)

Appendix 3. Medicines and Hallucinogens

Victor Turner has written in some detail on African medicines (1967, 191–202, 229–358, 367–70; 1968, 159–61, 185–91; 1969, 23–27, 53–63; and 1975a, 51–61, 117–19). A comprehensive list of Zimbabwe African medicines is given in Gelfand and coworkers (1985); Wilson (1959, 142–53) gives a chapter on Nyakyusa medicines; also Evans-Pritchard (1937, 177–204) has a chapter on Azande medicines. But in none of these reports do hallucinogens rank very highly. In my own analysis in this volume, I concentrate on the operational use of each medicine and the purpose of their multiple focusing action in the ritual. None of the properties I have been able to trace showed hallucinogenic effects. Nor was I able to distinguish which single medicine or combination of them might have caused my head temporarily to swim.

Richard Katz (1982) refers to the minor use of an indigenous drug, gaise noru noru, among the !Kung to induce *kia* trance when the learner has difficulty achieving it. "The drug experience itself becomes a preparation for kia, since both experiences are altered states of consciousness" (47–48). "The drug is supposed to help the students, not catapult them into another unknown and potentially frightening altered state" (283–94). This describes very much what the Ihamba medicines were accomplishing. Junod (1962) reported that Thonga "magicians employ *miri,* i.e., medicinal herbs or objects, drugs which, however, are all thought to possess special powers. I do not say 'supernatural' powers, as the notion conveyed by this word cannot exist in any definite form amongst people who have hardly a true conception of Nature. The stronger the *miri,* the stronger the magician" (517). Whisson (1964) described the treatment of a sick Luo man with steam: "The magician crushed some leaves and boiled them in a pot, William was put under a blanket and the covered pot put under it with him. The top was removed, and the steam rose into the blanket. He began to sweat freely and felt as if coils of rope were being unwound from his body and limbs" (293).

The point is further illuminated by Henry Munn in an essay on "The Mushrooms of Language" in Harner (1973), describing the eating of mushrooms at the seance of a Mazatec medicine woman. "The mushrooms are merely the means, in interaction with the organism, the nervous system, and the brain, of producing an experience grounded in the ontological-existential possibilities of the human, irreducible to the properties of a mushroom" (97). The Indians, he says, associate them with communication, with truth, and the enunciation of meaning, not with delusion (122). The shamanistic condition provoked by the mushrooms is intuitionary, not hallucinatory. He notes, "The Mazatec shamans eat the mushrooms that liberate the fountains of language to be able to speak beautifully and with eloquence so that their words, spoken for the sick one and those present, will arrive and be heard in the spirit world" (92). These "words" correspond to the Ihamba "*words*" of Meru and the others and to the divinatory propositions.

What happens in Ihamba is that medicines are used as loosening-up agents, as "coming-out" powers, not to provide a psychedelic trip. "Preparation," "help," "producing possibilities," "liberating" are the words used by Katz, Harner, Munn, and others to describe the function. "Protection" and "giving the ability to see spirits," are the virtues Singleton and Fideli claimed for their *nsompu* leaf medicine. Harner describes how a Jivaro shaman diagnoses illness. He drinks concentrated green tobacco water, and the consciousness-changing substance permits him to see into the body of the patient as if it were glass (1980, 17). "He had drunk, and . . . now he could see. Now he could find the truth. He stared at the stomach of the sick man. Slowly, it became transparent like a shallow mountain stream, and he saw within it, coiling and uncoiling, *makanchi*, the poisonous serpent, who had been sent by the enemy shaman. The real cause of the illness had been found" (Harner 1973, 15–16). However, in many cultures healers can see into the body without the use of drugs, usually while in a trance or comparable state.

Harner holds that "dancing, accompanied by drumming, is the far more common method employed by shamans throughout much of the primitive world to achieve a shamanic state of consciousness sufficient to have an experience" (1980, 60). But he warns anthropologists against underestimating the importance of drugs as affecting native ideology (1973, 17). Findings show that there exists a wide continuum between practitioners who take drugs continually in order to fall in a trance, and those who take none. I regard the events at Meru's Ihamba as falling somewhere in between; some quality of the medicine did make me momentarily dizzy and may have triggered and liberated a rarely-used faculty—as rarely used as childbirth muscles, but none the less real. I repeat that I did not merely intuit the spirit form emerging from Meru's back but saw it, *saw* it with my own eyes. This is different from intuition or imagination; it is nearer to seeing a ghost. What also made the experience possible was the broadly based social and long-term cultural support that surrounded me among the Ndembu. The simple explanation might be that my attempt at prayer along with Singleton at the greeting tree, and the complex ritual that followed, brought spirit help to make me see, which is how the Ndembu would explain it.

Appendix 4. Cupping with Horns

Apart from Victor Turner's study the literature on cupping with horns is hardly more than technical. Ackernecht (1971, 100) stated that "cupping with a horn over an incision is so generally applied in Africa that it has almost completely replaced scarification." However, documentation in any detail remains scarce, save for Michael Gelfand and W.F.P. Burton. Gelfand and coworkers (1985) describe the Shona traditional doctor applying *murumiko* horns to a patient using a cupping method identical to that in Ihamba:

> Application of a *murumiko* to a painful or swollen part is a common method of treatment. . . . The *murumiko* is applied especially in the treatment of rheumatism, pleurisy, painful abdominal conditions or other disorders in which severe and continuous pain is experienced. . . . The *murumiko* is said to suck out or remove impure blood from the infected parts or, in the case of *chitsinga* or *chipotswa* [troubles caused by poison planted by a witch], foreign bodies like insects, bones, and snakes . . . [ending with] spitting out . . . a bone . . . in front of the patient, showing that the trouble has been removed. (20–21)

Spiritual influences are identified beforehand by divination. The treatment is undertaken in the context of a consultation, not a public ritual. Gelfand includes a photograph of a consultation and treatment with a cupping horn (369).

W.F.P. Burton's account (1961, 84–85) of the Luba practice is almost exactly the same, even though the Shona and the Luba are eight hundred miles apart. The Luba cupping practitioner professes to tell by the shape and color of the blood clot in the horn how much pain he has drawn out of the sufferer. Burton's account omits references to extraction of objects or spirits connected with the treatment.

Eileen Krige (1936) relates that the favorite treatment among the Zulus is cupping: "Incisions are made on the skin with a sharpened iron and blood drawn by suction through a horn. Then ashes of medicinal roots are rubbed into the cuts" (332).

Barrie Reynolds (1963, 67–69) mentions that among the Barotse of

Zambia foreign bodies, either actual or supposed, may be extracted by cupping or sucking. Also Kohler (1941, 79) in an old but ever-fresh text on Zulu Izangoma diviners and their spirits briefly describes cupping. Whisson (1964) shows how among the Kenyan Luo: "The diviner would make small cuts on the body at the point paining the patient, place a horn over the cuts, suck and produce some half-digested food from his mouth, which, he would claim, he had sucked from the body of the patient" (288).

Christopher Taylor (personal communication) drew my attention to a variety of bloodletting and sucking techniques in Africa and even in Europe. He mentioned the *kurumika* cupping horn techniques of Kenya, where there is normally nothing found in the horn; the "capturing of spirits" in Ruanda, done not with horns but with ordinary glass tumblers used as sucking cups; the cupping with glasses done in France to take bad air out of the lungs, called *ventouser;* in France again, the bleeding of cows that have swellings, called *coup de sang;* and the former use of leeches in England and Europe, done to relieve a surfeit of blood—a process in which the leech actually injects anticoagulants into the blood in order to be able to draw blood, and possibly helping to prevent blood clots and thrombosis. Taylor distinguishes different types of cupping: simple bloodletting to let out bad blood, sucking out bad air, the capturing of spirits, taking out intrusive objects, taking out "object-spirits," and various combinations of these.

Ackernecht's statement about cupping is thus upheld by later research. Ndembu cupping itself is not an isolated case, but still the extraction of a tooth is rare in Africa. However, Judith Macdonald (1985) mentions a spirit tooth in Tikopia, Solomon Islands, that was used to rid a sick man of a spirit affliction:

> Once the medium had discovered the cause of the man's sickness he was able to call on a powerful clan spirit who had a detachable man-eating tooth. The tooth was sent to kill the two spirit children and, this accomplished, the man recovered. (80)

Appendix 5. Music and Drumming

Drums, Ngoma

The word for "drum," is used by most central and southern Africans as the same word "ritual" itself. It used to be unthinkable to hold a public ritual without drumming. The Ndembu drum is a large, tense vibrating emotional object, bongo-shaped, with a skin so tight that the least tap produces a rich sound. It is usually beaten with the palm of the hand. It awakens and attracts the spirits; at a ritual with the doctor Philip Kabwita, our drummer marched at the back of the procession to round up the laggard spirit as it accompanied our procession down to the river into which we were intending to cast the spirit (Turner 1986b, 32).

The drum entrains the singing, its mighty repeating "vertebral" structure of sound bears one along in time, its driving power hustles restless thoughts to one side to make way for wholehearted singing, then for trance and the release of a spirit. The drummer is in tune with the spirit so that his rhythm changes when he senses the spirit's advent, then both spirit and humans arrive at the climax at once.

Drumming in Ihamba
(Excerpted from William Blodgett's "Ihamba" 1986, 123–33.)

First, I preface the discussion with a brief exploration of the place of the drum in Ndembu culture. I shall give some notes on observations I made during Nyakanjata's Ihamba which I experienced prior to my exposure to neurobiology. And finally, I shall relate these observations to Neher's study (1962) concerning physiological explanations of unusual behavior involving drums, and to the findings of neurobiologists.

Among the Lunda, drums are made from five species of trees. These are ikamba dachihamba (*Cryptosepalum maraviense*), mukula (*Pterocarpus angolensis*), muyombu (*Kirkia acuminata*), chiputa mazala (*Erythrina tomentosa*), and kabanjibanji. Judging from my research, ikamba dachihamba seems to be the tree of preference. In the ritual of Chihamba, ikamba dachihamba was the ishikenu or "greeting" medicine. It was at one time "used as a war medicine to render warriors invulnerable to spears or musket balls" (Turner 1975a, 138). Its roots are compared to soaked cassava root, and sometimes cassava root is compared to the body of a person because it is both thick and round. In the context of Chihamba, ikamba dachihamba means the body of the Chihamba spirit. Concerning the tree's symbolism Victor Turner (1975a) wrote, "The whiteness of the root is of first importance and connects it with other white things typical of these rites. . . . Whiteness is goodness (*kuwaha*)" (168–69), which also means health, power (*ngovu*), remembering and meeting with ancestor spirits, life, huntsmanship, revelation (*kusolola*), sweeping clean, and washing.

Among the Ndembu there are seven types of drums, but three stand out as most important. In order of size, largest to smallest, these are the kayanda, the monfusa, and the musenki. According to my informant, Jose Chenza, each type of ritual has its own set of drum rhythms. He told me, "It's the rhythm that matters, not the drum itself because drums are scarce. The persons who have been making them are dying, and beating drums is discouraged by the missions." I myself attended a few rituals where the scarcity of drums was evident. In one performance of Kanenga, African stools were beaten. It was during this ritual that I was told that not only are the drum rhythms important but the song lyrics also. For in Kanenga, it is believed the afflicting shade will make the patient shake when it is pleased by the song. In this context, the ritual actors may suspect the shade is someone they once knew, and they will therefore sing songs known to have been favorites of the shade. But according to my older informants, notably Kasonda, the drum itself is of first importance, for drums are said to please ancestor spirits.

Just as we Westerners refer to a tree's "heartwood," the Ndembu refer to that part as *muchima*, "liver," the seat of the emotions and disposition. But with drums, of course, the heartwood is carved out. The muchima is made hollow. The drum head (*chitemba*) is made from the skin of a duiker killed (and therefore brought into public view, "revealed") by a hunter. When beaten the body of the drum vibrates. These vibrations are amplified within the drum, within the "hollow liver," and sounds are thereby produced.

The symbolism of the drum becomes apparent. In Chihamba, ikamba da Chihamba is likened to the body of the Chihamba spirit. Here, the word "spirit" refers to a named, known person. So in the generic sense, the drum is the body of a spirit. Then in ritual, the drum head is beaten and the body of the spirit vibrated thus causing the spirit to speak. And in a metaphorical sense, when a spirit talks, every "body" listens. As neurobiologists have shown us, it is quite impossible to "listen" and not be physiologically and emotionally affected by what is heard. In this sense, "spirit possession" makes great sense.

Now with reference to Nyakanjata's Ihamba, I will include the following observations that I made during the performance. As noted in Chapter 3, it was following Snodia's initial confession that collective group participation and the "circle of trust" truly became manifest. While the episodes (*kutachika*, "stations") became longer in duration and more complex, the songs became shorter in duration, but greater with respect to the number of songs sung in succession. And most interestingly, the melody lines became less ornate. As Singleton said, "Keep on helping. Come on! Ihamba songs! You know them all right, everybody knows them." To which Benwa replied, "You'd best have songs that are easy. Then they'll help you. It's hard to sing these difficult ones." What did Benwa mean by "difficult"? I did not have the opportunity to ask him. However, I have examined the lyrics and listened to the songs many times over. I conclude he was not referring to the rhythm of the song but rather the complexity of the lyrics and the accompanying melody. The singing style became more mantra-like with greater use of the call-and-answer technique.

One of the guiding principles may be along the following lines: with greater participation, there comes a need for greater focusing of the group. The greater the problem presented by the ku-tachika episodes, the more critical becomes the resolution of the problem. For the more "critical" a problem is, the more likely we are to describe it as being "complicated." And finally, the more complicated the problem, the more focused the effort must be. So we conclude that Ndembu songs unify the group in intention and, of course, in rhythm. We find in fact that rhythm and tone are adjusted in such a way as to maintain group cohesion. For example, after Singleton concluded that Sakutoha was the second ihamba afflicting Nyakanjata there followed a song which was soon interrupted by an argument between Njesi and Zinia. Amidst the shouting opponents, the ax-blade percussion continued (in my second attendance of Ihamba, I also noted this phenomenon). It should be noted that higher pitch and therefore frequency may have a more decisive and dramatic effect than lower pitches, which seem to have more of a bridging effect. Like the policeman's whistle and the fire-truck's siren, ax-blade percussion seems to have a shriller and more penetrating quality than the thunder-like sounds of the kayanda drum. It was only later I learned that the sound produced by ax-blade percussion is known as kukenkumwena (literally, "to address").

Again, I point out the above observations were made in the field at a time when I knew little about neurobiology. I stress this in order to show that the different methodological approaches offered by nonbiological sciences, on the one hand, and by biological and cognitive sciences, on the other hand, need not be seen as mutually exclusive. Rather, they should be seen as complementary approaches, the yin and the yang, through which the curious student must traverse and find the middle way. For as Victor Turner (1985) wrote, "an extreme ethological view of human society as rigidly genetically determined is as uninformative as an extreme behaviorist view of the human brain as a tabula rasa written on by experience" (271).

With this point in mind, I now turn to the neurobiologists to see what they have to offer to support my earlier observations. First, we ask ourselves what neurobiological explanation can we find for the appearance of songs of shorter duration but greater in the number and sung in succession. Part of the answer must lie in the fact that when a new song commences, the drum rhythms often shift markedly. I contend that the drummers are in fact attempting to elicit a trance from the patient. If the patient does not shake, it may indicate that the patient is not going to initiate a trance in response to the invocation. But at the same time, the absence of a trance may point to the possibility that the driving potential of the rhythms played is insufficient to elicit a trance. According to Andrew Neher (1962) who studied the ritual effects of drum rhythms,

> We expect to find from anthropological data: 1) A changing stimulus frequency to encompass the range of individual differences in brain rhythms, and 2) susceptibility to particular rhythms by particular individuals. . . . Rhythm compared with continuous stimulation [gives] time between pulses for nerve fatigue to dissipate. Nerves in the brain have a spontaneous firing rate that is reinforced by a rhythmic stimulus of similar frequencey . . . slightly below 8 to 13 cycles per second. . . . [In Africa] the Lala of Northern Rhodesia, the Sogo Dance of Ghana, and the dance of the Nsenga of Central Africa . . . have a frequency between 7 and 9 cycles per second. (151–54)

A similar cyclicity is found in the Northwest Coast of Canada:

> Recent research on the shamanistic spirit dances of the Salish Indians of the Northwest Coast supports Neher's findings on the capacity of rhythmic drumming to induce an altered state of consciousness. Jilek and Ormestad found

that drum beat frequencies in the theta wave EEG frequency range (four to seven cycles per second) predominated during initiation procedures using the Salish deer-skin drum. This is the frequency range, Jilek notes, that is expected to be most effective in the production of trance states. (Harner 1980, 52)

I have not as yet analyzed Ihamba music in this way, but it is my expectation that such an analysis would conform to these findings.

If in fact a trance state can be elicited from the patient involuntarily, then another possibility is that the drummer, either consciously or unconsciously, also responds to the invocation. He may in fact have a personal stake in the outcome of any invocation. In any case, the kutachika episode produces stress, and stress has been shown to increase susceptibility to rhythm. The greater number of songs in succession is likely to be accompanied by hyperventilation. Overexertion and fatigue result in increased adrenalin secretion and a lowering of the blood sugar level. Also, a chemical called adrenochrome has been isolated from adrenalin and has been shown to be "related chemically to every hallucinogen whose chemical composition has been determined" (Hoffer and Osmond 1967, 33).

A second question we must ask is whether or not there is a neurobiological advantage to songs in which the lyrics are more mantra-like? If we want to facilitate a trance state, the answer is yes. However, the choice of mantra is perhaps a misnomer, for Robert Ornstein (1972) describes mantra as "meaningless." On the other hand, students of Buddhist and Hindu philosophies contend that mantras are meaningful in "mystical senses." In certain meditation techniques, reduction of sensory inputs by means of repetition of a mantra, a mellifluous sound, has the effect of monopolizing the verbal-logical activities of the left hemisphere, leaving the right hemisphere to function freely. Conversely, response to the rhythms of chanting and singing, dancing, handclapping, and percussion instruments engages right-hemisphere capabilities, concomitantly evoking the "timeless" quality or the attendant experience (quoted in Lex, 1979, 126, from Ornstein 1972).

This is significant because it reflects the experience of the anthropologist. It is true the song lyrics became shorter, and sometimes individual lines of the lyrics were repeated over and over. To me these Ndembu songs appear mantra-like because I'm not a native speaker. But then Robert Ornstein is not a native Buddhist or Hindu either. The confusion may boil down to the fact that both the word "mantra" and "chant" are used thoughtlessly. Compare the *American Heritage Dictionary* definitions:

Mantra, a sacred formula believed to embody the divinity invoked and to possess magical power. It is used in prayer and incantation.

Chant, 1) a short, simple melody in which a number of syllables or words are sung on each note. 2) A song or canticle sung in this manner. 3) A song or melody. 4) A monotonous rhythmic voice.

Ndembu song texts are used in prayer and incantation, and the Ndembu do believe their songs have magical power. In some contexts such as the Kanenga ritual, songs are believed to have a relationship to the ancestral spirit or shade invoked. From this it would appear that one could describe Ndembu song lyrics as a mantra. On the other hand, the Ndembu songs to which we are referring often do have short and simple melodies. At present, there is no rule that each note of melody is assigned several syllables or words as we find in Gregorian chant. Furthermore, it is difficult to say whether or not these Ndembu songs are sung in a "monotonous rhythmic voice." Would it not be ethnocentric to do so? It is interesting to note that one of the Latin words related to chant is *os-cen,* meaning "a singing bird used in divination." In either case, trance is evoked, and individual feeling of oneness and integration temporarily achieved.

There is no need to rehash what has already been said about the collective tuning effect and entrainment of brain rhythms caused by drum rhythms. I point out: (1) a single drum beat contains many frequencies. Mixed sounds are transmitted along more nerve pathways in the brain than is a single frequency. (2) A drum beat contains mostly low frequencies. The low-frequency receptors of the ear are more resistant to damage than the delicate high-frequency receptors and can withstand higher amplitudes of sound before pain is felt. Therefore, drum music should transmit more energy to the brain than a stimulus of higher frequency (Neher 1962, 151–52).

Songs

In Nyakanjata's Ihamba there was a total of five grudge statements, thirteen invocations, and forty-three songs.

SUBJECT MATTER OF LYRICS

Principal spirit figures: hunters' spirits, ihamba spirits.
Principal human figures: hunters.

Relationships: fathers, mothers, brothers, sisters, children, wives, friends, guests, chief, orphans, strangers.

Animal themes: elephant, cow, owl, bees, eyes of animals.

Ihamba ritual themes: tooth, witchcraft familiars, coming out, divining, touching, marijuana.

Hunting themes: hunting, killing, guns, clothes, tattoos, hunting medicine.

Bush themes: walking, arriving, path, bush, bridge, setting sun.

Gardening themes: planting, eating, cassava mush, pumpkin, calabash.

Emotions: welcoming, blessing, boasting, crying, hunger, trouble, sickness, liver (seat of the emotions).

In these songs hunting themes predominated. Spirits were a strong concern. Kin were highly important as in all Ndembu songs. Food and the emotions had a strong place. All these themes contributed to the heightened mood of the assembly, so that along with other factors music became a vehicle of the spirit.

Appendix 6. The Extraction of Harmful Intrusions[1]

As reviewed in Appendix 4, bloodletting by means of cupping horns is widespread in Africa. Ihamba comes under the category of the extraction of something harmful. Some accounts of this practice among other African peoples are available. Gelfand and coworkers (1985, 369–77) illustrate cupping among the Shona with photographs. Here, unlike the Ndembu, the foreign object, often a bone, is spat out in front of the patient, showing that the trouble has been removed (20–21). Evans-Pritchard (1937, 102–4) wrote that he saw Azande witchdoctors remove spiders, grubs, or worms, by the trick of concealing them in the mouth or in poultices; caterpillars would be seen crawling on the patient which had been brought to the scene in the witchdoctor's horn. Evans-Pritchard confessed being distressed at the trickery used. Victor Turner believed that old Ihembi used trickery in the Ihamba of the 1950s but was not concerned because he was concentrating on the ritual process itself, the symbolic system arrayed in it, and the social drama underlying it. Here we are seeking closer understanding of the actual extraction.

Richard Katz (1982) gives a vivid picture of the "pulling-out" process among the !Kung.

> The pain involved in the boiling of the healers' num (spiritual energy), in the putting of that num into the one being healed, in the drawing of the other's sickness into their own body, and in the violent shaking of that sickness out from their body is acknowledged by the healers by crying, wailing, moaning, and shrieking. They punctuate and accent their healing with these sometimes ear-shattering sounds. As their breath comes with more difficulty, until they are rasping and gasping, the healers howl the characteristic kowhedili shriek, which sounds something like "Xsi—i! Kow-ha-di-di-di-di!" Some say the shriek forcibly expels the sickness from a spot on the top of the healers' spine. Others say the shriek marks the painful process of shaking the sickness out from the healers' hands. . . .
>
> The num is put into others to draw out the sickness and to activate more num, which among other things helps draw out the sickness. . . . Healing is a process where a substance called sickness is transformed by a substance called

num. It is not a mechanical process where one substance is replaced or erased by another. [Here Katz is grappling with the idea of transformation, just as I have been with the matter of the tooth or spirit form. It appears that the Ndembu idea of the tooth is a *tooth/spirit*, oscillating between the two in a way that is hard to catch.]

"What do you see when you pull?" [Katz asks the !Kung].

Kaha says . . . "I pull little pieces of metal out of my wife's legs and hips, like little pieces of wire. These bits of metal are tying her leg ligaments up. I pulled her dead father's testicles out of her heart. Then I told her dead father not to pursue her anymore."

"Can she see what you remove?"

"No. I tell her what I see." (107–10)

A similar example appears in a site partly within African cultural influence. Michael Lambek (1981, 44) who worked in Mayotte, a small island between Africa and Madagascar, describes the cure for a patient afflicted by sorcery. It consisted of the location and extraction from his body of a small rotting cloth packet filled with dirt, nailclippings, hair, broken glass, etc. This was done by squeezing the body. Lambek says it is shown to the patient to reassure him that his disease has left him.

We find in the reports on ethnic healing throughout the world many references to the extraction of harmful intrusions. Harner mentions, in addition to the methods of the Jivaro shamans, those of the Lakota Sioux medicine man who attracts the harmful object out of the patient's body with tobacco, and the Northwest Coast Salish shaman's method of letting the patient take his clothes off and the sickness with it, whereupon the shaman puts on those clothes, removing the sickness forever from the patient (Harner 1980, 130–34). The Chippewa Indians make use of a "sucking doctor" (Ritzenthaler 1963, 321–22). Maddox (1923, 190–92) lists many Native American peoples where the doctor sucks the affected part and exhibits some foreign body, mentioning the Florida Indians, the Sioux, Algonkin, Kernai, Ojibway, Apache, and Shingu Indians. He describes (80) how the Californian Karok doctor sucks the patient, then vomits up a frog; and how the Cumana Indians suck disease from the patient, then vomit a hard black ball (190). Maddox calls these claims absurd. Spencer and Gillen (1927, 516) described how Australian Aborigines extracted quartz, bone, bark, charcoal, or glass marble objects from their patients. Extraction by suction among the Paiute Indians is described by Beatrice Whiting (1950):

Sucking is part of nearly every ceremony. The doctor often sucks out some foreign object and thus effects a cure. He spits the object out of his mouth and shows it to the people. He then mixes it with dirt in his hands, rubs his hands

together, and the object disappears. Sometimes he vomits the object into a pan
of earth to make it disappear. (214)

Rogers (1982, 92–95) discusses a number of forms of extraction, rang-
ing from the symbolic removal of intangible objects to hand magnetism
and object removal "managed with a considerable degree of contrivance"
(93). Rogers, like Dow, believes that the techniques are basically psycho-
therapeutic and that faith in the powers of the shaman is of first importance.
Rogers also comments:

> In attempting to interpret the beliefs behind the object removal method of
> healing, it must be borne in mind that the items themselves may not necessarily
> be the objective cause of the illness. Sickness may be thought of as having been
> brought on by magic, which is an evil-working force that not only generates
> the sickness, but also manifests itself in the form of the foreign object. When
> the shaman removes the object, he breaks the magic spell and this sets the road
> toward recovery. The object is an outward sign of the magical force, a "mate-
> rialized impurity." (Lévy-Bruhl 1935, 252–53; Rogers 1982, 94)

Here Rogers himself is oscillating between magic and ordinary reality,
as do most anthropologists concerned with ritual and healing. That they are
sympathetic to this extent is a measure of their sensitivity and thus, in an
important sense, of their objectivity.

A couple of examples show how this form of healing tends to branch
out into odd particularities—as Ihamba does. Janice Reid (1983) wrote
down a young Yolngu woman's narrative:

> My brother's wife was attacked by a spirit which stabbed her in the back with
> a long fingernail. The *marrnggitj* healer extracted the fingernail. When he
> opened his hand, there it was. It had blood on it. I just looked at him. I
> believed him then. (68)

And Ludvigson (1985) gives this ethnographic passage from the Vanuatu Islands:

> The seers are the only healers to use a therapeutic technique called *avuavuti*
> "pull out." I saw a seer do this at Tonsiki on the far side of the valley. Squatting
> next to his patient, he picked up two large leaves in each hand. Then, holding
> the leaves flat against each hand with a thumb, he placed them next to each
> other on his patient's shoulder, pulling them down her arm and bringing them
> together in one movement, finally folding up the leaves and tucking them
> under the toes of his left foot. He repeated the treatment on the woman's other
> arm, legs, and back.

Another seer explained to me that when they *avuavuti,* they pull out "bits of rat food, bits of lizard food. They remove the things that are making the person ill—like blood, but it isn't blood. Like the spit of some bad thing that lives on the ground. Then the man's body gets well again."

Some seers were said to be able to remove *vezeveze* [sorcery] objects and produce them for an astonished audience to admire. (60)

So far, we have encountered in the way of extracted objects a tooth; a bloody tuft of down; spirit darts; quartz; bone; bark; charcoal; a glass marble; a frog; a hard round ball; pieces of metal such as wire; father's testicles; bad meat from cows, pigs, sardines, and chickens; a rotting cloth bag; snakes; insects; spiders; grubs; worms; caterpillars; a bloody fingernail; rat food; lizard food; half-digested food; and spit. Rogers (1982) adds to this catalogue stone, lizard, broken sticks, bits of sharpened bone or ice, and mice (93). Most of the objects imply pain and disgust. It is seers rather than plain herbalists that remove them, because they can see the spirit nature of the objects. Some of the accounts show a practitioner using sleight of hand or conjuring. Even so, it is clear that something harmful *has* been removed. Ambivalence exists in the anthropologist's mind about these cases; nevertheless, he or she can often mark where climax takes place and the spirit phase begins.

Appendix 7. A Composite Ihamba Scenario

This composite story of Meru's Ihamba would agree with what Ihamba doctors told Vic Turner and me in the 1950s and also what the later doctors told me in 1985.

Singleton Kahona owned a hunter's tooth. It had belonged to his father Kahona, and when the old headman died he left it to his son and apprentice Singleton. Singleton kept it in a small sealed calabash in his hut. His possession of the tooth was an honor, a means of good fortune, and a responsibility. Singleton succeeded Kahona and Benwa as full chiyanga in the Tooth Guild.

Something was wrong in the village. Before the development of Christianity, before pagan structures in the village were pulled down, the tiny calabash containing the tooth used to hang in its bag under a tall thatched shelter on stilts. In recent times Singleton had been forced to put the container on top of a mat slung under the rafters inside his hut. One could easily forget that it was there, tucked away out of sight. Singleton had forgotten to feed his ihamba tooth for a long time.

Meru, his sister through his older mother, lay in her hut tense and tossing; pain crept along her veins. One night Benwa came into her hut and put his ear on her upper back. He heard the gnawing. Singleton went immediately to his own hut and rummaged on top of his ceiling mat. He couldn't find the ihamba. Where was it? It was a dangerous thing to be at large. He couldn't find it. Meru was sick because of neglect of the tooth; it had not been respected, it needed blood, and had migrated to wherever blood was to be found, into Meru. An Ihamba ritual was needed to take the ihamba out.

Singleton went with his chiyanga doctors to the bush for medicine and spoke to his guild forebears and teachers at the Greeting Tree, and they came to him. The spirits of Kahona and the others led their erstwhile apprentice through the selection and focusing of medicines, through the drum calls, the divinatory communications, and his shouts of "Come out!" They guided his hand as he felt for the tooth on Meru's body. He sometimes grinned with the knowledge, the feeling that was going through him, and sometimes he was vastly irritated by interruptions in the ritual process. He was in the flow until at last the tooth answered the call, and the social integument of living and dead spirits gave birth. The spirit form appeared big and gray like a musalu ghost; he caught it and clutched it in his mongoose skin bag, then transferred it to the receiving can. He grabbed the receiving can and ran to the hut in the rain. The tooth, a solid object, was now in the can along with the blood.

After this, in Meru's hut, the solid tooth entered the phase of being respected, and it responded with a satisfied air when it was fed and nested in flesh. Meru was also anointed with the same blood. It protected her in the same way. Both she and the tooth spirit were well.

The givens of this story need not necessarily be reworked to correspond with Western ways of thinking; it is an Ndembu type of story, and relates to the facts according to a different logic.

Appendix 8. Old and New Ihamba Compared

1951	1985
One night sex taboo for patient and doctors	Same
Two rasps	One rasp
Song: Mukokey-ey	Song: Mukongu katukatu-ey
Gun and wallet carried	Nil
Man basket carrier	Woman basket carrier
Musoli is greeting tree	Mufungu is greeting tree
Money requested at greeting tree	Same
White clay line from base of tree	Red clay rubbed on trunk on east side, from base of tree, and on west side
Medicine taken from greeting tree	Medicine not taken from greeting tree, as it is "mother"

Medicines

Musoli	Mufungu
Mwangala	Musengu
Musengu	Mututambulolu
Mututambulolu	Chikwata
Kasasenji	Mukombukombu
Mukombukombu	Mucha
Muneku	Mutungulu
Ikunyi	Musoli
Mufungu	Mutuhu
Mutata	Mukandachina
Mutuhu	Muhotuhotu
Muchikachika	Musesi
Munjimbi	Munjimba tree at shrine
Mutalu	Nil
Musongusongu	Nil
Chikochikochi	Nil
Kapokomenena	Nil
Muhangandumba	Nil

Mushilambulu	Nil
Dust from crossroads and hut	Nil
Blood from mulundu bird	Blood from foot of rooster

Medicines in Common

Musoli	Musoli
Musengu	Musengu
Mukombukombu	Mukombukombu
Mufungu	Mufungu
Mutuhu	Mutuhu

Other Features

Shrine pole is kapwipu	Shrine pole is kapepi
Anthill spirit house	Same
Grass bundle on shrine pole	Nil
Musoli pegs for anthill	Nil
Firewood species not mentioned	Firewood is ironwood
Water poured beside mortar	Water poured on each side of mortar
Castor oil leaf lid for tooth receptacle	Castor oil leaf and mukosu bark lid for tooth receptacle
Beer sprinkled on anthill shrine and ax	Nil
Receptacle rests on maize stalks	Nil
Four cupping horns	Three cupping horns
Two blue duiker horns with isaku medicine	One blue duiker horn with isaku medicine
Beer for all	Beer only for doctors
Red clay beside eyes of assistants	Same
Doctor divines in mortar	Nil
Red lines on patient's back, chest, and across back of shoulders	Red patch on upper back of patient
White lines as above	Nil
Reed used to clean horn	Needle used to clean horn
Patient drinks from striped horn	Nil
Red parrot feather in hair of patient	Nil
Chicken dipped in medicine and thrown away	Same
Mpandwila leaf clapping	Same
Grudge, chitela	Words, mazu
Blood collected from ground	Nil
Dance pointing gun at patient to shoot ihamba	Nil

Nine musical instruments	Six musical instruments
Twenty to thirty people present	Same
Doctor circles patient's house dancing, to kitchen, to three crossroads, takes dust, also dust from threshold, dances around group	Doctor performs antelope dance
Addresses and invocations	Same
Divinatory proposals	Same
Two medicine purses	One medicine purse
Chewing and spitting medicine on patient	Chewing and spitting medicine into horn
Chant: Maheza, maheza, ngambu, yafwa, with variation: Mangameza, mafwa	Same, no variation
Extra ihamba teeth put in basket	Nil
Ihamba will not come out because patient looks at sun	Patient placed facing east toward where sun comes out
Two metal whistles blown	Nil
Grass torch carried around patient	Nil
Horn on finger of doctor	Nil
Ihamba stored in bag under small shelter	Ihamba tooth stored in Vaseline jar
Food taboo: catfish	Nil
Nil	Childbirth references
Nil	References to tutelary spirits

Appendix 9. Matriliny, Rituals, and Religions: The 1985 Ndembu

Changes in Matrilineal Residential Affiliation

	VILLAGE MEMBERSHIP	
	1951 *(%)*	*1985* *(%)*
Headman himself and his matrilineal kin	57	40
Descendants of headman	11	36
Children of male matrikin of headman	6	0
Patrikin	4	3
Affines and other kin	3	21
Nonrelated	19	0

Healing Rituals Experienced by eighteen persons, in Decades

	NUMBER OF RITUALS
1925–1935	3
1935–1945	4
1945–1955	2
1955–1965	4
1965–1975	9
1975–1985	14

Religions in the Kawiku Township of the Ndembu

	%
Traditional	37
Baha'i	24
Christian Fellowship	17
Catholic	9
Christian Mission to Many Lands	7
Apostles of John Maranke	6

Appendix 10. Maps

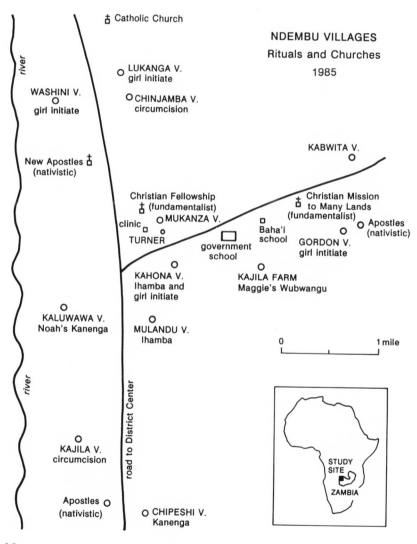

† Catholic Church

NDEMBU VILLAGES
Rituals and Churches
1985

○ LUKANGA V.
girl initiate

WASHINI V.
○
girl initiate

○ CHINJAMBA V.
circumcision

KABWITA V.
○

New Apostles †
(nativistic)

river

Christian Fellowship
† (fundamentalist)
○ MUKANZA V.
clinic □
TURNER □ ○

□ Baha'i
school

† Christian Mission
to Many Lands
(fundamentalist)
○ Apostles
(nativistic)

□
government
school

GORDON V.
girl intitiate

○
KAHONA V.
Ihamba and
girl initiate

○
KAJILA FARM
Maggie's Wubwangu

○
KALUWAWA V.
Noah's Kanenga

○
MULANDU V.
Ihamba

0   1 mile

river

road to District Center

○
KAJILA V.
circumcision

STUDY
SITE

ZAMBIA

Apostles ○
(nativistic)

○ CHIPESHI V.
Kanenga

Map 1.

KAHONA VILLAGE

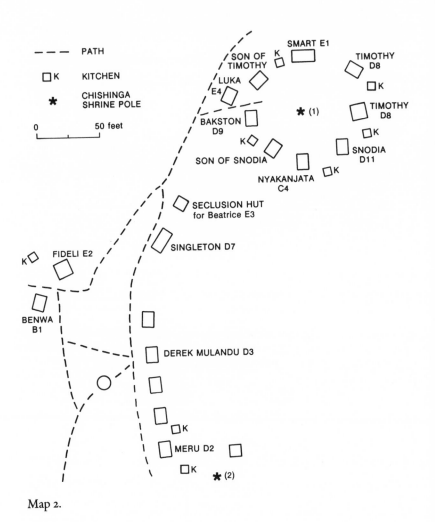

Map 2.

Appendix II. Abridged Genealogy of the Kahona Family

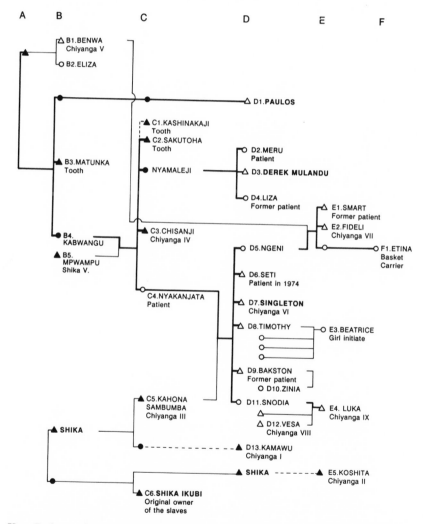

Key: Patients, doctors (chiyanga), and tooth afflictors are indicated. Thick lines show matrilineal links; dotted lines indicate probable matrilineal links. Headmen's names are indicated in bold. Siblings are not listed in order of age.

Notes

Introduction

1. I do not take credit for this. I am aware that the skills and sympathies of many anthropologists who have never had such an experience are currently bringing the discipline to life in a way that has never been done before.

The present book represents another radically different way of looking at ritual.

2. When I returned to America I sent many copies of Turner's books to the Ndembu. Previous to my 1985 visit no correspondence with them seemed forthcoming, so such consignments would have been useless. As it was, even from 1986 onward, no acknowledgement of receipt of the batches of books has reached me. Nevertheless, it is to be hoped the books found some readers.

3. Comparisons between the two eras are made in the course of the present study, and a chart of the two sets of medicines and points of ritual, old and new, is given in Appendix 8.

4. A word should be said about medical anthropology, to which category some readers might suppose this volume belongs. It would be flattering to think this were so. A great edifice of work has been built up consisting of careful studies of health problems and healing practitioners and rituals—many of them leaving open the way for further investigation into the detailed, even intimate, "close-to-the-body" means by which healing is effected. A number of them grant the traditional healer real credit for helping the sufferer, especially in the area of meaning assignment, which is a therapeutic requisite in itself. In any event, this work does constitute a study of one kind of healing in a typically African idiom. For reference to studies of spirit healing in Africa and elsewhere and of other cultural elements associated with my data, I refer the reader to Appendixes 1 to 6.

5. The anthropology of experience is further developing into a honing of the social senses so that the complex interconnections that are always threading through experience may be recorded. It is hard to predict how far this method, called radical empiricism, may take us.

Chapter 1: The Field Context of the Ihamba Rituals in 1985

1. Some claimed that Mulandu, a matrilineal cousin of the two, was actually headman.

2. The ihamba tooth is also called *nsongajama* ("sharp-pointed and deep-rooted").

Chapter 2: The Medicine Quest for the First Ihamba

1. The narrative has composite sources: (1) it is told from memory; (2) it draws from the field notes of Bill Blodgett and myself, written down both during the events themselves and further annotated each evening when more thought could go into the notes; (3) it is taken from Bill Blodgett's tape recordings of the live events (later transcribed and translated by Morie Kasonda, also Morie's son, age 16, and Jennifer Matooka, the two translations being carefully compared for accuracy); (4) it uses exegesis taken from the discussions with the traditional doctors that took place afterward, taped and later processed similarly; (5) it is informed by scrutiny of the photographs once they were brought home and processed; and (6) last but not least, it draws extensively from William Blodgett's manuscript "Ihamba: Holistic Treatment, Holistic Analysis," written on his return. This composite picture occasionally results in the effect of switched viewpoints, of seeing inside different people's heads at different times—in a sense what Bakhtin (1981) termed "heteroglossia," a narrative trick that has been developed throughout history, and Bakhtin explains its use in various forms of the novel. In such a composite narrative it is doubtful exactly who is the author. It is the same in this case.

There is a certain departure from chronological sequence in that I include in the story of the first medicine quest many of the uses and interpretations of herbs told us in consultation *after* the event. Rather than always refer to such later consultations, I supply the knowledge at the time of encountering the herb, making for a better narrative.

Generally, interpretations are made in the light of the earlier research in the 1950s, in the light of the work of other anthropologists, of Singleton, Fideli, and Benwa's interpretations, and later of the comments of colleagues in America. The conversations and addresses have been translated into English, first from the transcriptions of our assistants and then rendered in regular English for the sake of a flowing account. Pseudonyms have been used, where necessary, to protect the rights of individuals to their privacy.

2. Mufungu: *Arisophyllea boehmii.*

3. Such a helper, or tutelary spirit, has been termed by psychologists, an "internal self-helper" (a term which is descriptive rather than analytic). The phenomenon is now seen as fairly common cross-culturally. As for Singleton, he often referred admiringly to his father, Kahona Sambumba. We heard that Sambumba had been a respected hunter, a member of the Wuyanga guild, and a skilled chiyanga, that is, doctor for removing ihambas. Chisanji, whom I knew in the 1950s, had been a mine policeman, also a hunter, and generally a rather tough personality.

4. Musengu: *Ochna pulchra,* or African oak. It bears five shiny black fruit in a ring topped by a red calyx, very striking and beautiful in appearance. The Ndembu

said, "One flower bears many small fruits—twins are like one person" (Turner 1969, 58). There is no mention of hallucinogenic properties.

5. Mututambulolu: *Xylopia adoratissima*, or Congo pepper, related to soursop. Its bitter fruit helps to expel stomach gas and reduce fever. The Javanese variety produces vertigo. Xylopia bears fragrant flowers that trap pollinating beetles.

6. Chikwata: *Ziziphus macronata*, or jujube plant, related to the buckthorn. It bears spines. Interestingly enough Christ's crown of thorns was said to have been made from a related species, *Rhamnus paliurus spina-christi*. It is used as a purgative medicine and is not known to have hallucinogenic properties.

7. Mukombukombu: *Tricalysia angolensis* (*lepticina*), possibly *leptothyrsia*, a citrus, related to the rue, which is a medicine for faintness, cramps, hysteria, and diseases of the womb. A South American species promotes the flow of saliva and increases perspiration. This identification is not confirmed and should be treated with caution.

8. Mucha: *Parinari mobola*, or coco plum. No hallucinogenic property has been discovered.

9. Mutungulu medicine was used in the Ndembu twin ritual because it has many spreading roots. It was sometimes given so that a woman would have many children. Here in Ihamba, the ihamba may have many children inside the patient. The purpose is reversed: the plant is used to kill the ihamba children inside. The word *Ku-tungulu* also means "to speak of a person behind his back," or "backbiting." Perhaps the grudge comes from this (see also Turner 1968, 61).

10. Musoli: *Vangueropsis lanciflora*. This tree bears small pear-shaped fruit that fall in quantities around its base. The fruit are relished by antelope who emerge into sight from the bush to eat the fruit, and are thus "revealed" to the hunters.

11. Mubanga: *Afrormosia angolensis*, or ironwood, a very tall tree.

12. Kapepi: *Hymemocardia acida*.

13. Muhotuhotu: *Canthium venosum*.

14. Mukandachina: *Rhus longipes*, related to poison ivy.

15. Each different Ihamba ritual was "context sensitive," in the terms Victor Turner and Robert Ellwood (personal communication) used, because it was a healing ritual, with a different patient and social context on every occasion, unlike the weekly services of the religions of the Book, Islam, Judaism, and Christianity, where the context is general.

16. Kapwipu: *Swartzia madigascariensis*.

17. The Ndembu possess a small repertoire of numinous objects, of which nsomu is but one example. These were called fetishes by early travelers and missionaries. It is now clear that they evince extraordinary internal complexity and unify many disparate meanings.

18. Among the Ndembu of the 1950s, possession of rare amulets was linked with power over witches and spirits, and this was also the case in 1985. However, the "patent" aspect of the substance was added since the earlier time, deriving from the increasing individualism of healers. Traditional doctors rarely cooperate with each other any more and do not consult another healer during difficult cases. The new emphasis derives from the contemporary possessiveness over anything that has value. In the 1950s in the same group of villages, buying and selling, except to traders to raise the ten shillings a year tax, was considered ungenerous and mean. In

those early days the forest resources were not scarce but human beings were, and the cooperation of one's kin and neighbors was valued accordingly.

19. Mudyi: *Diplorryncus condylocarpon* of the *apocynaceae* family. It yields a milk-like latex. It is related to a species from which stropanthus, a heart remedy, is taken.

20. This was the anthropology of experience, as Vic Turner and I called it (V. Turner and Bruner 1986, 221–24). He wrote, following the philosopher Wilhelm Dilthey, that meanings are given to a primary experience *after* that experience. Thus all culture ultimately derives from experience, and therefore the role of an anthropologist is inseparable from experience.

21. It should be noted that leaves, roots, and bark were distinguished from each other. Leaves were crushed for a cold infusion; roots were stewed as separate or paired items; bark pieces were stewed all together. Some items were chewed and spat on horns and the like; some leaves were put between the fists for the clapping rite (see kupandwila). The pharmacopeia had its own rationale. The frequent switching from cold to hot in Ndembu treatment followed the common pattern of fever in the human body, especially in malaria.

22. About notes generally, there could be no substitute for taking them at this stage. Even if an anthropologist were lucky enough to have a movie camera operating continually one would need to write down the names of people, emphasize significant happenings and their meanings, record actions occurring in sectors at which the camera was not pointing, and jot down personal impressions.

Chapter 3: The First Ihamba: The Performance for Nyakanjata

1. For the degrees of hunters' initiation see Chapter 5.

2. Lambek (1981) notes that in Mayotte the spirit possessing one family member interacts with and may possess the rest. He terms such a system "dense connection" among spirits and hosts. "The spirit or its kin continues as a sign of the family, and the relationships of family members to the spirit and, through the spirit, to each other, are reproduced. . . . An identity relationship between their spirits suggests processes of identification and competition as well as cooperation between the hosts. . . . [The family branches] are asserting an equivalent, autonomous, and hence potentially independent relationship to the nodal ancestor" (720–21). This ambivalent sense of identity in common affliction, yet the individualizing effect of that affliction, emerges in the laughter at this stage of Ihamba.

3. An observation that could be a motto for anthropologists.

Chapter 4: Discussion of the First Ihamba

1. Virilocality refers to the domicile of a married woman in the village of her husband.

2. There are similar ambiguities in the zar possession cult of the Sudan: "The requests of *zayran* [zar spirits] are to be enjoyed by them through the senses of their human hosts. Yet, if it is the spirit who desires, it is not always the spirit who speaks or is thought to speak. Zaineb remarks that her uncle's wife's spirit said, 'I want . . . ,' but elsewhere that *she* said, in a deep (male) voice, 'Unless you put on a ceremony for her!' Again, 'she said, "You must make coffee for Him. . . ." They made Him coffee and *she* drank it.' [Boddy comments:] Thus, although the identities of host and spirit are distinct and even here remain functionally independent, it appears that they coalesce in possession trance" (Boddy 1989, 151).

Chapter 5: Background to the Second Ihamba

1. *Wajila:* "sacrosanct."
2. See Appendix 8 for a comparison of the medicines of the two eras.

Chapter 6: The Second Ihamba: The Performance for Meru

1. Musesi: *Erythrophloeum africanum,* or *Burkea africanum.*
2. Liver is used as we use heart.
3. An African-American anthropology graduate student from Harvard University.
4. The Grateful Dead synchronize drums with the other music like this, creating the sound of a single organism.
5. An opaque "plasma" might describe it. In William Blodgett's field notes of 1985, page 219, Philip Kabwita refers to the bad ghost *musalu.* "Munginju medicine makes musalu visible. You can only see musalu, which comes in smoke or mist, when you drink pounded leaf medicine."
6. Fideli here gave his father's African name Muhelwa.
7. Sangunja is Singleton's African name inherited from his distant uncle, Benwa's father. During this conversation Fideli sometimes used Singleton's exact words and sometimes spoke in his own right.
8. *Chimbanda* means "African doctor."
9. Singleton used the word *chinjikijilu,* which was translated by Windson as "symbol." The word "indicator" might give the sense of pointer to something unknown.
10. In the 1950s the purpose of the maize meal was to cool the ihamba and transform it from a moving and afflicting spirit into a quiet hunter's talisman (Turner 1968, 173).
11. That night after writing the diary entry for the feeding of the ihamba, I began to dream as I sat with the notebook. I saw a door open a little bit and light coming through it, which made me happy. I have had dreams of doors opening before.

Chapter 7: Ritual and the Anthropology of Experience

1. Ralph Wendell Burhoe, research professor emeritus in theology and the sciences at Meadville/Lombard Theological School, Chicago.

2. Victor Turner's book (1968) showed that the extraction of harmful extrusions is not limited to the Americas, Siberia, Oceania, or Australia, but is found in Africa as well (see Appendix 6). The distinction between shaman and spirit-guided healer has created confusion here. Singleton was not the kind of shaman defined as one who lies prone while his shamanic consciousness wanders forth to bring back the lost spirit to the sick person, but he was the kind of healer who is endowed with a tutelary spirit who guides him in his craft (see Appendix 2). Both types of healer are guided by a helping spirit. Among the Ndembu it is the patient who falls in a trance, and by lying passive her or his body responds to the medicinal and ritual "calling-out" effect so strongly focused upon her or him. A similar responsive state spreads to those gathered around the ritual core, a fact well known to the doctors, who medicate those who are closely concerned (as we were medicated) in order to give them the power to see the spirit and also for protection.

3. Compare the photograph of an Ihamba doctor holding his middle finger over a divining mortar in Turner 1968, 169.

4. Compare in Chapter 3, "Benwa's hands stroked the ihamba toward the cupping horn. All of a sudden Nyakanjata's hand spread convulsively."

5. Roy Wagner put it this way: "The body's construct is one step ahead, and perception one step behind the 'now'" (personal communication). Wagner's sophisticated understanding of past, future, and memory is the subject of his present writing.

Chapter 8: Seeing Spirits

1. This reference to direct perception needs explanation. I saw the spirit form with my own eyes, just as one can press keys on the word processor called "reveal codes" and actually see a screen where the workings, the inner dynamics of the processing of words are revealed. In Ihamba then, my perception of what was really going on was not at that moment mediated by the inhibiting "tidying up" process which, of course, we need in our daily lives. The perception was unmediated, immediate, direct. "Direct perception" is a useful term because it covers the other senses as well, not only sight, and may also include clairvoyance at a distance.

Appendix 6: The Extraction of Harmful Intrusions

1. This term is taken from Harner (1980, 113–34), who devotes a chapter to the subject.

References

Ackernecht, Erwin H. 1971 [1943]. *Medicine and Ethnology.* Baltimore: Johns Hopkins University Press.

d'Aquili, Eugene, C. Laughlin, and J. McManus, eds. 1979. *The Spectrum of Ritual: A Biogenetic Structural Analysis.* New York: Columbia University Press.

Ashby, W. Ross. 1960. *Design for a Brain, The Origin of Adaptive Behavior.* New York: Wiley.

Bakhtin, Mikhail. 1981. *The Dialogic Imagination,* Michael Holquist, ed. Austin: University of Texas Press.

Barnard, Alan. 1979. "Nharo Bushmen and Medicine Men." *Africa* 49: 68–80.

Beattie, John, and John Middleton. 1969. *Spirit Mediumship and Society in Africa.* New York: Africana.

Benveniste, Emile. 1971 [1956]. *Problems in General Linguistics.* Coral Gardens, Fla.: University of Miami Press.

Binsbergen, Wim van. 1979. *Religious Change in Zambia.* Haarlem: Knipscheer.

Blake, William. 1970 [1802]. Letter to Thomas Butts, 22 November 1802, in *The Poetry and Prose of William Blake,* ed. D. Erdman. Garden City, N.Y.: Doubleday.

Blodgett, William. 1986. "Ihamba: Holistic Treatment, Holistic Analysis." Unpublished manuscript.

Boddy, Janice. 1989. *Wombs and Alien Spirits: Women, Men, and the Zar Cult in Northern Sudan.* Madison: University of Wisconsin Press.

Bourguignon, Erica. 1973. *Religion, Altered States of Consciousness, and Social Change.* Columbus: Ohio State University Press.

Bowen, Eleanor. 1954. *Return to Laughter.* New York: Harper.

Bridgeman, P. W. 1959. *The Way Things Are.* Cambridge: Harvard University Press.

Buckley, Anthony. 1976. "The Secret—An Idea in Yoruba Medicinal Thought," in J. B. Loudon, ed., *Social Anthropology and Medicine.* London: Academic Press, pp 397–421.

———. 1985. *Yoruba Medicine.* Oxford: Clarendon.

Burhoe, Ralph W. 1974. "The Phenomenon of Religion Seen Scientifically," in Allan Eister, ed., *Changing Perspectives in the Scientific Study of Religion.* New York: Wiley, pp 15–39.

Burton, W. F. P. 1961. *Luba Religion and Magic in Custom and Belief.* Turveren, Belgium: Musée Royal de L'Afrique Centrale, Series 8, 35.

Camino, Linda. 1986. *Ethnomedical Illnesses and Non-Orthodox Healing Practices in a Black Neighborhood in the American South: How They Work and What They Mean.* Doctoral Dissertation, Department of Anthropology, University of Virginia.

Campbell, Alan Tormaid. 1989. *To Square with Genesis: Causal Statements and Shamanic Ideas in Wayapi*. Iowa City: University of Iowa Press.

Cawte, John. 1974. *Medicine Is the Law: Studies in the Psychiatric Anthropology of Australian Tribal Societies*. Honolulu: University of Hawaii Press.

Clifford, James. 1983. "Ethnographic Authority." *Representations* 1(2): 118–46.

Colson, Elizabeth. 1969. "Spirit Possession among the Tonga," in John Beattie and John Middleton, eds., *Spirit Mediumship and Society in Africa*. New York: Africana, pp 69–103.

Dawson, John. 1964. "Urbanization and Mental Health in a West African Community," in Ari Kiev, ed., *Magic, Faith, and Healing*. New York: Free Press, pp 305–42.

Deikman, A. J. 1969. "Experimental Meditation," in C. T. Tart, ed., *Altered States of Consciousness*. Garden City, N.Y.: Doubleday.

———. 1975. "Deautomization and the Mystic Experience," in R. Ornstein, ed., *The Psychology of Consciousness*. New York: Penguin Books, pp 200–20.

Deren, Maya. 1953. *Divine Horsemen—The Living Gods of Haiti*. London: Thames and Hudson.

Douglas, Mary. 1970. *Witchcraft Confessions and Accusations*. London: Tavistock Publications.

Dow, James. 1986. *The Shaman's Touch: Otomi Indian Symbolic Healing*. Salt Lake City: University of Utah Press.

Dwyer, Kevin. 1982. *Moroccan Dialogues*. Baltimore: Johns Hopkins University Press.

Edgerton, Robert B. 1977. "A Traditional African Psychiatrist," in David Landy, ed., *Culture, Disease, and Healing*. New York: Macmillan, pp 438–45.

Eliade, Mircea. 1964. *Shamanism*. Princeton, N.J.: Princeton University Press.

Evans-Pritchard, E. 1937. *Witchcraft, Oracles, and Magic among the Azande*. Oxford: Clarendon.

Fabian, Johannes. 1983. *Time and the Other*. New York: Columbia University Press.

Favret-Saada, Jeanne. 1980. *Deadly Words: Witchcraft in the Bocage*. Cambridge: Cambridge University Press.

Fisher, M. K. 1984. *Lunda-Ndembu Dictionary*. Ikelenge, Zambia: Lunda-Ndembu Publications.

Foster, G. M., and B. G. Anderson. 1978. *Medical Anthropology*. New York: Wiley.

Frankenberg, Ronald, and Joyce Leeson. 1976. "Disease, Illness and Sickness: Social Aspects of the Choice of Healer in a Lusaka Suburb," in J. B. Loudon, ed., *Social Anthropology and Medicine*. London: Academic Press, pp 223–58.

Geertz, Clifford. 1977. "Curing, Sorcery, and Magic in a Javanese Town," in David Landy, ed., *Culture, Disease, and Healing*. New York: Macmillan, pp 146–54.

———. 1986. "Making Experience, Authoring Selves," in Victor W. Turner and Edward M. Bruner, eds., *The Anthropology of Experience*. Urbana: University of Illinois Press, pp 343–80.

Gelfand, Michael, S. Mavi, R. B. Drummond, and B. Ndemera, eds. 1985. *The Traditional Medical Practitioners in Zimbabwe*. Kopje, Harare, Zimbabwe: Mambo.

Grossinger, Richard. 1980. *Planet Medicine: From Stone Age Shamanism to Post-Industrial Healing*. Boulder, Colo.: Shambhala.

Gussler, Judith. 1973. "Social Change, Ecology, and Spirit Possession among the South African Nguni," in Erica Bourguignon, ed., *Religion, Altered States of Consciousness, and Social Change*. Columbus: Ohio State University Press, pp 88–126.

Haar, Gerrie ter. 1987. "Religion and Healing: The Case of Milingo." *Social Compass* 34(4): 475–93.

Hamer, John, and Irene Hamer. 1977. "Spirit Possession and Its Sociopsychological Implications among the Sidamo of Southwest Ethiopia," in David Landy, ed., *Culture, Disease, and Healing*. New York: Macmillan, pp 367–75.

Harner, Michael. 1968. "The Sound of Rushing Water." *Natural History* 77(6): 28–33, 60–61.

———. 1972. *The Jivaro: People of the Sacred Waterfalls*. Garden City, N.Y.: Doubleday.

———. 1973. *Hallucinogens and Shamanism*. New York: Oxford University Press.

———. 1980. *The Way of the Shaman: A Guide to Power and Healing*. San Francisco: Harper and Row.

Harrison, Ira, and David Dunlop, eds. n.d. "Traditional Healers: Use and Non-use in Health Care Delivery." *Rural Africana* 26.

Herskovits, Melville J. 1948. *Man and His Works: The Science of Cultural Anthropology*. New York: Knopf.

Hoffer, Abram, and H. Osmond. 1967. *The Hallucinogens*. New York: Academic Press.

Holmer, Nils M., and Henry Wassén. 1947. *Mu-Igala or the Way of Muu, a Medicine Song from the Cunas of Panama*. Göteborg, Norway.

Hooper, Antony. 1985. "Tahitian Healing," in C. Parsons, ed., *Healing Practices in the South Pacific*. Honolulu: Institute for Polynesian Studies, pp 158–98.

Horton, Robin. 1967. "African Traditional Thought and Western Science." *Africa* 37: 50–71, 155–87.

Imperato, Pascal. 1974–75. "Traditional Medical Practitioners Among the Bambara of Mali and Their Role in the Modern Health-Care Delivery System." *Rural Africana* 26: 41–53.

Janzen, John. 1978. *The Quest for Therapy in Lower Zaire*. Berkeley: University of California Press.

———. 1982. *Lemba: 1650–1930: A Drum of Affliction in Africa and the New World*. New York: Garland.

Jung, Carl. 1928. *Two Essays in Analytical Psychology*. New York: Dodd and Mead.

Junod, Henri A. 1962 [1912]. *The Life of a South African Tribe, Volume II: Mental Life*. New York: University Books.

———. 1934. "Les cas de possession et l'exorcisme chez les VaNdau." *Africa* 7: 270–99.

Katz, Richard. 1982. *Boiling Energy: Community Healing among the Kalahari Kung*. Cambridge: Harvard University Press.

Kennedy, John G. 1977. "Nubian Zar Ceremonies as Psychotherapy," in David Landy, ed., *Culture, Disease, and Healing*. New York: Macmillan, pp 375–84.

Kiev, Ari, ed. 1964. *Magic, Faith, and Healing*. New York: Free Press.

Kleinman, Arthur. 1980. *Patients and Healers in the Context of Culture*. Berkeley: University of California Press.

Kohler, M. 1941. *The Izangoma Diviners*. Pretoria: Government Printer.

Krige, Eileen J. 1936. *The Social System of the Zulus*. London: Longmans Green.

Lambek, Michael. 1981. *Human Spirits: A Cultural Account of Trance in Mayotte*. Cambridge: Cambridge University Press.

Landy, David, ed. 1977. *Culture, Disease, and Healing*. New York: Macmillan.

Lévi-Strauss, Claude. 1963. *Structural Anthropology*. New York: Basic Books.

———. 1980. "The Sorcerer and His Magic," in D. Landy, ed., *Culture, Disease, and Healing*. New York: Macmillan, pp 445–53.

Lévy-Bruhl, Lucien. 1935. *Primitives and the Supernatural*. New York: Dutton.

———. 1985 [1910]. *How Natives Think*. Princeton, N.J.: Princeton University Press.

Lex, Barbara. 1979. "The Neurobiology of Ritual Trance," in E. d'Aquili, C. Laughlin, and J. McManus, eds., *The Spectrum of Ritual*. New York: Columbia University Press.

Lienhardt, Godfrey. 1961. *Divinity and Experience*. London: Oxford University Press.

Littleton, Scott. 1985. Introduction, in *How Natives Think* by Lucien Lévy-Bruhl. Princeton, N.J.: Princeton University Press, pp v–lviii.

Loudon, J. B., ed. 1976. *Social Anthropology and Medicine*. London: Academic Press.

Ludvigson, Tomas. 1985. "Healing in Central Espiritu Santo, Vanuatu," in Claire Parsons, ed., *Healing Practices in the South Pacific*. Honolulu: Institute for Polynesian Studies, pp 51–64.

Macdonald, Judith. 1985. "Contemporary Healing Practices in Tikopia, Solomon Islands," in Claire Parsons, ed., *Healing Practices in the South Pacific*. Honolulu: Institute for Polynesian Studies, pp 65–86.

Maddox, J. C. 1923. *The Medicine Man*. New York: Macmillan.

Margenau, Henry. 1960. "Truth in Science and Religion," in Harlow Shapley, ed., *Science Ponders Religion*. New York: Appleton-Century-Crofts, pp 100–16.

McCulloch, Merran. 1951. *The Southern Lunda and Related Peoples*. London: International African Institute.

Melland, Frank H. 1923. *In Witch-bound Africa*. London: Seeley, Service and Co.

Messing, Simon. 1976. "Traditional Healing and the New Health Center." *Conch* 8: 1 and 2: 52–64.

Milingo, E. 1984. *The World Between: Christian Healers and the Struggle for Spiritual Survival*. New York: Maryknoll.

Mindeleff, Cosmos. 1898. "Navaho Houses." *Bureau of American Ethnology Reports* 17: 475–517.

Morgan, William. 1977. "Navaho Treatment of Sickness: Diagnosticians," in David Landy, ed., *Culture, Disease, and Healing: Studies in Medical Anthropology*. New York: Macmillan, pp 163–69.

Munn, Henry. 1982. "The Mushrooms of Language," in M. Harner, ed., *Hallucinogens and Language*. New York: Oxford University Press, pp 86–122.

Nadel, S. F. 1946. "A Study of Shamanism in the Nuba Hills." *Journal of the Royal Anthropological Institute* 76: 25–37.

Needham, Rodney. 1967. "Percussion and Transition." *Man* 2: 606–14.

Neher, Andrew. 1962. "A Physiological Explanation of Unusual Behavior in Ceremonies Involving Drums." *Human Biology* 34: 126–44.

Ornstein, Robert. 1972. *The Psychology of Consciousness*. San Francisco: Freeman.

Overing, Joanna. 1985. *Reason and Morality*. London: Tavistock.

Parsons, Claire D. F., ed. 1985. *Healing Practices in the South Pacific*. Honolulu: Institute for Polynesian Studies.

Peters, Larry. 1981a. "Ecstasy and Healing in Nepal: An Ethnopsychiatric Study of Tamany Shamanism." *Other Realities* 4(179): 37–54.

———. 1981b. *Ecstasy and Healing in Nepal*. Malibu, Calif.: Undena.

Prince, Raymond. 1968. *Trance and Possession States*. Montreal: R. M. Bucke Memorial Society.

———. 1964. "Indigenous Yoruba Psychiatry," in Ari Kiev, ed., *Magic, Faith, and Healing*. New York: Free Press, pp 84–120.

Rainey, Froelich. 1947. *The Whale Hunters of Tigara*. New York: Anthropological Papers of the American Museum of Natural History, vol. 41, part 2.

Ramanucci-Ross, Lola. 1979. "On Analyses of Event Structures as Philosophical Derivations of the Investigating Cultures," in Bruce Grindal and Dennis Warren, eds., *Essays in Humanistic Anthropology*. Washington, D.C.: University Press of America, pp 53–67.

Reid, Janice. 1983. *Sorcerers and Healing Spirits*. Canberra: Australian National University Press.

Reynolds, Barrie. 1963. *Magic, Divination and Witchcraft among the Barotse of Northern Rhodesia*. London: Chatto and Windus.

Ridington, Robin. 1987–88. "A Tree that Stands Burning: Reclaiming a Point of View as from the Center." *Steward Journal* 17(1–2): 47–75.

Ritzenthaler, Robert. 1963. "Primitive Therapeutic Practices among the Wisconsin Chippewa," in Iago Galdston, ed., *Man's Image in Medicine and Anthropology*. New York: International Universities Press, pp 321–22.

Rogers, Spencer L. 1982. *The Shaman: His Symbols and His Healing Power*. Springfield, Ill.: C. C. Thomas.

Roure, Lucian. 1912. "Visions." *The Catholic Encyclopedia*, ed. C. Herbermann. New York: Appleton, 15: 477–78.

Sacks, Oliver. 1970. *The Man Who Mistook His Wife for a Hat*. New York: Summit, pp 7–23.

Schechner, Richard. 1985. *Between Theater and Anthropology*. Philadelphia: University of Pennsylvania Press.

Schwartz, Theodore. 1989. "Anthropological Observations of New Age Religion," in *Abstracts of the 88th Annual Meeting*. Washington, D.C.: American Anthropological Association, p 84.

Shukman, Ann. 1977. *Literature and Semiotics*. New York: North Holland Publishing Company.

Shweder, Richard. 1989. "The Future of Cultural Psychology." *Anthropology Newsletter* 30(7): 19.

Singer, Philip, ed. 1976. "Traditional Healing: New Science or New Colonialism?" *Conch* 8: 1–2.

Spencer, W. B., and F. J. Gillen. 1927. *The Arunta: A Study of a Stone Age People*. London: Macmillan.

Spring Anita. 1978. "Epidemiology of Spirit Possession," in J. Hotch-Smith and

A. Spring, eds., *Women in Ritual and Symbolic Roles*. New York: Plenum, pp 165–90.

———. 1980. "Faith and Participation in Traditional versus Cosmopolitan Medical Systems in Northwestern Zambia." *Anthropological Quarterly* 53(2): 130–41.

Stoller, Paul. 1984. "Eye, Mind, and Word in Anthropology." *L'Homme* 24(3–4): 91–114.

Stoller, Paul, and Cheryl Olkes. 1987. *In Sorcery's Shadow*. Chicago: University of Chicago Press.

Swartz, M. J., and Jordan, D. K. 1976. *Anthropology: Perspective on Humanity*. New York: Wiley.

Taylor, Christopher. 1987. "Milk, Honey, and Money: Concepts of Pathology in Ruanda." Paper read at Southeastern Regional Seminar in African Studies, University of Virginia.

Turner, Edith. 1986a. "Encounter with Neurobiology: The Response of Ritual Studies." *Zygon* 21(2): 219–32.

———. 1986b. "Philip Kabwita, Ghost Doctor: The Ndembu in 1985." *The Drama Review* 30(4): 4–35.

———. 1987a. *The Spirit and the Drum*. Tucson: University of Arizona Press.

———. 1987b. "Zambia's Kankanga Dances: The Changing Life of Ritual." *Performing Arts Journal* 30(3): 57–72.

———. "Bar Yohai, Mystic: The Creative Persona and His Pilgrimage," in Smadar Lavie, Kirin Narayan, and Renato Rosaldo, eds., *Creativity/Anthropology*. Ithaca, N.Y.: Cornell University Press, pp. 225–52.

Turner, Victor. 1957. *Schism and Continuity in an African Society: A Study of Ndembu Village Life*. Manchester, England: Manchester University Press.

———. 1962. *Chihamba, the White Spirit: A Ritual Drama of the Ndembu*. Rhodes-Livingstone Papers, 33. Manchester, England: Manchester University Press.

———. 1967. *The Forest of Symbols: Aspects of Ndembu Ritual*. Ithaca, N.Y.: Cornell University Press.

———. 1968. *The Drums of Affliction: A Study of Religious Processes Among the Ndembu of Zambia*. Oxford: Clarendon.

———. 1969. *The Ritual Process: Structure and Anti-Structure*. Chicago: Aldine.

———. 1974. *Dramas, Fields, and Metaphors*. Ithaca, N.Y.: Cornell University Press.

———. 1975a. *Revelation and Divination*. Ithaca, N.Y.: Cornell University Press.

———. 1975b. "Ritual as Communication and Potency: An Ndembu Case Study," in Carole Hill, ed., *Symbols and Society*. Athens, Ga.: Southern Anthropological Society, pp 58–81.

———. 1976. "The Bite of the Hunter's Ghost: Conscience and Community in an African Healing Ritual." *Parabola* 1(2): 42–49.

———. 1985. *On the Edge of the Bush,* ed. E. Turner. Tucson: University of Arizona Press.

———. 1992. *Blazing the Trail,* ed. E. Turner. Tucson: University of Arizona Press.

Turner, Victor, and Edward Bruner, eds. 1986. *The Anthropology of Experience*. Urbana: University of Illinois Press.

Twumasi, Patrick A. 1985. *The Professionalization of Traditional Medicine in Zambia*. Lusaka: University of Zambia.

Wagner, Roy. 1975. *The Invention of Culture*. Chicago: University of Chicago Press.
———. 1983. "Visible Ideas: Toward an Anthropology of Perceptive Values." *South Asian Anthropologist* (Essays in Honor of Victor Turner) 4(1): 1–8.
———. 1986. *Symbols that Stand for Themselves*. Chicago: University of Chicago Press.
Walens, Stanley. 1981. *Feasting with Cannibals*. Princeton, N.J.: Princeton University Press.
Walker, Sheila. 1972. *Ceremonial Spirit Possession in Africa and Afro-America*. Leiden: Brill.
White, C. M. N. 1949. "Stratification and Modern Changes in an Ancestral Cult." *Africa* 19(4): 324–31.
———. 1961. *Elements in Luvale Beliefs and Rituals*. Manchester, England: Manchester University Press.
Whisson, Michael G. 1964. "Some Aspects of Functional Disorders Among the Kenya Luo," in Ari Kiev, ed., *Magic, Faith, and Healing*. New York: Free Press, pp. 283–304.
Whiting, Beatrice. 1950. *Piaute Sorcery*. New York: Viking Fund Publications in Anthropology.
Willis, Roy G. 1977. "Pollution and Paradigms," in David Landy, ed., *Culture, Disease, and Healing*. New York: Macmillan, pp 278–85.
Wilson, Brian. 1970. *Rationality*. Oxford: Blackwell.
Wilson, Monica. 1959. *Communal Rituals of the Nyakyusa*. London: Oxford University Press for the International African Institute.
Wordsworth, William. 1977 [1850]. *The Prelude*. New York: Penguin.
Yoder, Paul. 1981. *Disease and Illness Among the Cokwe: An Ethnomedical Perspective*. Doctoral Dissertation, Department of Anthropology, University of California at Los Angeles.

Index

University of Pennsylvania Press
SERIES IN CONTEMPORARY ETHNOGRAPHY
Dan Rose and Paul Stoller, General Editors

Camille Bacon-Smith. *Enterprising Women: Television Fandom and the Creation of Popular Myth.* 1991

Robert D. Desjarlais. *Body and Emotion: The Aesthetics of Illness and Healing in the Nepal Himalayas.* 1992

John D. Dorst. *The Written Suburb: An American Site, An Ethnographic Dilemma.* 1989

Douglas E. Foley. *The Heartland Chronicles.* 1995

Douglas E. Foley. *Learning Capitalist Culture: Deep in the Heart of Tejas.* 1990

Kirin Narayan. *Storytellers, Saints, and Scoundrels: Folk Narrative in Hindu Religious Teaching.* 1989

Sally Ann Ness. *Body, Movement, and Culture: Kinesthetic and Visual Symbolism in a Philippine Community.* 1992

Dan Rose. *Patterns of American Culture: Ethnography and Estrangement.* 1989

Paul Stoller. *The Taste of Ethnographic Things: The Senses in Anthropology.* 1989

Lawrence J. Taylor. *Occasions of Faith: An Anthropology of Irish Catholics.* 1995

Edith Turner, with William Blodgett, Singleton Kahona, and Fideli Benwa. *Experiencing Ritual: A New Interpretation of African Healing.* 1992

Jim Wafer. *The Taste of Blood: Spirit Possession in Brazilian Candomblé.* 1991

This book has been set in Linotron Galliard. Galliard was designed for Mergenthaler in 1978 by Matthew Carter. Galliard retains many of the features of a sixteenth century typeface cut by Robert Granjon but has some modifications that give it a more contemporary look.

Printed on acid-free paper.